CATULLUS
The Shorter Poems

Edited with an Introduction, Translation and Commentary by
John Godwin

Aris & Phillips is an imprint of
Oxbow Books, Oxford, UK

ISBN 9780856687150

First published 1999. Reprinted 2007.

A CIP record for this book is available from the British Library.

Printed and bound by CPI Group (UK) Ltd, Croydon, CR0 4YY

To Bren
uxori carissimae

Contents

Preface

Catullus expresses the wish (1.10) that his 'little book' may last r
generation, and he would surely be gratified to see yet anothe
translation of his work to add to the groaning shelves of such book
libraries. This poet has hardly been neglected by scholars and reader:
and translations of his work continue to be produced – so why
Certainly I have learned a good deal from the work which has gone be1
to the commentaries of Kroll, Fordyce, Quinn, Goold and Syndikus i
is obvious – and I have also tried to discuss some of the massive second
on the poet which appears every year in books and journals around tl
again my debt to their work will be obvious to those familiar with the li
   My primary purpose in producing this edition has been to try to b1
of the literary beauty and interest of a poet whose appeal is clearly
whose techniques and preoccupations may seem at times remote from
these poems have often been imitated and anthologised, while others
find a place in standard editions such as that of Fordyce; and this edi
find value in all the poems of Catullus – the scatological and the sava
the poems of love and friendship. Catullus, after all, produced all these
we find some of the texts puzzling and repellent then we have to wor
our literary criteria are wide enough to encompass this poet at all. Th
the second volume of a complete edition of the entire poetry of Catul
volume (*Poems 61-68*) having appeared in 1995.
   James Morwood read the entire book in draft form and was a:
generous with his time in correcting errors and alerting me to areas whe
made myself clear or where I was clearly wrong. All mistakes that rer
own.

J(

Shrewsbury,]

Bibliography

This is the list of the works which I have found most useful in preparing this edition. Where abbreviations are used in the commentary, these are indicated after the title's listing below.

Works of Reference:

A.P.	*Anthologia Palatina*
OCD	*The Oxford Classical Dictionary* (3rd edition, Oxford, 1996)
OLD	*The Oxford Latin Dictionary* (Oxford, 1982)
CHCL	*The Cambridge History of Classical Literature* vol 1 (1985), vol 2 (1982)
CIL	*Corpus Inscriptionum Latinorum* (1863)
LSJ	*A Greek-English Lexicon* Liddell and Scott (revised Jones) (9th edition, Oxford 1968)

Major editions of Catullus include:

Aldine edition (1502)
Muretus (1554)
Achilles Statius (1566)
Voss (1684)
Lachmann K. (1829)
Baehrens, E. (Leipzig, 1885)
Ellis, Robinson (Oxford, 1889)
Munro, H.A.J. *Criticisms and Elucidations of Catullus* (London, 1905)
Lenchantin de Gubernatis, M. (Turin, 1953)
Mynors, R.A.B. (Oxford Classical Text 1958) (OCT)
Fordyce, C.J. (Oxford 1961)
Pighi, G.B. (Verona, 1961)
Kroll, W. (5th edition, Stuttgart 1968)
Bardon, H. (Brussels 1970)
Quinn, K. (London 1970)
Thomson, D.F.S. (Chapel Hill 1978)
Goold, G.P. (London 1983)
Lee, G. (Oxford, 1990)
Garrison, D.H. (London 1991)
Godwin, J. *Poems 61-68* (Warminster, 1995)

Books and Articles:

Adams   Adams, J.N., *The Latin Sexual Dictionary* (London, 1982)
Austin   Austin, R.G.(ed.), Virgil *Aeneid 4* (Oxford, 1955)
Brunt   Brunt, P.A. '*Amicitia* in the late Roman Republic' *Proceedings of the Cambridge Philological Society* n.s. 11 (1965) 1-20
Conte   Conte, G.B., *The Rhetoric of Imitation* (Ithaca, 1986)
Copley   Copley, F.O., 'Catullus *c*. 4: the world of the poem' *Transactions of the American Philological Association* 89 (1958) 9-13 (=Quinn (1972b) 129-135)
Costa   Costa, C.D.N., *Lucretius* de rerum natura V (Oxford, 1984)
Dodds   Dodds, E.R., *The Greeks and the Irrational* (California, 1951)
Doubrovsky   Doubrovsky, S, *The New Criticism in France* (trans. D. Coltman, Chicago and London 1973 from *Pourquoi la nouvelle critique?* Paris, 1966)
Dover   Dover, K.J., *Aristophanes* Frogs (Oxford, 1993)
Ferguson   Ferguson, J. *Catullus* (Greece and Rome New Surveys in the Classics 20) (Oxford 1988)
Fitzgerald   Fitzgerald, W., *Catullan Provocations: Lyric Poetry and the Drama of Position* (California, 1995)
Fowler 1989   Fowler, D.P., 'First Thoughts on Closure: Problems and Prospects' *Materiali e Discussioni per l'analisi dei testi classici* 22 (1989) 75-122
Fowler 1993   Fowler, D.P., 'Postmodernism, Romantic Irony and Classical Closure' in: De Jong and Sullivan (eds) *Modern Critical Theory and Classical Literature* (*Mnemosyne* Supplement 130) (Leiden, 1993)
Fraenkel 1956   Fraenkel, E., 'Catulls Trostgedicht für Calvus' *Wiener Studien* 69 (1956) 278-88
Fraenkel 1957   Fraenkel, E., *Horace* (Oxford, 1957)
Griffin 1976   Griffin, J. 'Augustan Poetry and the Life of Luxury' *Journal of Roman Studies* 66 (1976) 87-105
Griffin 1980   Griffin, J., *Homer on Life and Death* (Oxford, 1980)
Griffin 1985   Griffin, J., *Latin Poets and Roman Life* (London, 1985)
Griffith   Griffith, M., *Aeschylus* Prometheus Bound (Cambridge, 1983)
Harrison   Harrison, S.J. *Virgil: Aeneid 10* (Oxford, 1991)
Henderson   Henderson, J., *The Maculate Muse: Obscene Language in Attic Comedy* (Oxford, 1991)
Hinds   Hinds, S., *Allusion and Intertext: Dynamics of Appropriation in Roman Poetry* (Cambridge, 1998)
Hopkins   Hopkins, K., *Death and Renewal* (Cambridge, 1983)
Hutchinson   Hutchinson, G.O., *Hellenistic Poetry* (Oxford, 1988)

Kaster   Kaster, R.A., 'A note on Catullus c.71.4' *Philologus* 121 (1977)
                      308-12
Kenney 1970   Kenney, E.J., 'Doctus Lucretius' *Mnemosyne* 23 (1970) 366-
                      392
Kenney 1971   Kenney, E.J., *Lucretius* de rerum natura III (Cambridge, 1971)
Kenney 1982   Kenney, E.J., *The Cambridge History of Classical Literature*
                      vol 2, part 1 pp. 3-32 ('Books and Readers in the Roman
                      World') (Cambridge, 1982)
Knox 1968   Knox, B.M.W., 'Silent Reading in Antiquity' *Greek, Roman
                      and Byzantine Studies* 9 (1968) 421-35
Knox 1985   Knox, B.M.W., 'Books and Readers in the Greek World' in
                      Cambridge History of Classical Literature vol. 1 (1985) 1-16
Lyne 1978   Lyne, R.O.A.M., 'The Neoteric Poets' *Classical Quarterly* 28
                      (1978) 167-187
Lyne 1979   Lyne, R.O.A.M., 'Servitium Amoris' *Classical Quarterly* 29
                      (1979) 117-130
Lyne 1980   Lyne, R.O.A.M., *The Latin Love Poets* (Oxford, 1980)
McKie   McKie, D.S., *The Manuscripts of Catullus: Recension in a
                      Closed Tradition* (Diss. Cambridge University 1977)
Macleod   Macleod, C.W. ,'Catullus 116' *Classical Quarterly* 23 (1973)
                      304-9
Mankin   Mankin, D., *Horace: Epodes* (Cambridge, 1995)
Martin   Martin, C., *Catullus* (Yale, 1992)
Mayer   Mayer, R., *Horace,* Epistles *Book 1* (Cambridge, 1994)
Morgan   Morgan, J.D., 'The Waters of the Satrachus (Catullus 95.5)'
                      Classical Quarterly 41 (1991) 252-3
Morton Braund   Morton Braund, S., *Juvenal Satires Book 1* (Cambridge 1996)
Most   Most, G. 'Neues zur Geschichte des Terminus "Epyllion"'
                      Philologus 126 (1982) 153-6
Nisbet 1961   Nisbet, R.G.M., *Cicero* In Pisonem (Oxford, 1961)
Nisbet and Hubbard   Nisbet, R.G.M., and Hubbard, M., *A Commentary on Horace:
                      Odes Book 1* (Oxford, 1970)
Nisbet 1978   Nisbet, R.G.M., 'Notes on the Text of Catullus' *Proceedings of
                      the Cambridge Philological Society* NS 24 (1978) 92-115 =
                      Collected Papers on Latin Literature (Oxford, 1995) 76-100
Nisbet 1995   Nisbet, R.G.M., *Collected Papers on Latin Literature* (Oxford,
                      1995)
Ogilvie   Ogilvie, R.M. *The Romans and their Gods* (London, 1969)
Paoli   Paoli, U.E., *Rome, its People Life and Customs* (London 1963)
Peden   Peden, R., 'Endings in Catullus' in: Whitby, Hardie, Whitby
                      (eds): *Homo Viator: Classical Essays for John Bramble*
                      (Bristol, 1987)

BIBLIOGRAPHY

Powell   Powell, J.G.F., *Cicero* Cato Maior de Senectute (Cambridge, 1988)

Quinn   see in major editions of Catullus above

Quinn 1959   Quinn, K., *The Catullan Revolution* (Cambridge, 1959)

Quinn 1972a   Quinn, K., *Catullus: an Interpretation* (London, 1972)

Quinn 1972b   Quinn, K., (ed.), *Approaches to Catullus* (Cambridge, 1972)

Rawson   Rawson, E., *Intellectual Life in the Late Roman Republic* (London, 1985)

Roberts   Roberts, D.H., Dunn, F.M. and Fowler, D.P., *Classical Closure: Reading the End in Greek and Latin Literature* (Princeton, 1997)

Ross   Ross, D.O. Jr., *Style and Tradition in Catullus* (Harvard, 1969)

Russell 1972   Russell D.A. and Winterbottom, M., *Ancient Literary Criticism* (Oxford, 1972)

Russell 1981   Russell D.A., *Criticism in Antiquity* (London, 1981)

Segal   Segal, Erich, *Roman Laughter* (Harvard, 1968)

Sharrock   Sharrock, A. *Seduction and Repetition in Ovid's* Ars Amatoria *II* (Oxford, 1994)

Syme   Syme, R., *The Roman Revolution* (Oxford, 1939)

Syndikus   Syndikus, H-P., *Catull: eine Interpretation* (3 vols, Darmstadt, 1984-7)

Thomas   Thomas, R.F., 'Catullus and the polemics of poetic reference (64.1-18)' *American Journal of Philology* 103 (1982) 144-164

Thomson   Thomson, D.F.S., 'Catullus 95.8' *Phoenix* 18 (1964) 30-36

Treggiari   Treggiari, S., *Roman Marriage* (Oxford, 1991)

Veyne   Veyne, P., *Roman Erotic Elegy* trans. D. Pellauer (Chicago-London, 1988) from *L'Élegie érotique romaine* (Paris, 1983)

Wilamovitz   Wilamovitz-Moellendorff, U., *Hellenistische Dichtung in der Zeit des Kallimachos* (2 vols, Berlin, 1924)

Williams   Williams, G., *Tradition and Originality: Roman Poetry* (Oxford, 1968)

Winterbottom   Winterbottom, M., *Roman Declamation* (Bristol, 1980)

Wiseman 1969   Wiseman, T.P., *Catullan Questions* (Leicester, 1969)

Wiseman 1985   Wiseman, T.P., *Catullus and his World: a Re-appraisal* (Cambridge, 1985)

Introduction

CATULLUS' LIFE AND TIMES

Catullus certainly lived in 'interesting times'. During his lifetime the military leaders who controlled Rome's army began to assume an increasingly dominant role in society: the aristocrat Sulla took over the state and attempted to impose a constitution which would give the Senate dominant power and (he thought) stability to the state, but his constitution crumbled within a few years of his death. There followed a period of thirty years in which military leaders, senators and urban demagogues vied with each other for power, culminating in the Civil War which began in 49 B.C. and which left Julius Caesar in total control. Frequently towards the end of Catullus' lifetime elections were held late (e.g. 55 B.C.) or abandoned because of violence and corruption, and the history of the period is peopled with few heroes and many villains: Catiline, whose abortive attempt at revolution in 63 B.C. gave Cicero his hour of glory but almost brought down the state, Clodius, whose popularity was secured by a blend of demagogy and thuggery and who met his end in a street brawl in 52 B.C., Verres, the rapacious governor of Sicily, and so on. One of the interesting features of Catullus' work for the modern reader is the small amount of direct political comment we find there: there is abuse of politicians (Caesar, Mamurra, Memmius etc.), but precious little of what we might call political ideals. Catullus had no answers to the evils of late-republican government: but he seems to have had neither faith nor interest in it either. Catullus' great contemporary Lucretius denounced the corrupt world of politics and advocated an apolitical Epicurean stance, even attempting to persuade Catullus' sometime praetor Memmius to follow his example: Catullus responded to the political chaos in a different manner.

On the one hand, then, there is no evidence that Catullus ever engaged in political life in Rome or anywhere else, and he only mentions politicians to abuse them either by insult (57), irony (49), studied indifference (93) or mockery (84). He also insults his 'friends' and so we should not take his abuse as itself a political gesture, but it does show him making no sign of any attempt to ingratiate himself with men who might have helped his political career. On the other hand, Catullus clearly believed that his poetry would have a future (1.10) and he seems to have channelled his energies into his art, carving out for himself and his friends a haven of poetry, friendship and love which eschewed the world of politics: and to mark this rejection of the world of politics he used the vocabulary of politics for the workings of love. Ross (83) perhaps overstates the case in saying that the poet used the '(almost technical) terminology of the workings of party politics and political alliances in Rome', but the Roman reader would have been in no doubt that words like *amicitia, fides, foedus* were found more often in the forum than the bedroom. Lyne (1980, 25-6) contests Ross' case and points out that in Rome the state was largely in the hands of the amateur – which meant the aristocrat – and that such people naturally used the vocabulary of 'aristocratic commitment and obligation': so it is not Catullus taking over the language of 'politics' but rather politicians and Catullus alike taking over the language of the prevailing governing class. This is no doubt true, but the issue is not greatly affected: Catullus does not use the language of politics to talk about politics but rather to talk about love, and his use of such 'public' terms as *amicitia, foedus, fides* in a private context of sexual love is arguably to some extent at least a reaction against the world of politicians who thundered high ideals in public but were guilty of all manner of corruption behind the scenes, just as his life of love is a reaction against the 'disapproving old men' of poem 5.

Of the external details of Catullus' life there is little independent evidence, and some of it is not especially reliable. St Jerome informs us simply that Catullus was born in Verona in 87 B.C. and died in 57 B.C.; the second date is disproved easily by the poet's reference to Caesar's invasion of Britain in 55 B.C. (11.9–12). Catullus does not refer to events after 54 B.C., and so it is tempting to locate his death in that year: Ovid mentions that he died young (*Am.* 3.9.61). The problem is neatly sewn up if we assume that Jerome mistook the year of Catullus' birth by placing it in Cinna's first consulship when in fact it was his fourth consulship (84 B.C.) – this allows Catullus to live for thirty years and die in 54 B.C. and is thus accepted by Goold (2). A more extreme view is that of Wiseman (1985,183-198), who believes that our poet went on to live after 54 and became a writer of mimes for the theatre – a theory which is not inherently implausible but which cannot be regarded as proven.

Some evidence has also been derived from the poems themselves, especially where they mention known individuals. Gaius Memmius, for instance, of whom a good deal is known, is named as the praetorian governor on whose staff the poet served in Bithynia; and his governorship can be securely dated from a letter of Cicero (*Q Fr.* 1.2.16) which tells us that Memmius was elected to be praetor in 58 B.C. If Memmius stayed in Rome for his year of office and then went to his province (as was usual), he will have been in Bithynia with Catullus from 57 B.C. until 56 B.C.

More famous even than Memmius are other names which we find on the pages of this poet: he wrote a poem addressed to Cicero, the finest orator of the period and a man of refined literary taste who knew a Neoteric hexameter line when he saw one (*Att.* 7.2) and who wrote poetry himself. More impressive still is the textual evidence linking Catullus with Julius Caesar, the future dictator of Rome: Suetonius records (*Iul.* 73) that Caesar was a friend of Catullus' father – which suggests, as Wiseman points out (Wiseman 1985, 100) that Catullus *père* was an important man – presumably in business circles. What is interesting is that the poet felt relaxed enough with Caesar to compose grossly insulting poetry about his personal life (29 and especially 57) without fear of reprisal – Suetonius uses Caesar's pardoning of Catullus as an example of his famous clemency, and one can only wonder what would have become of Catullus if he had writen such verses fifty years later under a harsher regime.

The love poems appear so heartfelt and 'sincere' that few scholars have ever dared but take them at face value. The identity of the 'real' Lesbia was stated, according to Wiseman (1985, 51-2), within a single generation of the poet's death by Julius Hyginus who was Librarian of the Palatine Library; it is stated as a matter of fact by Apuleius (*Apologia* 10) that Catullus gave Clodia the false name of Lesbia, a name with the same metrical scansion as her real name and a practice apparently common in love-poetry of the time. Scholars quickly inferred that this Clodia must have been the most famous woman of that name alive at the time – Clodia Metelli, sister of the popular activist (and enemy of Cicero) Publius Clodius and wife of Metellus Celer. This fits nicely with other facts: Catullus' mistress was married (68. 145-6 is unambiguous on that point), Metellus Celer was indeed governor of Cisalpine Gaul (where Verona is) in 62 B.C., and Cicero, in defending Marcus Caelius Rufus against Clodia's accusation of attempted murder, paints a scandalous portrait of this woman as having had an affair with Caelius and been subsequently spurned by him. All in all she appears rich, loose and thoroughly dangerous to know – exactly the sort, one feels, who would impress a sensitive poet and trample on his feelings in the heartless manner described in poems 11, 75, 76, etc. Add to that the name Caelius which appears in poems where the poet lays claim to 'our Lesbia' (58) and one might swiftly arrive at the certainty of the 1966 edition of the *Oxford Companion to Classical Literature* which states categorically (s.v. 'Caelius') that Caelius 'supplanted Catullus as lover of Clodia'. Such neat coincidence is extremely appealing, but it is quite possibly wrong. For one thing, the Caelius referred to in poem 58 is a sick man with gout and smelly breath, while Cicero's client was nothing if not young and healthy.

We will never know for certain. Even if Apuleius is correct in giving Lesbia the name Clodia, there were other women of the same name at the same time and of the same family – Clodia Metelli's two sisters, for instance. The pseudonym theory is itself open to serious questioning: the references to 'Lesbia' might have denoted a Greek courtesan of that name (although Griffin ((1985) 28), who argues forcibly that Roman poets loved Greek girls, still regards Catullus' Lesbia as an 'amateur' (i.e. a Roman lady)), or at least be intended to disguise her as one, and it is even possible that 68.145-6 which refers to the woman's husband without naming her may be describing another woman altogether, although poem 83 has Lesbia speaking in the presence of her husband. The connotations of the name 'Lesbia' were also very different to the ancient world than they are to us; *lesbiazein* as a verb in Greek meant 'to give oral sex' (Henderson 183-4, Mankin 211), and so to call this Roman lady by this name was hardly the 'innocent-sounding substitute for the mistress' real name' (Quinn) or the bluestocking soubriquet ('Roman Sappho' or some such) which many scholars imagine, but rather a risqué nickname more appropriate to a prostitute. The two poems (11 and 51) composed in Sapphics lend credence to the 'poetic' significance of the name, while the obscene connotations of the name itself tend away from this; as often in Catullus, the use of the pseudonym raises questions and leaves the text quizzical and teasing. We do not (of course) need biographical facts to appreciate the love-poetry he composed, and anyway the poet chose to hide the object of his feelings behind a pseudonym. The literary tradition of Elegy and Iambus in Greek poetry for instance abounds in cases where the poet is almost certainly adopting a *persona* as a literary mouthpiece rather than as a confessional voice (cf. *CHCL* vol.1, 118). We would do better to look at the poems on their own terms, as poetry.

POETRY AS PERFORMANCE

Ancient culture was predominantly an oral culture. Homer was possibly an oral performer whose epics were only written down much later, drama – tragedy and comedy – was written to be performed on the stage, oratory (both political, forensic and also epideictic) was composed for delivery in public. This habit of hearing ancient literature rather than silent reading went beyond these obviously public genres: the historians gave recitations of their work (Livy only attracted small audiences, we are told: Tacitus tells us that audiences wanted to go home with memorable phrases in their minds), as did the poets: Virgil was a formidable reciter of his own poetry, reading out the whole of his *Georgics* to the young Octavian over several days in 29 B.C., and Juvenal complains that one cannot escape the endless recitations given by poets at parties and in the baths (see further Wiseman 1985, 124–6). Audience response, said Aristotle, was the key element in determining the speech's purpose (*Rh.* 1358b2-4) and ancient education (at least higher education) was in the main rhetorical education to produce confident and competent public speakers, and in which teachers would set specimen topics for their students to debate (cf. Petronius 48, Seneca *Controv.*) or else set them to write speeches to be delivered by a historical figure (*suasoria*): one favourite of this genre was the question of whether Sulla ought to resign his powers (for examples of all these see Winterbottom).

Clearly this highly public manner of reception differs vastly from the predominant method employed in modern literary society, where the text is usually taken home and read silently by an individual in private. Reading today is a private matter to stay in for: in the ancient world literature was more often a reason to go out. As Kenney (1982, 12) puts it: 'a book of poetry or artistic prose was not simply a text in the modern sense but something like a score for public or private performance', although we do also see evidence of people 'reading' texts to themselves (e.g. Aristophanes *Frogs* 52-3, and Caecilius' unnamed girlfriend in poem 35: see further Knox 1985, 9). What is notable is that even private reading was not usually silent: when Caesar was found to be reading silently it was commented on as something extraordinary (Knox 1968).

Roman poets like Catullus, unlike dramatists or orators, did not have a natural opportunity to display their works in public and so had to arrange readings if they were to have a 'public' at all. They could hire a hall and perform to anybody who cared to come: they could recite their works at dinner-parties (as Trimalchio recites verse at his dinner in Petronius' *Satyricon*): or they could have their works recited in the baths or even on the street. Reciting poems to a small group of friends and inviting their critical comments was a well-established custom (cf. Cicero *Q. Fr.* 3.5; Horace (*Ars P.* 386-390) recommends nine years of such informal 'advice' before letting the work loose on a wider public). Publishing in the modern sense of producing multiple copies of a text was of course also done – but the exercise was costly in terms of both money and of needing educated slave copyists. Cicero's friend Atticus was perhaps the first Roman to go into publishing as a business venture, and there were large libraries both private (e.g. that of Piso or Lucullus) and public (the first one being the Pollio library founded in 39 BC). Poetry could be bought and sold: Horace claims that no bookseller will let *his* poems be mauled by sweaty hands (*Sat.* 1.4.71-2): and might even (horror of horrors) end up as a school text-book (Horace *Epist.* 1.20.17-18); Propertius speaks of Virgil's *Aeneid* becoming a classic text (2.34.65-6) before Virgil was dead. Catullus (14.17) talks of buying up the works of bad poets from the bookstalls. The advantage of being published in book form is that the writer reaches a much wider audience than recitation could find – libraries were later placed all over the Roman world and carried Roman literature as far as St Albans, and so Catullus' confidence that Cinna's *Zmyrna* will travel far (poem 95) may not be misplaced or hyperbolic – but had the disadvantage that the author lost control of the reception of his text which might be 'mauled' in performance just as Horace fears the book will be mauled at the bookshop. Horace (as often) puts the matter neatly: *nescit uox missa reuerti* – 'once sent out, the voice cannot come back' (*Ars P.* 390: cf. *Epist.* 1.20.6, Martial 1.3). Once the text was in the public domain, it became the property of the public and left authorial control for ever so that anyone who wanted could get a text copied for himself: plagiarism was an ever-present danger in a society with no such thing as copyright law, although (paradoxically) publication did at least assert the authorship of the text and might actually protect against plagiarism (Kenney 1982, 19, citing Pliny *Ep.* 2.10.3, Martial 1.29, 1.66, 2.20); and the only way in which corrections could be made to a text once published was to issue a new text going back on the first.

Writers throughout the ages have complained of being poorly paid, and one wonders why they bothered to have their work published at all as the financial rewards in the Roman world were so derisory. Horace (*Ars P.* 345) and Martial (10.74.7) lament the fact that the publisher makes money from their text but they see precious little of it, and there were really only the following options for the Roman writer: either 1) enjoy patronage and be paid for producing work which the patron wanted (or writing poems which decline to do so (*recusationes*)), such as seems to have happened in the case of Maecenas with his generous support of the poets Horace, Virgil, Propertius and others; or 2) have private income and not need the money; or else 3) suffer poverty and live off the dole like any other *cliens* (Juvenal 1.134). Most scholars assume that Catullus fell into the second category: his background and life-style seems to have been well-to-do (full details in Fordyce ix–xiv) – although he pleads poverty (13.8) – and he found himself moving in the circles of political figures such as Memmius and Caesar. His dedicatee is Cornelius Nepos but it is generally believed that Nepos was a literary supporter rather than a financial backer. Wiseman (1985, 126) goes so far as to say: 'Catullus was a man of substance, far from the necessity of earning patronage by his pen; he wrote for a cultured élite, and despised the popular taste (95.10)'.

Catullus, to be sure, does not refer in his poems to recitation as the mode of reception, but then neither does Virgil. Catullus does refer to his poems being written down as notes on wax-tablets (e.g. 42, 50) but the tone of these poems makes it clear that the notes are sketches rather than the finished item which was produced as a proper book 'polished with pumice-stone' (1.2). The whole point of poem 42 is that the poet is angry that his first jottings have left his safe keeping and may be being mocked or copied elsewhere, the additional irony being that this poem is itself a finished product even though it treats of first jottings. We are surely justified in assuming that the text we have is the finished product and that these poems were to be received by a listener rather than a silent reader of the book. All ancient writers wrote for an audience, and these poems are as much as performance as any other ancient text.

NEOTERIC POETRY

Catullus was hardly a lone poetic voice in Rome at the time, nor was he the first. There was abundant literature before him in Latin – epic poetry, satire, comedy, tragedy, farce, historical writing, etc. – and before that there was the massive – and the massively influential – wealth of literature from Greece. It was not uncommon for poets to claim originality (cf. Lucretius 1.926-30, Horace *Odes* 3.30.13-14) and the Catullan circle of poets which we now know as the 'New Poets' (*noui poetae*, the Neoterics) clearly felt that they were writing literature of a new and original kind, but it is worth recalling (however briefly) some of the literary predecessors whose work they must have read and imitated.

One obvious source of influence on Catullus was the sort of poetry written in Greek Elegy and Iambus in the seventh and sixth centuries B.C. Poets such as Archilochus and Hipponax in particular established a style of composition which Catullus imitates and develops: Hipponax invented the metrical scazon (used frequently by Catullus) and used it to devastating effect in poems of sexual frankness and outspoken abuse of his enemies, abuse ranging from relatively mild charges against his friends to stronger accusations against his enemies, and Archilochus writes with frankness of his own (sometimes disreputable) behaviour such as throwing away his shield (cf. Mankin 6–9, CHCL vol.1, 117–128, 158–64). Archilochus' verbal assault on Lycambes and his daughters caused them all (so the story runs) to hang themselves in shame: and even though this story is dubious it does at least credit poetry with a power which is surprising and shocking. So when Catullus attacks his friends for minor indiscretions such as taking a napkin (12) or his enemies for a range of sexual perversions (the Gellius and Mamurra poems, for example) we might be reading the attacks of an Archilochus or Hipponax against his *bête noire* Bupalus: and when Catullus describes his meeting with his mistress in poem 68 or looks forward to 'nine consecutive fuckifications' with Ipsitilla in poem 32, he is working in a tradition of sexual frankness of which an early example turned up in 1974 in the 'Cologne fragment' of Archilochus (fr. 196a West); a text in which the poet describes his seduction of the younger sister of his former beloved; this fragment interestingly combines the account of the poet's sexual conquest with abuse of the older sister (as promiscuous and past it) which in turn looks forward to the 'abuse-poems' of Catullus (43, 58-9 etc.) and Horace (e.g. *Epod.* 8 and 12). In poem 40 Catullus uses the literary term *iambos* to denote precisely this sort of Archilochean verse attack on his enemies: and we know that this poetry (now only fragmentary) was still very much read in the Alexandrian period and later.

The poets of the Early Greek Elegy and Iambus were capable, as we have seen, of astonishing obscenity and frankness: they could also write with feeling and emotion. Archilochus' description of the passion of love stands comparison with Sappho and Catullus 51:

'I lie struck down by desire, lifeless, penetrated through my bones by the bitter pains of the gods' (fr. 193)

and the Cologne fragment manages to convey both delicate tenderness and erotic directness with blithe unselfconsciousness:

'Taking the girl I laid her down among the flowers, covered her with a soft cloak, holding her neck in the crook of my arm ... she like a fawn ... I gently touched her breasts with my hands where my assault bared the new skin of her youth for me: feeling all her beautiful body I shot my white strength, just touching her blonde hair.'

Catullus will also have been familiar with the lyric poetry of Sappho, Alcaeus, Anacreon, Ibycus and so on, poets whose works combine a deceptively 'honest' tone suggesting 'real' feelings with the high artistry of the professional singer and performer. Both traditions were fully studied and developed in what is very much the crucible for much of Roman literature, the literary world of Alexandria.

The Egyptian city of Alexandria (founded by Alexander the Great) was, in the time of Catullus, 'the greatest city in the world' (Wiseman 1985, 54). In the period from 280 to 240 B.C., as the cultural centre of the Greeks, Alexandria was the birthplace of some of the greatest literature produced in the ancient world. Poets such as Callimachus, Theocritus and Apollonius Rhodius reacted to the literature which preceded them and determined to be more than mere epigones: and it was their poetics and their example which inspired the Neoterics in Rome two centuries later.

Reading Alexandrian literature is not always easy. These writers expected their readers to have a wide vocabulary and an even wider range of background knowledge with which to understand their works. The techniques of allusion to other literature and sometimes recondite periphrases to denote people and places suggests that this was literature meant for 'literati', not for the man in the street. Finally, the Alexandrian writers appear to have cultivated an aesthetic of 'art for art's sake' which was in conscious reaction against the didacticism of earlier poetry, whose usefulness was traditionally accounted for in terms of the good advice or moral instruction it provided (Russell 1981, 84-98). Paradoxically, the Alexandrians produced the most thoroughly didactic poets of all – Nicander of Colophon's didactic epics on *Venomous Reptiles* and *Antidotes to Poisons* for instance – but the studied didacticism of these works fooled nobody. They were hardly manuals for the hill-walker, but ingenious and artistic exercises designed to show off the skill of the poet in his ability to transform anything into refined verse. No longer did the poet concern himself with 'high' style and 'high' society, telling great tales of kings and heroes, either: the Alexandrians show a keen interest in the feelings and the everyday lives of 'ordinary' people. Alexandrian poetry gave its readers a new angle on old legends, the delightful detail rather than the thunder of grandeur, the artistic word-order and exquisite euphony which repays repeated readings, the arch periphrases and allusions, the refusal to employ a straight linear narrative and the complex symmetry of construction.

So who were the poets whom we call 'neoterics'? We only have the term 'New Poets' from a critical remark of Cicero; in 50 B.C., Cicero wrote to Atticus (*Att.* 7.2.1) 'We came to Brundisium on the 24th November after having your special luck in seafaring – so fair for me

> *flauit ab Epiro lenissimus Onchesmites*
>
> ('blew from Epirus the gentlest Onchesmites').

That verse with its spondaic ending you could pass off as yours or any of the 'newer poets' you like.'

The word Cicero uses for 'new poets' is Greek, and the word he uses for 'spondaic' is also in Greek: this immediately suggests that the poets referred to used Greek terminology and Greek literary ideas in their writing. When we look at the line which Cicero composed, it displays the following features which (again) we can ascribe to the poets he is parodying: it is a line of hexameter verse (the metre used for epics both great and small) and it has an unusual spondaic fifth foot (see below on metres): the final two feet are entirely occupied by a single four-syllable word – in fact the entire line consists of only four words (counting *ab-Epiro* as a single item). There is the choice of vocabulary, with Onchesmus in Epirus being used to coin a word (only found here) to denote a breeze from that south-western part of Epirus, a coinage which relies on the reader's knowledge to make the line make sense: there is the gentle alliteration of the letter *s* to support the blowing of the breeze. It is as good a line as many which we find in the extant remains of the New Poets, and it is hardly surprising that Cicero (who wrote poetry himself) was quietly proud of it. If we examine the text of Catullus we find similar features to the ones which Cicero produced: the fifth-foot spondee (76.15, 64.3), the learned reference (95.5), the line created out of a very few words (6.11, 38.8, 100.1), the long proper name to conclude a line (116.2, 66.66), and so on.

The group of poets around Catullus of whom we know the names were: Calvus, Cinna, Cato and Cornificius, and of their works only fragments remain. That they formed a 'school' is open to doubt (see Lyne (1978) who argues that they were not unique in their choice of poetic practice) but they certainly seemed to have composed a similar range of poetry: epigrams, wedding-songs, occasional verse in a variety of metres with erotic, obscene, humorous or satirical content. The poetic form most obviously favoured by these poets was the new form (in Latin) of the short epic or *epyllion* (on the history of the term see Most) such as poem 64 of Catullus or the *Zmyrna* of Cinna, the *Io* of Calvus, the *Glaucus* of Cornificius, the *Diana* of Valerius Cato, the *Dindymi Dominam* of Caecilius (mentioned in poem 35): this sort of poem was minutely crafted in form (the *Zmyrna* took nine years to write, according to Catullus (95.1-2)) and would be original in content – looking at a familiar story from an unfamiliar viewpoint, as had been done in Callimachus' *Hecale*, or switching to another story by means of an *ecphrasis* as in the Theseus and Ariadne episode in Catullus poem 64. The subject matter was often love, especially 'pathological' love such as that of a girl for her father (*Zmyrna*) or of a mortal for a sea-nymph (Catullus 64), or of a merman sea-god who fell for the nymph Scylla (*Glaucus*), or the mysterious world of Cybele as expounded in Caecilius' *Dindymi Dominam* (and by Catullus in 63), all the sort of stories which could be found in the Greek poet Parthenius' *erotica pathemata*, a work with a great influence on poets of this generation. The interest in pathological love which we find in these short epics is mirrored also in the pathological love which we also find in the short poems where the poet expresses the sort of feelings which elsewhere (e.g. 64.132-201) are put into the mouths of mythological heroines and heroes.

The short epic does not aim to tell the whole story, but rather expects the reader to know the whole story and to be able to appreciate the artistry of the poet who has sculpted what appears to be a miniature fragment of it in such unfragmentary perfection. This leads us on to another major Alexandrian feature: learning (*doctrina*). Alexandrian literature demands knowledge of history, geography and mythology and teases and flatters the reader with its arch allusive style: Catullus, who was later termed *doctus* by Martial (1.61.1, 14.100) and Ovid (*Am.* 3.9.63), alludes to such things as literary history (e.g. *Battiades* 116.2), geography (4.6-15, 7.4, 11.5-12), mythology (e.g. *Thyonianus* in 27.7). More striking still is the poet's use of contrasting themes (faithful friends vs unfaithful woman, for instance, in 11) and his interest in the bizarre (90), the obscure (66), the unexpected (the shifts of feeling and perspective in 8, the self-mockery in 10), and the aesthetic concentration on the poems as things in themselves which can wound (12.10-11, 40.2) or bless with immortality (6.16-17) or curse with notoriety (40) and whose creation can render the poet sleepless with excitement (50) and the reader mad with lust (35). It is worth lingering over the poems in which Catullus speaks of poetry itself to develop a picture of his notion of the importance of poetry and of the interaction with other poets.

Many literary 'groups' define themselves negatively by contrasting their own practice with that of other (inferior) writers, as Callimachus famously did in his influential preface to the *Aitia*. Catullus defines the 'good poetry' of himself and his friends primarily by contrast to the 'poor poetry' of long-winded, bombastic epic which (he claims, as Horace also claims later (*Sat.* 1.4)) was turned out by the yard by inferior poets with no talent except stamina. In poem 36 he (effectively) calls the *Annals* of Volusius a waste of paper (cf. 95.8 where the same point is made wittily) and the contrast of their style is evinced in the Catullan style of prayer (36.11-15) with its learned religious references over against the poetry of Volusius which is (he says) 'full of the countryside'. Catullus is (at it were) showing off how Volusius should be writing. Suffenus is similarly derided in poem 22 for the elegant (and expensive) appearance of his book hiding the 'rustic' contents which are prodigiously long: another waste of good money and paper (although the ending of this poem is interestingly modest and rather reduces the polemical tone). A parcel of such bad poetry is seen in poem 14 as deserving a counter-blast both in the poem itself and in a return parcel of named bad poets. In poem 50 we see the poet recalling a session of poetry-writing with Calvus and the emphasis throughout is on the contrast between the 'lightness' (*uersiculos*) and 'playfulness' (*lusimus*) of the verse and the very serious effects it had on the poet whose passionate response (*dolorem*) is one more appropriate to a lover. This sort of verse may be 'slender' and light, but that does not mean it is not to be taken seriously – quite the reverse, for all the poet's self-effacing talk of 'trifling efforts' (*nugas* 1.4). Poetry is called for when in a depressed state (38) or is needed to punish the wrongdoer (40). Poem 35 is a brilliant combination of the 'invitation' poem with praise of the poet's friend's success with the girls and also praise of his poetry: Caecilius is called a *poeta tener* ('love-poet' a term applied later by Horace (*Ars P.* 333) to Propertius) who writes *uenuste* – and so inspires love (of which Venus was the goddess) in his female readers. The contrast of the slender elegant miniature epic (which will travel far and live long) with the flatulent epic of lesser poets (which will get no further than the local river and end up wrapping mackerel) is made explicit in poem 95 where Cinna's *Zmyrna* is contrasted with (again) Volusius' *Annales*. Interestingly, the poem also contrasts the new poetry with Greek poetry of several centuries before: Antimachus, whose poem *Lyde* was described by Callimachus (fr. 398Pf) as 'fat and inelegant' is said by Catullus to be 'swollen' (*tumido*). What this shows is that Greek poetry was very much still in constant circulation, and that Callimachus' opinion on Antimachus was copied word for word by Catullus. This contrast of the elegant literature of a Callimachus and the boorish alternative is the note on which our collection ends, as Catullus expresses his determination to use the weapons of the mudslinger rather than throw pearls before swine. The book thus closes with a further affirmation of the Callimachean literary values of elegance, wit, grace, brevity and charm. We receive the impression that Catullus formed a bond of solidarity with other poets of like mind (*sodalis* 95.9) and they established a bond of hostility towards poets who did not share their Alexandrian love of the exquisite miniature.

Key words mark out the aesthetic landscape which Catullus and his fellow-poets inhabit. Most Roman poets aspire to the Alexandrian quality of 'learning' (*doctrina*) and Catullus is no exception: but he also uses a range of aesthetic terms which are characteristic of his group. Terms such as *lepidus* ('delightful') and *uenustus* ('lovely') occur twelve and eleven times respectively, *bellus* ('pretty') turns up fifteen times; these indicate a policy of *l'art pour l'art* rather than any didactic message. Wit and cleverness are vital: the poet praises *sal* ('salt', metaphor for 'wit') nine times and the term *facetus* ('clever') occurs six times, as the poetry strives to impress for its originality and humour as much as for its technique – note also the approving use of *nouus* ('new') right at the start of the first poem. The opposites of these terms are heaped as insults on the heads of the poets and people who are not in the same circle – so *illepidus, inuenustus, insulsus, infacetus* are all applied to people who cross the poet's path artistically (e.g. 22.14) or who offend for their stupidity (e.g. 17.12) or behaviour (10.32, 12.5). Constantly in the poems the polar opposition is drawn between the city and the country: good poets and clever people are *urbanus* (39.10) while the dolt and the blockhead is *rusticus* (e.g. 22.9–10, 36.19).

This poet distances himself and his work from the simple and blunt and lays claim to refinement and artistry, even when (as often) the obscene content of the text strikes many modern readers as far more 'blunt' and crude than 'refined' and 'urbane'. As we have seen, this tradition of poetic obscenity goes back a long way to the early Greek poets of the 7th century B.C., and we find poetry both personal and public (Old Comedy, for instance) using obscene words and concepts freely. The sexual world of the Romans, as described by Wiseman (1985, 10–14) and Fitzgerald (61–4), seems to have been markedly different from our own and the expression of sexual and excremental humour certainly seems to have been uninhibited and not restrained by the same taboos as apply to many modern societies. Some of the obscene language used in this text is threatening – the poet (or his subjects) bringing male sexual aggression to express anger and a desire to dominate their enemies, such as in poems 15, 16 and 28. Some of it imputes sexual impotence – or incompetence – to the poet's enemies so that they are cuckolded (e.g. 17, 78); and some of it accuses the enemy of engaging in scatological acts which both amuse and disgust the reader (e.g. poems 88, 98) or engaging in incest (89-91) or passive homosexuality (112). The 'unclean mouth' (cf. Fitzgerald 63) is a regular theme in these obscene poems (e.g. 80, 97), as is the use of obscenity to provide 'punch-lines' with which to end poems (e.g. 56). The composition of erotic poetry was not something to be ashamed of – even Pliny indulges in this pastime (*Ep.* 5.3.2) and names plenty of other Romans who shared his interest – but neither was it to be taken as evidence of a *louche* lifestyle.   ˍ

INTERPRETATIVE STRATEGIES

Reading poetry is a many-sided business, and all critics have their own stance and attitude towards the text they claim to serve. This section will discuss the different strategies adopted by editors towards these poems and will seek to justify the critical stance which has been adopted in this edition.

The easiest way to read a poem is to see it simply as a record of the poet's own life. If Catullus writes a rude poem to Gellius, then he must have fallen out with a real man called Gellius and been spurred into composing this poem to declare it. His poetry expresses feelings which are real and the situation which they describe is also real. There must have been a 'real' Lesbia to inspire these love-poems and we can chart his affair with her from the poems. This 'biographical' school of criticism treats the poems as documents of real life and has had a good deal of attention paid to it: Quinn, for instance, can confidently assert on poem 103 that it is 'a note of complaint to Silo, a pimp who has turned nasty. C. offers him an alternative ...'. In its most developed form it prompts scholars to try to map out the life-story of the poet from his poetry, as in the well-known theory that poem 51 was the first missive from Catullus to 'Lesbia'. It is hard to imagine a poet composing an elegy to a dead brother if his brother had not died: and many scholars have been so impressed by the passion and self-effacing honesty of his love-poetry that they state quite categorically that 'Catullus' love-poetry springs from his life' (Lyne (1980) 20).

This line of approach is seriously flawed as a strategy for interpreting poetry. Much of the space in the existing commentaries concerns itself with trying to identify the 'real' Gellius or especially the real Lesbia, and one can often come away with the impression that we are then engaged in historical rather than literary research. We all like to learn facts about the lives of writers and artists, but this activity should not be confused with critical assessment of their works. Nobody, for instance, would treat biographical information about Mozart as a guide to one of his symphonies. For another thing, the assumption that poem 103 is an adequate response to a dishonest brothel-keeper is naive in the extreme: do brothel-keepers read poems? Would such a man be stung into playing the game because of a few elegiac couplets circulated among a few poets? Just as it is hard to believe that the *Epistles* of Horace -- or Pliny for that matter – are 'real' letters like those of Cicero, so also it is difficult to allow the documentary view of Catullus to be seen as an adequate response to the text. Poets, like artists, need something to write about, and their success or failure as artists does not depend in any way on the 'truth' of their words but on the artistic criteria which they set themselves and which are set for them by the reading public. Catullus in fact explicitly denies that his 'art' has anything to do with his private life in poem 16 where he comically threatens his detractors who draw conclusions about the man from his works. Poets *qua* people are bound by moral standards, but poems are not. In the final analysis, poets are ultimately wordsmiths who create poetry, not exhibitionists who parade their lives in public. The romantic assumption that poets are possessed by a feeling and then seek to give this expression in a poetic form is not necessarily true to life: often the poet will experiment with a form (the Sapphic stanza, say, or the hendecasyllabic) and need to find an appropriate 'feeling' to put into it. If in the course of doing so he uncovers 'genuine' feelings inside himself (of which he may have been unaware) that is something else: but his writing of poetry can be motivated by artistic rather than personal reasons.

This is not to deny, however, the New Historicist view that texts are in some measure written against a social and political background of power-structures. Catullus, we noted earlier, does not write theoretical texts on political matters: but his choice of subject matter is hardly neutral and indicates a certain apolitical stance which can be read as a gesture of impatience with the futility of political action in the age of the generals. Indeed it could easily be argued that the aggression of his tone is the voice of a poet seeking to wound with words in an age where weapons gleamed – and his studied indifference to Caesar (poem 93) is anything but genuine indifference (which does not bother to write poems) but rather a conscious attempt to wound the pride of the man who commanded such respect elsewhere – and that the 'soft' image of the poet masks a need to assert his power as a writer. Similarly, what he has to say about sexual politics – both heterosexual and homosexual – has its own subtext which reflects his position in a historical milieu which Wiseman has well described (Wiseman 1985, 1–14). Male sexuality is seen as aggressive and threateningly violent and the poet sees himself as passively 'shafted' by Memmius (poem 28.9-10) as well as actively shafting others (16.1–2, 56.6–7). His adoration of the girl whom he calls Lesbia or the youth Iuventius contradicts this machismo somewhat by presenting them as either his equal (poem 5) or else someone whose power over him he resents and despises himself for (8, 76, 99). The poetry can be read against the background of Roman society as an expression of a culture many of whose aspects we no longer share. At a more basic level the picture which the poetry presents of a *jeunesse dorée* ardent in love and poetry tells us something about the *otium* which poem 51 bemoans, and the awareness of earlier Latin and Greek literature tells us a good deal about the level of literary education available to a young man of the time.

Other features of the poetry have the effect of distancing the poet and his reader from any direct contact with either the life of the poet or of his age. The intertextual context of these poems is of great interest to the critic and something which no commentary can afford to ignore. If – to take an obvious example – a writer in English were to have a character suddenly say 'to be or not to be' we are at once alerted to a level of irony in what he is saying. Catullus was writing for an educated audience who would similarly pick up at once when he refers to the works of earlier writers in Latin and Greek, and the parallel passages which the commentary cites are to make these intertextual references clear to the reader as they would have been to the poet's Roman audience. The echoing of earlier works is not plagiarism of their work – as if the poet could pass the lines off as his own original work – but rather engaging with the past in a conscious attempt to mark out the poet's own contribution to the literary tradition, as is most easily seen in the opening of 64 with its repeated allusions to earlier versions of the Argo legend, (a legend which poem 64 is going to subvert) as seen by Thomas and discussed by Hinds (2, 18) or else in his rereading of Sappho in poem 51 (well discussed in Fowler 1993, 245-8). The *doctrina* which we discussed earlier is no idle parade of learning but a statement of literary principle which places Catullus in a stance of commitment to a whole set of Alexandrian ideals and which has the effect of filtering the 'story' being told through the lens of irony.

There is then the ordering of the poems within the book. If one examines the collection as it has come down to us it falls into three sections: polymetric poems (1-60), 'long poems' (61-68) and elegiac poems (69-116). Within these broad groupings the poet seems to have consciously produced contrasts of tone and style between adjoining poems. Poems 5 and 7 (love-poems addressed by the poet in his own *persona*) are separated by poem 6 (the lover Flavius as seen by others), giving an ironic view of the poet himself by comparison and contrast with Flavius who is to Catullus as 'Catullus' is to us. Similarly poem 96 (a highly emotional consolation to the bereaved Calvus) is followed by the humorous and scatological poem 97: 'life must go on ...'. Sometimes there is ironic distance between poems – the same Catullus who disapproves so strongly of adultery in 61. 97-99 is himself a happy adulterer in 68. 145-6 – sometimes within a single poem different attitudes are struck (the heroic *virtutes* in 64.51 turn out to be far from heroic in the depiction of Theseus). There are sequences of poems – the Lesbia poems and the Iuventius poems, for instance – but the reader is not allowed to linger on any one person or theme for long and the writer studiously avoids monotony in his ordering of the collection. In the collection as a whole our expectations are constantly being foiled.

There is also the matter of closure which is a vital 'framing' device much discussed at present (see Roberts, Dunn and Fowler 1997). Many of the poems end, for instance, with the poet himself, leaving us with a note of ironic self-reference as a closural gesture which is almost his signature at the foot of the page as it leaves the reader in awe both of the 'enclosed' perfection of the art and therefore also of the skill of the artist: see for instance the generalising endings of poem 22, the summarising ending of poem 45, the cartoon ending of poem 39 (where we finally discover just why Egnatius' teeth are so white) or 88, the exclamatory ending of 43, the personal ending to the 'impersonal' epyllion 64 or the impersonal ending to the personal poem 70, ring-composition as in poem 16 and 99, and so on (on this see Peden). There is also the device of false closure where we think that the poem has finished when in fact it will continue (see e.g. poem 8, discussed by Fowler 1989, 98-101) or else where we find a poem promising 'future' poems at the end of the whole collection (poem 116). The constant revaluation of stances and sentiments which the collection of separate poems yields has the effect of making all the poems within it 'open' and (in particular) open to further comment later on: the poet who expresses love in one poem (5) will later express hatred (85) and then love again (87). Above all, the poet's habit of addressing or referring to himself as 'Catullus' creates an openness which resists the easy option of seeing the text as transparent and enclosed: the very artificiality of the self-address calls attention to the pose being struck. As Veyne powerfully expressed the matter: 'Catullus calls to himself under the name Catullus, but this is just a fiction, for after all, we really do not address ourselves by name and say to ourselves "Listen, Veyne, stop this foolishness". Catullus took his own name, Catullus, as his stage name.' (Veyne, 174, quoted Fowler 1993, 246). The comparison is made of the poet's use of his name with that of the pop-singer, who appears to be voicing his deepest feelings but who is in fact performing for an audience an artificial piece which may have no relation to his own life.

Reading the text in this way as an ironic artefact can preserve the awareness of the artistry involved while avoiding the danger of seeing the whole thing as merely intellectual play: sure, the poet has 'made it all up' – but then so do all lovers and all artists. The slippage between stances adopted, the self-awareness of having both said and heard it all before and of the artifice involved in writing this sort of poetry is a given of the writer's condition then as much as it is now, and the ironic attitude is thus the recognition of this and the exploration of the only 'reality' – i.e. contingent, fluid appearances – which is available to any of us. Part of the peculiar fascination and value of these poems lies precisely in the fluidity and inscrutability of the stances adopted, even where – especially where – they seem most 'moral' and didactic, as at the end of poem 64 or in poem 76. The stance may be 'sincere' in the old-fashioned sense (in that it may accord with a genuine feeling of the poet's), but its expression in a work of high art can never be interpreted without consideration of the form in which the feelings are couched, its context set in a sequence of poems and its intertext – which almost always set the sentiments expressed in a distanced frame of irony. This reading forces the content of the poems to lack 'foundation' in that they are here not being presented simply as 'facts' but visions and fantasies spun in words and encountered in two-dimensional shape on the page: and the words themselves are loose and insubstantial, constantly open to questions of meaning and tone, frequently slipping into invisible quotation marks as attitudes are struck and images cast. This method of reading does not, however, follow the principles of the

New Criticism to its ultimate end, whereby the poem is not to be judged by reference to any criteria beyond itself, if only because the resonance of many of the words used by Catullus (*amicitia* for instance, or *pietas*) cannot be appreciated without reference to criteria of historical and philosophical enquiry and because the individual poet is not an island entire unto himself but a member of a large intertextual procession. If, after all, the old style of 'biographical' criticism – which saw the text as the 'confessions' of the author – tended to produce authors without works, the New Criticism, by refusing to allow the historical and literary setting of the author any place at all in the interpretation of his works, produced works without authors, as Doubrovsky well put it (Doubrovsky 114).

THE METRES

Latin poetry is written in a fairly rigid system of metres, all of which in turn relies on the 'quantity' of each vowel as being either long or short, a long vowel being reckoned to take twice as long to pronounce as a short vowel. A syllable is reckoned to be a single vowel sound, followed either by nothing (an 'open' syllable) or by a consonant (a 'closed' syllable): usually a single consonant following a vowel is reckoned to be the first consonant of the following syllable (e.g. *ca-li-gi-ne*) and does not affect the length of the vowel: but where two or more consonants follow a vowel, the first one is included in the first syllable (*men-sa*) which is thus 'closed' and becomes lengthened – the exceptions being combinations of mute and liquid consonants (*b, c, g, p, t* followed by *r; c, p, t,* followed by *l*) are considered as belonging to the following syllable (*ma-tris*) and need not lengthen the vowel. Diphthongs (*ae, eu, au,* etc.) are always long by nature: single vowels may be long or short by nature and may vary with inflection (e.g. the final -*a* of *mensa* is long by nature in the ablative case, short in the nominative) or they may be lengthened by position when followed by two or more consonants as indicated above (e.g. 83.4 *esset nunc* where the (short) final *e* of *esset* is followed by *tn*- and so lengthened). In cases where a word ending with a vowel (or a vowel + *m* such as *iustam*) is followed by a word beginning with a vowel or *h*, the two syllables usually merge ('elide') into a single syllable, as at 59.4 *deuolutum ex* is scanned as *deuolut(um) ex* (four syllables).

This collection of poems employs many different metres, the main ones being: hendecasyllabics (all but 17 of poems 1-60) and elegiac couplets (69-116). In what follows the following signs are used:

—   means a long syllable
∪   means a short syllable
x   means a syllable which may be either long or short
//   means the caesura (word-end in the middle of a foot of a hexameter).

Elegiac couplets
This metre, as its name suggests, composes lines in pairs: the first line of the couplet is always a hexameter, while the second is a pentameter. This metre was used a great deal by earlier Greek poets.

The **hexameter** is the 'epic' metre used by Homer and all later epic poets. The line is divided into six 'feet', each of which is either a dactyl (a long syllable followed by two short syllables (–∪∪ in conventional notation)) or a spondee (two long syllables (– –)). The last foot is always dissyllabic, the last syllable of all being either long or short. Thus a 'typical' hexameter line will run:

–∪∪/–   –/–   //   –/– – / – ∪∪ /– –/

Péliacó quondám // prognátae uértice pínus

where the ´ sign indicates the stressed syllable at the beginning of a foot and the // sign shows the 'caesura' – the word-break in the middle of a foot – usually the third.

Latin also had a stress accent, whereby most words were stressed on the penultimate syllable, or on the antepenultimate if the penultimate were a short vowel. Thus the first line of poem 85 would be spoken:

ódi ét ámo; quáre íd fáciam fortásse requíris

but 'scanned' metrically as:

ódi et amó; quare íd faciám fortásse requíris

Quite how the two ways of reading Latin verse blended or competed is unclear: one notes that in hexameters there is a tendency for the stress accent and the metrical ictus to collide in the earlier and middle parts of the line but to coincide at the end – a tendency which is however abruptly broken when the line ends with a monosyllable as at 83.5.

The **pentameter** is literally five feet, but is conventionally composed in two halves, each of two dactylic/spondaic feet followed by a single syllable. The second half of the pentameter is in the overwhelming majority of cases dactylic (i.e. two dactyls followed by a single syllable). The pentameter thus runs:

– –/ – –/– // –∪∪ /–∪ ∪/∪

ét dis / ínuit/is // désinis / ésse mi/sér

Elegiac couplets tend to be complete sense-making units; enjambement from the hexameter to the following pentameter is common (cf. e.g. 76.1–2) but only rarely do we find enjambement from the pentameter into the next hexameter (110.6–7, 66. 24-5 are examples).

Glyconics/Pherecrateans
This is the metre used in the Marriage Song 61 and the hymn to Diana in 34. It is made up of three glyconics followed by a pherecratean. The basic colon is the choriamb (–∪∪–), found in both the glyconic and the pherecratean, metres very similar in form as follows:

Glyconic: –X –∪∪– ∪–
Pherecratean: –X –∪∪– –

In practice, the second syllable of both metres is virtually always short, although there are exceptions (e.g. 61.175).

    – **x**– ∪ ∪   – ∪ – (glyconic)
montium domin(a) ut fores...
    – **x** – ∪ ∪ – – (pherecratean).
amniumque sonantum

Catullus – like his predecessor Anacreon but unlike Horace later on – observes strict synaphea both in 61 and 34 – i.e. the stanza is the metrical unit, with no hiatus between lines except at the ending of a stanza, lines ending with a vowel eliding into the next line within the stanza (e.g. 34.11-12, 61. 135-6); the few occasions where synaphea is not observed make one wonder (at the risk of *petitio principii*) whether the text is sound. There is even one example of a word split across two lines (61. 46-7).

Priapean is used once in this collection (poem 17) and consists of a glyconic followed by a pherecratean as follows:

    – **x** –∪∪ – ∪ – (glyconic)   – **x** – ∪∪ – – (pherecratean)
o colonia quae cupis   *ponte ludere longo*

Some editors (e.g. Lee) print the text of this poem in 'half-lines' as above.

Sapphic stanza
This is used in two poems (11, 51) and consists of three sapphics followed by an adonean, as follows:

    –∪ – – – ∪ ∪– ∪ – –
ille mi par esse deo uidetur
    – ∪ – – – ∪ ∪ –∪ –∪ –
ille si fas est superare diuos
    – ∪ – – – ∪ ∪ –∪ – –
qui sedens adversus identidem te
    – ∪ ∪ – **x**
spectat et audit

Hendecasyllabics
The majority of the 'polymetric' poems (1-60) are composed in this metre, an eleven-syllable line similar to the glyconic and the sapphic and scanned as follows:

    x x – ∪∪ – ∪ – ∪– **x**
cui dono lepidum nouum libellum

The first two syllables are either –∪, – –, or else ∪– (but never ∪∪).

Iambic trimeters are found in poems 4, 29, 52: in poems 4 and 29 the scheme is:

    ∪ –/∪ –/∪ –/ ∪ –/∪ –/ ∪ **x**
phaselus ille quem uidetis hospites

whereas in poem 52 the scheme allows slightly more metrical freedom:

x –/ ∪ –/ x   –/∪ – / ∪ –/∪x
per consulatum peierat Vatinius

Choliambics or Scazons ('limping iambics') are used in poem 8, 22, 39, 44, 59, 60 and consist of five iambs followed by either a trochee or a spondee. The metre was invented by the Greek poet Hipponax, and the final reversal of metrical stress places a sudden emphasis on the final two syllables of the line.

x –/ ∪–/ x   –/∪–/∪– / – x
miser Catulle, desinas inep/tíre

Iambic tetrameter catalectic is found only in poem 25. The term 'tetrameter' indicates that the line is made up of four 'metra' each of two iambs: 'catalectic' indicates that the final syllable of the last iamb is suppressed, as follows:

x – / ∪ –/ ∪ –/ ∪–/ x –/∪–/ x – / x
cinaede Thalle mollior cuniculi /capil/lo

Greater Asclepiad is only found here in poem 30:

– –   – ∪ ∪ –   – ∪∪– – ∪ ∪ –∪x
Alfen(e) immemor atq(ue) unanimis false sodalibus

THE TRANSMISSION OF THE TEXT

We have no certain knowledge of the form of Catullus' original text. He describes his work as a 'little book' (1.1) which rather suggests that the text we have was originally divided up into books – most obviously into three sections: 1-60 (about 900 lines of polymetric poems), 61-64 (840 lines: long poems) and then 65-116 (660 lines of elegiacs). Any one of these groups would make a 'little book' (*libellus*) while the whole collection would be far too big to deserve the name. This (of course) presupposes that the poet himself 'edited' and 'published' his work – another assumption in need of evidence. There is ample evidence of care in the ordering of the these poems, but of course that ordering need not have been carried out by the poet himself.

Our texts of Latin and Greek literature have in many cases survived only by near-miracles. The original written texts of the poet were copied laboriously by hand by scribes in the Roman world, and when the West entered what we now call the Dark Ages the copying of texts became the job of monasteries. Some authors survived comfortably with large numbers of manuscripts still extant: others only made it by the skin of their teeth. Catullus was one of the latter.

Poem 62 was very lucky: there is one manuscript surviving from the ninth century which contains it, the *codex Thuaneus* (*T*) now kept in Paris. This was an

anthology of passages from Catullus, Martial, Juvenal and Seneca belonging to a
certain Jacques-Auguste de Thou.   For the rest we are indebted to a single
manuscript of the poems which came to the poet's home town of Verona at the start
of the fourteenth century. This manuscript, now known as *Codex Veronensis* or *V*,
contained everything we have of Catullus and its loss would have destroyed almost
all of the text of this poet. It was written in France in the late twelfth century and
had these verses attached to it, verses written allegedly by Benvenuto Campesani
(1255–1323):

> ad patriam uenio longis a finibus exul;
> > causa mei reditus compatriota fuit,
> scilicet a calamis tribuit cui Francia nomen
> > quique notat turbae praetereuntis iter.
> quo licet ingenio uestrum celebrate Catullum,
> > cuius sub modio clausa papirus erat.
> (I come to my native land, an exile from distant lands;
> > the reason for my return was a fellow-citizen.
> He to whom France has given a name from reeds
> > and who marks the journeying of the passing crowd.
> Celebrate your Catullus with whatever appreciation you can,
> > Catullus whose book had been hidden under a bushel.')

V was copied by a scholar (manuscript A) but this too was lost – as was the copy
of A known as manuscript X. (For the existence of A see McKie 38–95). V, A and
X did not survive, but A was copied again in the second half of the fourteenth
century and this copy is kept in the Bodleian Library in Oxford, from which it
derives its name *Codex Oxoniensis* ('the Oxford Manuscript') or *O*. X was then
copied twice: the first copy (*G*) being kept in Paris, the second (*R*) in Rome. So far,
then, the descent is as follows:

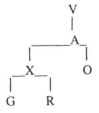

O, G and R are the basis of all modern texts: from a close comparison of their
similarities and differences we can be reasonably sure of the text of V: and the
much earlier testimony of T agrees with V sufficiently to make us fairly sure that T
and V derive from a common ancestor. O, G and R were themselves copied many
times, and there are occasions where these humanists' copies have an inspired

correction of the tradition of V (e.g. 68.11, 66.18), but their emendations are based on no other knowledge of the textual tradition than is available to ourselves. There are over 100 of these later manuscripts before 1472 when the first printed edition appeared in Venice, an edition based on one single manuscript – with all its imperfections – out of the many, and destined to fix the printed text of Catullus for a long time to come. It has been estimated that V contained at least 1000 errors (Goold 11): renaissance humanists managed to rectify about half of them (460) before 1472: and since then scholars have continued to worry at the remaining half. Some of these emendations involve no change of reading but merely one of orthography (most famously, A.E. Housman's reading of V's *Emathiae tutamen opis, carissime nato* as the eminently sensible *Emathiae tutamen, Opis carissime nato* (64.324)), while some of them reflect palaeographic confusions in the distant past (e.g. confusion of 'f' and 's' in V's reading *fundanti* for *sudanti* at 64.106, or *fragrantem* for *flagrantem* at 68.139, or a confusion of *i* and *l* at 23.19 where V reads *cuius* for *culus*) or a failure to recognise a proper name (e.g. *cuma est gravis* for *Cinna est Gaius* at 10.30). Nor have we finished this task: the text still contains what are called cruces – passages such as 55.9-12 where the tradition is certainly wrong but where no convincing emendation has yet been thought up, and which are conventionally bracketed with a symbol of a cross (*crux*, †), as well as a whole range of passages where the received text has excellent credentials but still raises problems of meaning (e.g. 94.2, 68.10), of whether fragments should be 'replaced' into other poems (Goold for instance puts 58b into 55: and most editors run 95 and 95b into a single poem) or of identity (who is *Amarunsia uirgo* at 64.395?) or of 'simple' sense (e.g. the ending of poem 1 and the place of the Muses, which Bergk emended out). Where the difference of opinion is far from obvious and the difference matters I have printed the various readings at the foot of the page in the *apparatus criticus* – for a fuller account of the readings see the *apparatus* in Mynors' Oxford Text. Throughout this edition I have printed what I consider to be the most convincing readings – some of which were suggested in the fourteenth century within a few years of V, some of which (e.g. 85.4) were suggested as recently as 1978. Work continues to be done on the history of the text (see e.g. McKie); and there is still ample scope for the reader of Catullus to continue the long process of cleaning up what was in 1350 a hideously corrupted text and try to discover what the poet himself wrote. The skills of the textual critic are often seen as 'scientific' and arid, when in fact the ultimate arbiter of the printed text is our historical imagination and our sensitivity to the poetry being transmitted.

SIGLA

CODICES:

    V= archetypum (codex Veronensis s. xii: fons communis O et X)
    O= Oxoniensis Canonicianus
    X= fons communis G et R
    G= Parisianus lat. 14137 anni MCCCLXXV
    R= Vaticanus Ottobonianus lat. 1829 s. xiv ex.
    T= Parisinus lat. 8071 s. ix (*continet carmen lxii*)

FONTES CONIECTURARUM MANU SCRIPTI:

    r = corrector(es) cod. R
    g = corrector(es) cod. G
    f = corrector anno MCCCCLVII
    $\zeta\eta$ = nescio quis ante annum MCCCCLX
    i = corrector anno MCCCCLXV

CATULLUS
THE SHORTER POEMS

I

cui dono lepidum nouum libellum
arida modo pumice expolitum?
Corneli, tibi: namque tu solebas
meas esse aliquid putare nugas
iam tum, cum ausus es unus Italorum   5
omne aeuum tribus explicare cartis
doctis, Iuppiter, et laboriosis.
quare habe tibi quidquid hoc libelli
qualecumque quidem est, patroni ut ergo
plus uno maneat perenne saeclo.   10

9 qualecumque quidem est, patroni ut ergo *Bergk:* qualecumque, quod patrona virgo *V*

II

passer, deliciae meae puellae,
quicum ludere, quem in sinu tenere,
cui primum digitum dare appetenti
et acris solet incitare morsus,
cum desiderio meo nitenti   5
carum nescio quid lubet iocari
credo, ut cum grauis acquiescet ardor   8
sit solaciolum sui doloris,   7
tecum ludere sicut ipsa posse
et tristis animi leuare curas   10
tam gratum est mihi quam ferunt puellae
pernici aureolum fuisse malum,
quod zonam soluit diu ligatam.

7 sit *Munro:* et *V*
8 ut...acquiescet *Guarinus:* et..acquiescat *V*
7f *transposuit Munro*

1

To whom am I giving an elegant new little book
just polished off with dry pumice-stone?
To you, Cornelius; for you used to
think my trifling efforts were something
even then, when you were the only Italian who had the nerve   5
to unroll the whole of history in three rolls –
learned ones, by Jupiter, and hard work.
So please accept this little book, whatever it is
and whatever its quality, so that, thanks to its patron it may remain
longlasting for more than one generation.   10

2

Sparrow, darling of my girl,
who she often plays with, who she holds in her lap,
to whom she is in the habit of giving the tip of her finger as it pecks
and stir you to bite her sharply,
when she is gleaming with longing for me   5
and wants to do some unspecified fooling about
so that when her heavy burning passion rests, I think
she can enjoy a little solace for her pain;
to be able to play with you, like the mistress,
and to raise up the sad passions of my heart,
is as welcome to me as (they say)   10
the fast girl found the little golden apple
which undid her girdle that had been tied for a long time.

III

lugete o Veneres Cupidinesque,
et quantum est hominum uenustiorum:
passer mortuus est meae puellae,
passer, deliciae meae puellae,
quem plus illa oculis suis amabat.   5
nam mellitus erat suamque norat
ipsam tam bene quam puella matrem,
nec sese a gremio illius mouebat,
sed circumsiliens modo huc modo illuc
ad solam dominam usque pipiabat.   10
qui nunc it per iter tenebricosum
illuc, unde negant redire quemquam.
at uobis male sit, malae tenebrae
Orci, quae omnia bella deuoratis:
tam bellum mihi passerem abstulistis   15
o factum male! o miselle passer!
tua nunc opera meae puellae
flendo turgiduli rubent ocelli.

IV

phaselus ille, quem uidetis, hospites,
ait fuisse nauium celerrimus,
neque ullius natantis impetum trabis
nequisse praeterire, siue palmulis
opus foret uolare siue linteo.   5
et hoc negat minacis Hadriatici
negare litus insulasue Cycladas
Rhodumque nobilem horridamque Thraciam
Propontida trucemue Ponticum sinum,
ubi iste post phaselus antea fuit   10
comata silua; nam Cytorio in iugo
loquente saepe sibilum edidit coma.
Amastri Pontica et Cytore buxifer,
tibi haec fuisse et esse cognitissima

3

Mourn, O Venuses and Cupids
and all you men of finer feeling!
The sparrow of my girl is dead
the sparrow, darling of my girl,
whom she loved more than her eyes;   5
for it was honey-sweet and knew its mistress
as well as a girl knows her mother,
and it would not move from that woman's lap
but hopping around, now this way and now that,
it would chirp constantly to the mistress alone.   10
Now it goes along a shady journey
the journey to that place from which they say nobody returns.
But as for you, curses be upon you, evil shades
of Orcus, who eat up all pretty things.
so pretty is the sparrow you have stolen from me.   15
Evil doing, as, o poor little sparrow,
it's your doing that my girl's
little eyes are swollen and red with weeping.

4

That yacht, which you see, guests,
says that it is the fastest of ships,
and that the force of no swimming beam
could pass it, whether it was required
to fly with its little palms or with canvas.   5
It claims that this is not denied by the shore of the threatening
Adriatic and the islands of the Cyclades
and honourable Rhodes and bristling Thracian
Propontis and the rough Pontic gulf,
where that which was later a yacht, was earlier   10
long-haired woods; for often on the ridge
of Cytorus she uttered a sound with her speaking hair.
Pontic Amastris and box-bearing Cytorus,
the yacht says that these things have been and are

ait phaselus: ultima ex origine   15
tuo stetisse dicit in cacumine,
tuo imbuisse palmulas in aequore,
et inde tot per impotentia freta
erum tulisse, laeua siue dextera
uocaret aura, siue utrumque Iuppiter   20
simul secundus incidisset in pedem;
neque ulla uota litoralibus deis
sibi esse facta, cum ueniret a mari
nouissimo hunc ad usque limpidum lacum.
sed haec prius fuere: nunc recondita   25
senet quiete seque dedicat tibi,
gemelle Castor et gemelle Castoris.

V

uiuamus mea Lesbia, atque amemus,
rumoresque senum seueriorum
omnes unius aestimemus assis!
soles occidere et redire possunt:
nobis cum semel occidit breuis lux,   5
nox est perpetua una dormienda.
da mi basia mille, deinde centum,
dein mille altera, dein secunda centum,
deinde usque altera mille, deinde centum.
dein, cum milia multa fecerimus,   10
conturbabimus illa, ne sciamus,
aut ne quis malus inuidere possit,
cum tantum sciat esse basiorum.

VI

Flaui, delicias tuas Catullo,
ni sint illepidae atque inelegantes,
uelles dicere nec tacere posses.
uerum nescio quid febriculosi

very well-known to you; from its furthest origin   15
it says that it stood on your summit,
dipped its little palms in your waves,
and from there through so many powerful straits
it bore its master, whether the left-hand breeze
was calling or the right, or whether a favourable Jove   20
fell upon both sheets at once;
and no vows had been made by it
to the shore gods when it came from
the nearest sea right up to this limpid lake.
But these were all beforehand; now it ages   25
in secluded peace and dedicates itself to you,
Castor twin and twin of Castor.

5

Let us live, my Lesbia, and let us love
and let us count the gossip of over-strict
old men as all worth one penny!
The sun can set and return again;
when our short light has once set   5
it is one eternal night to be slept through.
Give me a thousand kisses, then a hundred,
then another thousand, then a second hundred,
then at once another thousand, then a hundred.
Then, when we have made many thousands   10
we will muddle up the accounts, so we do not know
or so that no evil person can give us the evil eye
when he knows that there are so many kisses.

6

Flavius, you would want to tell Catullus of your darling
if she were not unsophisticated and uncouth –
you would not be able to keep quiet about her.
You are in love with some hot little tart

scorti diligis: hoc pudet fateri.   5
nam te non uiduas iacere noctes
nequiquam tacitum cubile clamat
sertis ac Syrio fragrans oliuo,
puluinusque peraeque et hic et ille
attritus, tremulique quassa lecti   10
argutatio inambulatioque.
nam nil ista ualet, nihil tacere.
cur? non tam latera ecfututa pandas,
ni tu quid facias ineptiarum.
quare, quidquid habes boni malique,   15
dic nobis. uolo te ac tuos amores
ad caelum lepido uocare uersu.

12 nam nil ista *Lachmann*: nil perstare *Skutsch*: nam inista pervalet *V.*

VII

quaeris, quot mihi basiationes
tuae, Lesbia, sint satis superque.
quam magnus numerus Libyssae harenae
lasarpiciferis iacet Cyrenis
oraclum Iouis inter aestuosi   5
et Batti ueteris sacrum sepulcrum;
aut quam sidera multa, cum tacet nox,
furtiuos hominum uident amores:
tam te basia multa basiare
uesano satis et super Catullo est,   10
quae nec pernumerare curiosi
possint nec mala fascinare lingua.

VIII

miser Catulle, desinas ineptire,
et quod uides perisse perditum ducas.
fulsere quondam candidi tibi soles,

and are ashamed to admit it.   5
For the fact that you are not lying through celibate nights
is shouted out by your bed, which keeps silent for no reason,
smelling of garlands and Syrian olive,
and the pillow dented evenly on one side and the other
and the shaken creaking of the rickety bed   10
and its way of walking across the room.
It is no use, no use at all keeping quiet about it.
Why? You would not show such shagged out limbs
if you were not doing some fooling about.
So tell us whatever you have, good or bad.   15
I want to summon you and your girlfriend
to the heavens in charming poetry.

7

You ask, how many kissifications
of yours are enough and more than enough for me.
As great a number as the Libyan sands that
lie on silphium-bearing Cyrene
in between the oracle of sweltering Jove   5
and the holy tomb of old Battus;
or as many as the stars which see, when night is silent,
the stolen love-affairs of people;
that is how many kisses are enough and more
than enough for you to kiss love-mad Catullus   10
a number which the nosy could not count
nor evil tongue bewitch.

8

Love-sick Catullus, stop being a fool
and regard as lost what you see has died.
Once beautiful suns shone on you

cum uentitabas quo puella ducebat
amata nobis quantum amabitur nulla.   5
ibi illa multa cum iocosa fiebant,
quae tu uolebas nec puella nolebat,
fulsere uere candidi tibi soles.
nunc iam illa non uult: tu quoque impotens noli,
nec quae fugit sectare, nec miser uiue,   10
sed obstinata mente perfer, obdura.
uale puella, iam Catullus obdurat,
nec te requiret nec rogabit inuitam.
at tu dolebis, cum rogaberis nulla.
scelesta, uae te, quae tibi manet uita?   15
quis nunc te adibit? cui uideberis bella?
quem nunc amabis? cuius esse diceris?
quem basiabis? cui labella mordebis?
at tu, Catulle, destinatus obdura.

IX

Verani, omnibus e meis amicis
antistans mihi milibus trecentis,
uenistine domum ad tuos penates
fratresque unanimos anumque matrem?
uenisti. o mihi nuntii beati!   5
uisam te incolumem audiamque Hiberum
narrantem loca, facta nationes,
ut mos est tuus, applicansque collum
iucundum os oculosque suauiabor.
o quantum est hominum beatiorum,   10
quid me laetius est beatiusue?

X

Varus me meus ad suos amores
uisum duxerat e foro otiosum,
scortillum, ut mihi tum repente uisum est,

when you kept coming and going wherever the girl led
loved by us as much as no girl will be loved.   5
When then those many entertaining things happened
which you wanted and the girl did not say no,
then truly beautiful suns shone on you.
Now she does say no; say no also, you weakling,
and do not chase after one who flees and do not live love-sick,   10
but harden your mind, endure, become firm.
Goodbye, girl. Catullus is now firm
and will not be looking for you nor asking you against your will.
But you will be hurt when you are asked by nobody.
Poor fool, alas for you, what life is left you?   15
Who will approach you? To whom will you seem pretty?
Whom will you love? Whose girl will you be said to be?
Whom will you kiss? Whose lips will you bite?
But you, Catullus, be resolved and firm.

9

Veranius, out of all my friends
you stand out by three hundred thousand miles,
have you come home to your household gods
and your brothers of one mind and your old mother?
You have come. O what happy news to me!   5
I shall see you safe and I shall hear you telling – as is your custom –
of the places, exploits and tribes of Spain
and drawing your neck to me
I shall kiss your sweet mouth and eyes.
Of all the happier people   10
who is happier or more lucky than me?

10

Varus had taken me from out of the forum,
when I had nothing better to do, to see his girlfriend,
a little tart, as I observed at once,

non sane illepidum neque inuenustum,
huc ut uenimus, incidere nobis 5
sermones uarii, in quibus, quid esset
iam Bithynia, quo modo se haberet,
et quonam mihi profuisset aere.
respondi id quod erat, nihil neque ipsis
nec praetoribus esse nec cohorti, 10
cur quisquam caput unctius referret,
praesertim quibus esset irrumator
praetor, nec faceret pili cohortem.
'at certe tamen,' inquiunt 'quod illic
natum dicitur esse, comparasti 15
ad lecticam homines.' ego, ut puellae
unum me facerem beatiorem,
'non' inquam 'mihi tam fuit maligne
ut, prouincia quod mala incidisset,
non possem octo homines parare rectos.' 20
at mi nullus erat nec hic neque illic
fractum qui ueteris pedem grabati
in collo sibi collocare posset.
hic illa, ut decuit cinaediorem,
'quaeso' inquit 'mihi, mi Catulle, paulum 25
istos commoda: nam uolo ad Serapim
deferri.' 'mane' inquii puellae,
'istud quod modo dixeram me habere,
fugit me ratio: meus sodalis –
Cinna est Gaius – is sibi parauit. 30
uerum, utrum illius an mei, quid ad me?
utor tam bene quam mihi pararim.
sed tu insulsa male et molesta uiuis,
per quam non licet esse neglegentem.'

XI

Furi et Aureli comites Catulli,
siue in extremos penetrabit Indos,
litus ut longe resonante Eoa

but not without charm or sex-appeal.
When we got here, various topics of conversation   5
cropped up, among them Bithynia nowadays – how it was,
what state it was in, what sort of money it had made me.
I told the truth in reply, that there was nothing for the Bithynians
nor the praetors themselves nor their staff, no reason for any of them
                                                        to bring back
a head better oiled, especially when we had a praetor   10
who was a right bastard and didn't give a fig for the staff.
'But even so' they say 'you picked up
men for the litter chair – the sort of thing produced there.'
To make myself better-off in the eyes of the girl
I say 'Things were not so bad for me that
just because I got a bad province
I could not get eight men who can stand up straight.'   20
In fact I had nobody, either here or there,
who could put the broken foot of an old camp-bed on his neck.
At this she – as you would expect of a tart –
said 'Please, my Catullus, lend me them for a little;   25
for I want to be carried to Serapis.'
'Wait' I said to the girl
'that which I just said that I had,
it slipped my mind; my friend –
Gaius Cinna – he got them for himself.   30
But what does it matter whether they are his or mine?
I use them as if I had got them for myself.
But you are a damn nuisance and a pain
for not letting a fellow forget himself.'

11

Furius and Aurelius, companions of Catullus
whether he will venture into the furthest Indies
where the shore is beaten by the far-resounding

tunditur unda,
siue in Hyrcanos Arabesue molles,   5
seu Sagas sagittiferosue Parthos,
siue quae septemgeminus colorat
    aequora Nilus,
siue trans altas gradietur Alpes,
Caesaris uisens monimenta magni,   10
Gallicum Rhenum horribiles quoque ulti-
    mosque Britannos,
omnia haec, quaecumque feret uoluntas
caelitum, temptare simul parati,
pauca nuntiate meae puellae   15
    non bona dicta.
cum suis uiuat ualeatque moechis,
quos simul complexa tenet trecentos,
nullum amans uere, sed identidem omnium
    ilia rumpens;   20
nec meum respectet, ut ante, amorem,
qui illius culpa cecidit uelut prati
ultimi flos, praetereunte postquam
    tactus aratro est.

11 horribiles quoque *Wilkinson* horribilesque *V* horribile aequor *Haupt*

XII

Marrucine Asini, manu sinistra
non belle uteris: in ioco atque uino
tollis lintea neglegentiorum.
hoc salsum esse putas? fugit te, inepte:
quamuis sordida res et inuenusta est.   5
non credis mihi? crede Pollioni
fratri, qui tua furta uel talento
mutari uelit: est enim leporum
differtus puer ac facetiarum.
quare aut hendecasyllabos trecentos   10

Eastern wave,
or whether he will go to the Hyrcanians or the effeminate Arabs   5
or the Sagae and the arrow-bearing Parthians,
or the waves which the seven-fold Nile
stains,
or whether he will cross the high Alps
seeing the memorials of great Caesar   10
the Gallic Rhine and the shaggy Britons
at the end of the world,
as you are prepared to attempt all this,
whatever the will of the heavenly ones will bring,
announce to my girl a few   15
unkind words.
Let her live and thrive with her lovers
whom she grips in her embrace three hundred at a time
loving none of them truly but again and again
breaking the balls of all,   20
and let her not look back as she once did to my love
which has fallen thanks to her badness like a flower
at the edge of the meadow, after it has been touched
by the passing plough.

12

Marrucinian Asinius, you do not use your left hand
nicely; when we are joking and drinking
you steal the napkins of those who are not watching.
Do you think this is smart? You are wrong, you fool;
It is a totally dirty and uncouth thing to do.   5
Don't you believe me? Believe Pollio
your brother, who would like to change
your thefts and would give as much as a talent to do it;
he is a boy stuffed full of wit and jokes.
So either expect three-hundred hendecasyllables   10

exspecta, aut mihi linteum remitte,
quod me non mouet aestimatione,
uerum est mnemosynum mei sodalis.
nam sudaria Saetaba ex Hiberis
miserunt mihi muneri Fabullus   15
et Veranius: haec amem necesse est
ut Veraniolum meum et Fabullum.

XIII

cenabis bene, mi Fabulle, apud me
paucis, si tibi di fauent, diebus,
si tecum attuleris bonam atque magnam
cenam, non sine candida puella
et uino et sale et omnibus cachinnis.   5
haec si, inquam, attuleris, uenuste noster,
cenabis bene; nam tui Catulli
plenus sacculus est aranearum.
sed contra accipies meros amores
seu quid suauius elegantiusue est: 10
nam unguentum dabo, quod meae puellae
donarunt Veneres Cupidinesque,
quod tu cum olfacies, deos rogabis,
totum ut te faciant, Fabulle, nasum.

XIV

ni te plus oculis meis amarem,
iucundissime Calue, munere isto
odissem te odio Vatiniano:
nam quid feci ego quidue sum locutus,
cur me tot male perderes poetis?   5
isti di mala multa dent clienti,
qui tantum tibi misit impiorum.
quod si, ut suspicor, hoc nouum ac repertum
munus dat tibi Sulla litterator,

or send me the napkin back,
which does not bother me for its price,
but it is a memento of my friend.
For Fabullus and Veranius sent me
Saetaban napkins from Spain as a gift;   15
I must love these just as I love
my little Veranius and Fabullus.

13

You will dine well, my Fabullus, at my house
in a few days, if the Gods are favourable to you,
if you bring with you a good and plentiful
dinner, not without a pretty girl
and wine and salt and all the guffaws.   5
If, I say, you bring these things, my dear friend,
you will dine well: for your Catullus'
purse is full of cobwebs.
In return you will get undiluted love
or something more pleasurable and charming: 10
for I will give you a perfume which the Venuses
and Cupids gave to my girl
and when you smell it you will ask the gods
to make you, Fabullus, all nose.

14

If I did not love you more than my own eyes,
o sweetest Calvus, I would hate you
with a Vatinian hate for that present;
for what have I done, what have I said
to explain why you destroy me badly with so many poets?   5
May the gods give many evils to that client
who sent you such a crowd of unholy men.
But if, as I suspect, it is Sulla the schoolmaster
who gives you this new and exquisite gift,

non est mi male, sed bene ac beate,   10
quod non dispereunt tui labores.
di magni, horribilem et sacrum libellum!
quem tu scilicet ad tuum Catullum
misti, continuo ut die periret,
Saturnalibus, optimo dierum!   15
non non hoc tibi, false, sic abibit.
nam si luxerit ad librariorum
curram scrinia, Caesios, Aquinos,
Suffenum, omnia colligam uenena.
ac te his suppliciis remunerabor.   20
uos hinc interea ualete abite
illuc, unde malum pedem attulistis,
saecli incommoda, pessimi poetae.

XIVb

si qui forte mearum ineptiarum
lectores eritis manusque uestras
non horrebitis admouere nobis,

XV

commendo tibi me ac meos amores,
Aureli. ueniam peto pudentem,
ut, si quicquam animo tuo cupisti,
quod castum expeteres et integellum,
conserues puerum mihi pudice,   5
non dico a populo-- nihil ueremur
istos, qui in platea modo huc modo illuc
in re praetereunt sua occupati–
uerum a te metuo tuoque pene
infesto pueris bonis malisque.   10
quem tu qua lubet, ut lubet moueto
quantum uis, ubi erit foris paratum:
hunc unum excipio, ut puto, pudenter.

I am not unhappy but glad and pleased   10
that your labours are not in vain.
Great gods, what a dreadful and untouchable little book!
Presumably you sent it to your Catullus
so that he would die on the spot,
on the best of days, the Saturnalia!   15
No, you will not get away with it, you scallywag.
For when it gets light I shall run to the stall of the booksellers
and gather together Caesii, Aquini, Suffenus and all the poisons
and repay you with these torments.   20
Meanwhile farewell and go away
to that place, from where you brought your evil foot,
you burdens of the age, worst of poets.

14b

If you readers of my foolish things
will not shrink from putting your hands
on us,...

15

I entrust to you myself and my love,
Aurelius. I ask for a modest favour,
that if you have ever desired in your heart
to keep anything pure and untouched,
then preserve the boy modestly for me.   5
I do not mean safe from the people – I have no fear
of those men who go up and down in the streets
occupied in their own business –
but I fear you and your penis
a menace to boys both good and bad.   10
Move it about where and how you like
as much as you want when you get an opportunity outside;
I make this one exception – a modest one, I think.

quod si te mala mens furorque uecors
in tantam impulerit, sceleste, culpam,   15
ut nostrum insidiis caput lacessas.
a tum te miserum malique fati!
quem attractis pedibus patente porta
percurrent raphanique mugilesque.

XVI

pedicabo ego uos et irrumabo,
Aureli pathice et cinaede Furi,
qui me ex uersiculis meis putastis,
quod sunt molliculi, parum pudicum.
nam castum esse decet pium poetam   5
ipsum, uersiculos nihil necesse est;
qui tum denique habent salem ac leporem,
si sunt molliculi ac parum pudici,
et quod pruriat incitare possunt,
non dico pueris, sed his pilosis   10
qui duros nequeunt mouere lumbos.
uos, quod milia multa basiorum
legistis, male me marem putatis?
pedicabo ego uos et irrumabo.

XVII

o Colonia, quae cupis ponte ludere longo,
et salire paratum habes, sed uereris inepta
crura ponticuli axulis stantis in rediuiuis,
ne supinus eat cauaque in palude recumbat:
sic tibi bonus ex tua pons libidine fiat,   5
in quo uel Salisubsali sacra suscipiantur,
munus hoc mihi maximi da, Colonia, risus.
quendam municipem meum de tuo uolo ponte
ire praecipitem in lutum per caputque pedesque,
uerum totius ut lacus putidaeque paludis   10

But if your evil mind and frenzied madness
drive you, you wicked man, to so great a sin   15
as to ensnare my head in a trap,
ah woe will be you, and your destiny one of suffering!
For with your feet pulled up and your door open
radishes and mullets will run you through.

16

I will bugger you and fuck your mouths,
Aurelius the pansy and Furius the pervert,
for you thought from the evidence of my little poems
that I was not modest enough because they are slightly unmanly.
For the holy poet ought to be pure   5
himself, but his little poems need not be like that;
they do at least have wit and charm
even if they are slightly unmanly and insufficiently modest
and can arouse something to give people the urge –
I do not mean boys but these hairy men   10
who cannot shift their stiff loins.
You, because you read many thousands of
kisses, do you think me lacking in manliness?
I shall bugger you and fuck your mouths.

17

O Colony, who want to play on a long bridge
and are ready to dance but fear the ill-fitting
legs of the little bridge standing on recycled posts
in case it falls flat on its back and sinks in the hollow mire;
may you get a good bridge to suit your desires   5
on which even the rites of Salisubsalus may be performed,
but give me this gift, Colony, of maximum laughter.
I want a certain townsman of mine to go from your bridge
headfirst into the mud head over heels,
just where of all the lake and the smelly marsh   10

liuidissima maximeque est profunda uorago.
insulsissimus est homo, nec sapit pueri instar
bimuli tremula patris dormientis in ulna.
cui cum sit uiridissimo nupta flore puella
et puella tenellulo delicatior haedo,   15
adseruanda nigerrimis diligentius uuis,
ludere hanc sinit ut lubet, nec pili facit uni,
nec se subleuat ex sua parte, sed uelut alnus
in fossa Liguri iacet suppernata securi,
tantundem omnia sentiens quam si nulla sit usquam;   20
talis iste meus stupor nil uidet, nihil audit,
ipse qui sit, utrum sit an non sit, id quoque nescit.
nunc eum uolo de tuo ponte mittere pronum,
si pote stolidum repente excitare ueternum,
et supinum animum in graui derelinquere caeno,   25
ferream ut soleam tenaci in uoragine mula.

XXI

Aureli, pater esuritionum,
non harum modo, sed quot aut fuerunt
aut sunt aut aliis erunt in annis,
pedicare cupis meos amores.
nec clam: nam simul es, iocaris una,   5
haerens ad latus omnia experiris.
frustra: nam insidias mihi instruentem
tangam te prior irrumatione.
atque id si faceres satur, tacerem:
nunc ipsum id doleo, quod esurire   10
meus iam puer et sitire discet.
quare desine, dum licet pudico,
ne finem facias, sed irrumatus.

11 meus iam 1473: me me V

the abyss is bluest and deepest.
He is a total idiot, and has not the brains of a two-year-old
child asleep on the rocking arm of his father.
Even though his wife is a girl of tenderest bloom
a girl more capricious than a sweet little kid   15
to be looked after more carefully than the blackest grapes,
he lets her fool about as she wants and does not care a jot,
and he does not raise himself for his part but lies
like an alder in a ditch hamstrung by the Ligurian axe,
perceiving everything as if there was nothing to perceive.   20
That is what this dolt of mine is like – sees nothing, hears nothing
not even who he is, doesn't even know whether he exists or not.
I want to send him headlong from your bridge
to see if it is possible to awake his stupid lethargy
and leave behind his lazy soul in the heavy mire   25
as a mule leaves behind its iron shoe in the sticky mud.

21

Aurelius, father of famines
and not only these but all those which have been
or are or will be in other years;
you desire to bugger my beloved.
Nor are your desires secret: you are with him,   5
joking together sticking to his side and trying everything.
It's all in vain; you can lay down traps against me
but I will get you first by fucking your mouth.
If you were doing this with a full stomach, I would keep quiet;
as things are I am cross about the fact that   10
the boy will learn to starve and thirst from you.
So stop it, while you may do so with modesty intact,
in case you make an end but with your mouth fucked.

XXII

Suffenus iste, Vare, quem probe nosti,
homo est uenustus et dicax et urbanus,
idemque longe plurimos facit uersus.
puto esse ego illi milia aut decem aut plura
perscripta, nec sic ut fit in palimpsesto   5
relata: cartae regiae, noui libri,
noui umbilici, lora rubra membranae,
derecta plumbo et pumice omnia aequata.
haec cum legas tu, bellus ille et urbanus
Suffenus unus caprimulgus aut fossor   10
rursus uidetur: tantum abhorret ac mutat.
hoc quid putemus esse? qui modo scurra
aut si quid hac re scitius uidebatur,
idem infaceto est infacetior rure,
simul poemata attigit, neque idem umquam   15
aeque est beatus ac poema cum scribit:
tam gaudet in se tamque se ipse miratur.
nimirum idem omnes fallimur, neque est quisquam
quem non in aliqua re uidere Suffenum
possis. suus cuique attributus est error;   20
sed non uidemus manticae quod in tergo est.

XXIII

Furi, cui neque seruus est neque arca
nec cimex neque araneus neque ignis,
uerum est et pater et nouerca, quorum
dentes uel silicem comesse possunt,
est pulcre tibi cum tuo parente   5
et cum coniuge lignea parentis.
nec mirum: bene nam ualetis omnes,
pulcre concoquitis, nihil timetis,
non incendia, non graues ruinas,
non facta impia, non dolos ueneni,   10
non casus alios periculorum.

22

That man Suffenus, Varus, whom you know well,
is a man of charm and articulate and civilised
and the same man composes by far the greatest quantity of verse.
I think he has ten thousand or more
written up, and not (as one does) put down   5
on re-used paper but imperial paper, new books,
new bosses, red ribbons for the wrapper,
all straightened up with lead and smoothed with pumice.
When you read this, that nice civilised
Suffenus seems any old goatherd or ditch-digger   10
once again; he is so out of character and changes.
What are we to think of this? The man who was just now a wit
or whatever seemed more refined than this,
the same man is more of a bumpkin than the country bumpkin,
as soon as he touches poetry, nor is he ever so happy   15
as when he is writing a poem;
so much does he rejoice in himself and admire himself.
Sure enough, this is a delusion we all suffer from, nor is there anyone
in whom you could not see a Suffenus in some respect.
Everyone has his own fault assigned to him;   20
but we do not see the part of the bag which is on our back.

23

Furius, who has neither slave nor money-box,
nor bug nor spider nor fire,
but you do have a father and stepmother, whose
teeth could eat even flintstone,
you manage pretty well with your parent   5
and with your parent's wooden wife.
No wonder: for you are all in good health,
your digestion is excellent, you fear nothing,
no fires, no houses collapsing and crushing,
no unholy deeds, no plots to poison you,   10
no other chances of dangers.

atque corpora sicciora cornu
aut siquid magis aridum est habetis
sole et frigore et esuritione.
quare non tibi sit bene ac beate? 15
a te sudor abest, abest saliua,
mucusque et mala pituita nasi.
hanc ad munditiem adde mundiorem,
quod culus tibi purior salillo est,
nec toto decies cacas in anno; 20
atque id durius est faba et lapillis.
quod tu si manibus teras fricesque,
non umquam digitum inquinare posses
haec tu commoda tam beata, Furi,
noli spernere nec putare parui, 25
et sestertia quae soles precari
centum desine: nam sat es beatus.

XXIV

o qui flosculus es Iuuentiorum,
non horum modo, sed quot aut fuerunt
aut posthac aliis erunt in annis,
mallem diuitias Midae dedisses
isti, cui neque seruus est neque arca, 5
quam sic te sineres ab illo amari.
'qui? non est homo bellus?' inquies. est:
sed bello huic neque seruus est neque arca.
hoc tu quam lubet abice eleuaque:
nec seruum tamen ille habet neque arcam. 10

And yet you have bodies drier than horn
or whatever is drier still
thanks to the sun and cold and fasting.
How could you be anything other than well and prosperous?   15
You have no sweat, saliva,
no catarrh or nasty nasal snot.
To this cleanness add something even more clean,
that your arse is cleaner than a salt-cellar
and you do not shit ten times in a whole year;   20
and when you do it is harder than a bean or pebbles
which you could rub with your hands and crumble it
and yet not ever be able to dirty a finger.
Do not despise such splendid blessings as these, Furius
and do not think them of little account   25
and stop praying for a hundred sestertia,
as you often do; for you are well-off enough.

24

O little flower of the Iuventii,
not only of these but of all that have been
or will be later in other years,
I would prefer you had given the riches of Midas
to that man who has neither slave nor purse   5
than that you should let yourself be loved by him.
'What? Is he not a lovely man?' you will say. He is:
but this nice man has neither slave nor purse.
Discard and make as little of that as you want:
but he still has neither slave nor purse.   10

XXV

cinaede Thalle, mollior cuniculi capillo
uel anseris medullula uel imula oricilla
uel pene languido senis situque araneoso,
idemque, Thalle, turbida rapacior procella,
cum diua Murcia arbitros ostendit oscitantes,　　　　5
remitte pallium mihi meum, quod inuolasti,
sudariumque Saetabum catagraphosque Thynos,
inepte, quae palam soles habere tamquam auita.
quae nunc tuis ab unguibus reglutina et remitte,
ne laneum latusculum manusque mollicellas　　　　10
inusta turpiter tibi flagella conscribillent,
et insolenter aestues, uelut minuta magno
deprensa nauis in mari, uesaniente uento.

5 Murcia *Munro*: arbitros *MacKay*: mulier aries *V*

XXVI

Furi, uillula uestra non ad Austri
flatus opposita est neque ad Fauoni
nec saeui Boreae aut Apheliotae,
uerum ad milia quindecim et ducentos.
o uentum horribilem atque pestilentem!　　　　5

XXVII

minister uetuli puer Falerni
inger mi calices amariores,
ut lex Postumiae iubet magistrae
ebriosa acina ebriosioris.
at uos quo lubet hinc abite, lymphae　　　　5
uini pernicies, et ad seueros
migrate. hic merus est Thyonianus.

25

Pansy Thallus, more effeminate than rabbit's fur
or nice goose-down or little ear-lobe
or the drooping penis of an old man or a dirty cobweb,
the same man, Thallus, more rapacious than a violent storm
when the goddess of sloth shows him guests are off their guard,　　5
send me back the cloak which you have seized upon
and the Saetaban napkin and the Bithynian tablets\handkerchiefs,
you fool, which you keep on public display like heirlooms.
Unglue these now from your claws and send them back and send them
　　　　　　　　　　　　　　　　　　　　　　　　　　back,
or else the whips will to your shame brand and scribble on　　11
your downy haunch and your pansy little hands
and you will pitch like you are not used to pitching, like a tiny
ship caught on the great sea when the wind is raging.

26

Furius, your little country-house is facing not
the blasts of the South wind nor those of the West wind
nor those of the savage North or the East,
but rather to a blast of 15,200.
What a dreadful and plague-ridden wind!　　5

27

Slave, steward of old Falernian wine,
pour for me cups that are bitterer
as the rule of our Mistress Postumia decrees,
drunker as she is than the drunken grape.
You, waters, go away from here to where you wish,　　5
you spoiler of wine, and go to live with the puritans.
This is the Thyonian undiluted.

XXVIII

Pisonis comites, cohors inanis,
aptis sarcinulis et expeditis,
Verani optime tuque mi Fabulle,
quid rerum geritis? satisne cum isto
uappa frigoraque et famem tulistis?   5
ecquidnam in tabulis patet lucelli
expensum, ut mihi, qui meum secutus
praetorem refero datum lucello?
o Memmi, bene me ac diu supinum
tota ista trabe lentus irrumasti.   10
sed, quantum uideo, pari fuistis
casu: nam nihilo minore uerpa
farti estis. pete nobiles amicos!
at uobis mala multa di deaeque
dent, opprobria Romuli Remique.   15

XXIX

quis hoc potest uidere, quis potest pati,
nisi impudicus et uorax et aleo,
Mamurram habere quod Comata Gallia
habebat ante et ultima Britannia?
cinaede Romule haec uidebis et feres?   5
et ille nunc superbus et superfluens
perambulabit omnium cubilia,
ut albulus columbus aut Adoneus?
cinaede Romule, haec uidebis et feres?
es impudicus et uorax et aleo.   10
eone nomine, imperator unice,
fuisti in ultima occidentis insula,
ut ista uestra diffututa mentula
ducenties comesset aut trecenties?
quid est alid sinistra liberalitas?   15
parum expatrauit an parum elluatus est?
paterna prima lancinata sunt bona,

28

Companions of Piso, empty-handed entourage,
with your tidy little knapsacks light to carry,
Veranius best of men and you, my Fabullus,
how are you doing? Have you endured enough
cold and hunger with that scum? 5
Is there any clear profit in the account books
in the red, as I found when I followed my
praetor and count my small expenses as a tiny profit?
Memmius, well and long did you screw me slowly
as I lay on my back, with all of that beam of yours! 10
But, so far as I see, you have been in the same
situation: you have been stuffed with no
less a tool. 'Find friends of good background indeed!'
But may the gods and goddesses grant many misfortunes
to you, you shame on Romulus and Remus. 15

29

Who can see this, who can allow it –
unless he is shameless and greedy and a gambler –
Mamurra having all that Long-haired Gaul
and furthest Britain used to have before?
Queer Romulus, will you see this and endure it? 5
Will he now, proud and prodigal,
walk round the marriage-beds of everybody
like a white dove or Adonis?
Queer Romulus, will you see this and endure it?
You are shameless, greedy and a gambler. 10
Was it on that account, o general without peer,
that you were on the furthest island of the west,
so that that shagged-out prick of yours
might gobble up twenty or thirty million?
If that isn't idiotic generosity, then what is? 15
Has he not screwed and gourmandised enough already?
First his father's goods were mangled,

54   CATULLUS

secunda praeda Pontica, inde tertia
Hibera, quam scit amnis aurifer Tagus:
eine Galliae optima et Britanniae?   20
quid hunc malum fouetis? aut quid hic potest
nisi uncta deuorare patrimonia?
eone nomine urbis o piissimi
socer generque, perdidistis omnia?

4 ante *Statius*: uncti *Faernus*: cum te V
20 eine..optima *Baehrens* hunc..timet V
23 o piissimi *Haupt* opulentissime V

XXX

Alfene immemor atque unanimis false sodalibus,
iam te nil miseret, dure, tui dulcis amiculi?
iam me prodere, iam non dubitas fallere, perfide?
nunc facta impia fallacum hominum caelicolis placent,
quos tu neglegis ac me miserum deseris in malis?   5
eheu quid faciant, dic, homines cuiue habeant fidem?
certe tute iubebas animam tradere, inique, me
inducens in amorem, quasi tuta omnia mi forent.
idem nunc retrahis te ac tua dicta omnia factaque
uentos irrita ferre ac nebulas aereas sinis.   10
si tu oblitus es, at di meminerunt, meminit Fides,
quae te ut paeniteat postmodo facti faciet tui.

4 nunc *Baehrens*: nec V
5 quos *Guarinus* quae V

XXXI

paene insularum, Sirmio, insularumque
ocelle, quascumque in liquentibus stagnis
marique uasto fert uterque Neptunus,
quam te libenter quamque laetus inuiso,
uix mi ipse credens Thuniam atque Bithunos   5

then the Pontic loot, then thirdly
the Spanish stuff which the gold-bearing river Tagus kno
is it he who now has the best bits of Gaul and Britain?
Why the hell do you nurture this man? What can he do
except gobble up fat inheritances?
Is that the reason, o holiest men of the city,
father-in-law and son-in-law, that you have wasted everything?

30

Alfenus, thoughtless and treacherous to loyal friends,
do you feel no pity now, hard-hearted one, for your sweet friend?
Now do you not hesitate to betray me, now to deceive me, traitor?
Do the wicked deeds of liars please the heaven-dwellers now –
gods whom you ignore as you abandon me, unhappy, in my
misfortune?
Alas, what are men to do, tell me, whom are they to trust?   6
you certainly kept telling me to surrender my soul, you wicked man,
leading me into your love as if all were safe for me.
Now, despite that, you pull back and allow the winds and the clouds of
the air
to carry off all your words and deeds making them useless.   10
Even if you forgot, still the gods remember. Honesty remembers;
she will later on make you repent of your action.

31

Sirmio, little eye of peninsulas and islands
all the ones which either of the Neptunes bears
in liquid pools and in the vast sea –
how gladly and how happily I see you,
scarcely believing that I have left Thynia and the Bithynian   5

neoteric poets.

liquisse campos et uidere te in tuto.
o quid solutis est beatius curis,
cum mens onus reponit, ac peregrino
labore fessi uenimus larem ad nostrum,
desideratoque acquiescimus lecto?   10
hoc est quod unum est pro laboribus tantis.
salue, o uenusta Sirmio, atque ero gaude
gaudente, uosque, o Lydiae lacus undae,
ridete quidquid est domi cachinnorum.

XXXII

amabo, mea dulcis Ipsitilla,
meae deliciae, mei lepores,
iube ad te ueniam meridiatum.
et si iusseris, illud adiuuato,
ne quis liminis obseret tabellam,   5
neu tibi lubeat foras abire,
sed domi maneas paresque nobis
nouem continuas fututiones.
uerum si quid ages, statim iubeto:
nam pransus iaceo et satur supinus   10
pertundo tunicamque palliumque.

XXXIII

o furum optime balneariorum
Uibenni pater et cinaede fili
(nam dextra pater inquinatiore,
culo filius est uoraciore),
cur non exilium malasque in oras   5
itis? quandoquidem patris rapinae
notae sunt populo, et natis pilosas,
fili, non potes asse uenditare.

fields and that I now see you in safety.
O what is more pleasant than when worries are dissolved
when the mind lays down its burden and tired with
foreign toil we come to our own household
and rest in our familiar bed?   10
This is the one thing which makes up for such great toils.
Hail, o lovely Sirmio, and rejoice with your rejoicing master
and you, o waves of the Lydian lake,
laugh all the guffaws you have at home!

32

Please, my sweet Ipsitilla,
my darling, my charming girl,
tell me to come to you after lunch,
and (if you give the word) help me by seeing
that nobody bolts the street door,   5
and that you don't decide to go out,
but rather stay at home and make ready for us
nine consecutive fuckifications.
If there's any chance, give me the order right now:
for I am lying down on my back, fed full,   10
banging through my cloak and tunic.

33

O best of the bath-house thieves,
Vibennius the father and poofter son of his,
(for the father is the one with the filthier hand,
the son the one with the greedier arsehole),
why will you not go into exile and to Hell?   5
You might as well – the thieving of the father
is well known to the people and you, son,
cannot sell your hairy buttocks for a penny.

XXXIV

Dianae sumus in fide
  puellae et pueri integri:
Dianam pueri integri
  puellaeque canamus.

o Latonia, maximi   5
  magna progenies Iouis,
quam mater prope Deliam
  deposiuit oliuam,
montium domina ut fores
siluarumque uirentium   10
saltuumque reconditorum
  amniumque sonantum:
tu Lucina dolentibus
Iuno dicta puerperis,
tu potens Triuia et notho es   15
  dicta lumine Luna.
tu cursu, dea, menstruo
metiens iter annuum,
rustica agricolae bonis
  tecta frugibus exples.   20
sis quocumque tibi placet
sancta nomine, Romulique,
antique ut solita es, bona
  sospites ope gentem.

XXXV

poetae tenero, meo sodali,
uelim Caecilio, papyre, dicas
Veronam ueniat, Noui relinquens
Comi moenia Lariumque litus.
nam quasdam uolo cogitationes   5
amici accipiat sui meique.
quare, si sapiet, uiam uorabit,
quamuis candida milies puella

34

We are in the trust of Diana
we girls and untouched boys:
untouched boys and girls we
sing of Diana.
O daughter of Lato, great   5
offspring of greatest Jove,
whom your mother bore
near the Delian olive-tree,
so that you might be the mistress of the mountains
and of the green forests   10
and of the distant glens and
of the sounding rivers:
you are called Juno Lucina
by child-bearing women in pain,
you are called powerful Lady of the Crossroads and Moon   15
with her bastard light.
You, goddess, with your monthly course
measure out the anuual journey
and fill up the country buildings of the farmer
with good crops.   20
May you be holy by whatever name you please
and as you have been accutomed of old,
with good help safeguard the
race of Romulus.

35

Papyrus, I would like you to tell Caecilius,
the love-poet and my friend,
to come to Verona, leaving behind the walls
of Novum Comum and the Larian shore.
For I want him to take on board some meditations   5
of a friend of mine and his.
So, if he has any sense, he will eat up the road
even though a pretty girl calls him back

euntem reuocet, manusque collo
ambas iniciens roget morari.   10
quae nunc, si mihi uera nuntiantur,
illum deperit impotente amore.
nam quo tempore legit incohatam
Dindymi dominam, ex eo misellae
ignes interiorem edunt medullam.   15
ignosco tibi, Sapphica puella
musa doctior; est enim uenuste
Magna Caecilio incohata Mater.

XXXVI

Annales Volusi, cacata carta,
uotum soluite pro mea puella.
nam sanctae Veneri Cupidinique
uouit, si sibi restitutus essem
desissemque truces uibrare iambos,   5
electissima pessimi poetae
scripta tardipedi deo daturam
infelicibus ustulanda lignis.
et hoc pessima se puella uidit
iocose lepide uouere diuis.   10
nunc o caeruleo creata ponto,
quae sanctum Idalium Vriosque apertos
quaeque Ancona Cnidumque harundinosam
colis quaeque Amathunta quaeque Golgos
quaeque Durrachium Hadriae tabernam,   15
acceptum face redditumque uotum,
si non illepidum neque inuenustum est.
at uos interea uenite in ignem,
pleni ruris et inficetiarum.
annales Volusi, cacata carta.   20

a thousand times as he makes to go, and putting
both hands around his neck begs him to stay a while.   10
If what I am told it true, this girl
is wasting away with helpless love for him.
For ever since she read his unfinished
Mistress of Dindymus, ever since then the poor little girl
has had fires eating out the inside of her bone-marrow.   15
I don't blame you, girl more scholarly
than the Muse of Sappho; that's a lovely start
to Caecilius' *Great Mother*.

36

Volusius' *Annals*, paper full of crap,
pay out a vow for my girl.
For she vowed to Cupid and holy Venus
that if I were given back to her
and stopped hurling fierce verses   5
that she would give choicest writings of the worst poet
to the slow-footed god
to be burnt up in unhappy firewood.
This the worst of girls saw as
a witty and elegant vow to make to the gods.   10
So now, goddess born of the sky-blue sea,
who lives on holy Idalium and open Urii
Ancona and reedy Cnidus
Amathus and Golgi
and Dyrrachium, the tavern of the Adriatic,   15
receive this vow and enter it as paid out,
if it is not lacking in wit and elegance.
As for you, meanwhile, come into the fire,
stuffed full of boorishness and charmless features,
Volusius' *Annals*, paper full of crap.   20

XXXVII

salax taberna uosque contubernales,
a pilleatis nona fratribus pila,
solis putatis esse mentulas uobis,
solis licere, quidquid est puellarum,
confutuere et putere ceteros hircos?   5
an, continenter quod sedetis insulsi
centum an ducenti, non putatis ausurum
me una ducentos irrumare sessores?
atqui putate: namque totius uobis
frontem tabernae sopionibus scribam.   10
puella nam mi, quae meo sinu fugit,
amata tantum quantum amabitur nulla,
pro qua mihi sunt magna bella pugnata,
consedit istic. hanc boni beatique
omnes amatis, et quidem, quod indignum est,   15
omnes pusilli et semitarii moechi;
tu praeter omnes une de capillatis,
cuniculosae Celtiberiae fili,
Egnati. opaca quem bonum facit barba
et dens Hibera defricatus urina.   20

5 putere *Hermann*: putare *V*

XXXVIII

malest, Cornifici, tuo Catullo
malest, me hercule, et laboriose,
et magis magis in dies et horas.
quem tu, quod minimum facillimumque est,
qua solatus es allocutione?   5
irascor tibi. sic meos amores?
paulum quid lubet allocutionis,
maestius lacrimis Simonideis.

37

Randy tavern and you tavern-men
ninth pillar from the hat-wearing brothers,
do you think that you alone have pricks,
that you alone have the right to fuck whatever
girls there are and that the rest of us are stinking goats? 5
Or, because you sit there witless in a never-ending line
one or two hundred of you, do you think I wouldn't dare
fuck all your mouths as you just sit there, all two hundred at once?
Go on thinking that: I will scrawl
on the front of the entire tavern with pricks. 10
For my girl, who has run away from my embrace,
beloved by me as no girl will ever be loved,
for whom great wars have been fought by me,
she has taken her seat there. You all love her,
you great and rich men, and also (shameful thing) 15
all you wimps and backstreet perverts.
And you above all, unique among the long-haired men,
son of rabbit-filled Celtiberia
Egnatius, whose dark beard makes him respectable
and his teeth brushed in Spanish urine. 20

38

Cornificius, your Catullus is in a bad way
in a bad way by Hercules and finding it heavy going,
more and more as the days and hours pass.
Have you consoled him with any words of consolation,
although it is the least and the easiest thing to do? 5
I am livid with you. Is this how you treat your beloved?
Send me any little words of consolation you like,
sadder than the tears of Simonides.

XXXIX

Egnatius, quod candidos habet dentes,
renidet usque quaque. si ad rei uentum est
subsellium, cum orator excitat fletum,
renidet ille; si ad pii rogum fili
lugetur, orba cum flet unicum mater,   5
renidet ille. quidquid est, ubicumque est,
quodcumque agit, renidet: hunc habet morbum,
neque elegantem, ut arbitror, neque urbanum.
quare monendum est te mihi, bone Egnati.
si urbanus esses aut Sabinus aut Tiburs   10
aut pinguis Vmber aut obesus Etruscus
aut Lanuuinus ater atque dentatus
aut Transpadanus, ut meos quoque attingam,
aut quilubet, qui puriter lauit dentes,
tamen renidere usque quaque te nollem: 15
nam risu inepto res ineptior nulla est.
nunc Celtiber es: Celtiberia in terra,
quod quisque minxit, hoc sibi solet mane
dentem atque russam defricare gingiuam,
ut quo iste uester expolitior dens est,   20
hoc te amplius bibisse praedicet loti.

11 pinguis *Lindsay*: parcus *V*

XL

quaenam te mala mens, miselle Rauide,
agit praecipitem in meos iambos?
quis deus tibi non bene aduocatus
uecordem parat excitare rixam?
an ut peruenias in ora uulgi?   5
quid uis? qualubet esse notus optas?
eris, quandoquidem meos amores
cum longa uoluisti amare poena.

39

Because Egnatius has brilliant teeth,
he beams all the time. If it's a case for the defendant's
bench, when the barrister is doing the tear-jerking,
he beams. If there is mourning at the pyre of a devoted
son, when the bereaved mother is weeping for her only son,   5
he beams. Whatever it is, wherever it is
whatever he is doing, he beams. This is a disease he has,
and not, I think, an attractive or a civlised one.
So I have to give you some advice, good Egnatius.
If you were from the city or a Sabine or Tiburtine   10
or a podgy Umbrian or a fat Etruscan
or a Lanuvine, swarthy and with good teeth,
or a Transpadane – to get to my own people as well –
or anyone who washes his teeth in a clean manner
I would still not want you to beam all the time,   15
since there is nothing dafter than a daft grin.
As it is, you're Celtiberian: and in Celtiberia
in the mornings everyone generally uses whatever he has pissed
to rub down his teeth and his red gums,
so that the more polished those teeth of yours are   20
the more deeply does this tell us you have drunk of your own piss.

40

What bad thinking, forlorn little Ravidus,
drives you head-first into my lampoons?
What god have you invoked unwisely
to make you stir up a lunatic quarrel?
Is it so that you might get a public audience?   5
What do you want? Do you wish to be famous for anything?
You will be famous, since you have desired to love
my beloved and will do so with a long penalty.

XLI

Ameaena puella defututa
tota milia me decem poposcit,
ista turpiculo puella naso,
decoctoris amica Formiani.
propinqui, quibus est puella curae,   5
amicos medicosque conuocate:
non est sana puella, nec rogare
qualis sit solet aes imaginosum.

XLII

adeste, hendecasyllabi, quot estis
omnes undique, quotquot estis omnes.
iocum me putat esse moecha turpis,
et negat mihi nostra reddituram
pugillaria, si pati potestis.   5
persequamur eam et reflagitemus.
quae sit, quaeritis? illa, quam uidetis
turpe incedere, mimice ac moleste
ridentem catuli ore Gallicani.
circumsistite eam, et reflagitate,   10
'moecha putida, redde codicillos,
redde putida moecha, codicillos!
non assis facis?' o lutum, lupanar,
aut si perditius potes quid esse.
sed non est tamen hoc satis putandum.   15
quod si non aliud potest ruborem
ferreo canis exprimamus ore.
conclamate iterum altiore uoce.
'moecha putide, redde codicillos,
redde, putida moecha, codicillos!'   20
sed nil proficimus, nihil mouetur.
mutanda est ratio modusque uobis,
siquid proficere amplius potestis:
'pudica et proba, redde codicillos.'

41

Ameaena, fucked-out girl,
has demanded a cool ten thousand from me,
that girl with the rather disgusting nose,
girlfriend of the bankrupt from Formiae.
Relatives, you who who have responsibility for the girl,   5
summon her friends and doctors:
the girl is not right, and is not in the habit of asking
the mirroring brass for what she is really like.

42

Come here, Hendecasyllables, all of you there are,
however many you are from wherever you come, all of you.
A foul tart thinks that I am a joke
and says that she will not give me back my
writing tablets, if you can stand that.   5
Let us chase her and shame them out of her.
Who is she, you ask? The woman you see
who has the disgusting way of walking, laughing
like an actress and a pest, with the face of a little Gallic dog.
Surround her and shame them out of her: 10
'Disgusting tart, give the tablets back!
Give the tablets back, you disgusting tart!
You don't give a damn?' The filth, the whorehouse,
or whatever can be more depraved than that.
But we must not think that that is enough.   15
If nothing else can do it, let us squeeze a blush
from her brassy bitch face.
Shout again raising your voice:
'Disgusting tart, give the tablets back!
Give the tablets back, you disgusting tart!'   20
We are making no progress. She is unmoved.
You need to change the plan and the method,
to see if you can make any better progress:
'Modest and chaste woman, give the tablets back!'

XLIII

salve, nec minimo puella naso
nec bello pede nec nigris ocellis
nec longis digitis nec ore sicco
nec sane nimis elegante lingua,
decoctoris amica Formiani.   5
ten prouincia narrat esse bellam?
tecum Lesbia nostra comparatur?
o saeclum insapiens et infacetum!

XLIV

o funde noster seu Sabine seu Tiburs
(nam te esse Tiburtem autumant, quibus non est
cordi Catullum laedere; at quibus cordi est,
quouis Sabinum pignore esse contendunt),
sed seu Sabine siue uerius Tiburs,   5
fui libenter in tua suburbana
uilla, malamque pectore expuli tussim,
non inmerenti quam mihi meus uenter,
dum sumptuosas appeto, dedit, cenas.
nam, Sestianus dum uolo esse conuiua,   10
orationem in Antium petitorem
plenam ueneni et pestilentiae legi.
hic me grauedo frigida et frequens tussis
quassauit usque, dum in tuum sinum fugi,
et me recuraui otioque et urtica.   15
quare refectus maximas tibi grates
ago, meum quod non es ulta peccatum.
nec deprecor iam, si nefaria scripta
Sesti recepso, quin grauedinem et tussim
non mihi, sed ipsi Sestio ferat frigus,   20
qui tunc uocat me, cum malum librum legi.

43

Hail, girl who has neither a small nose
nor pretty foot nor black eyes
nor long fingers nor a dry mouth
and certainly not a tongue which is too elegant,
girlfriend of the bankrupt from Formiae.   5
Is it you that the region claims is pretty?
Is it with you that our Lesbia is compared?
O what a tasteless and witless generation!

44

O farm of mine, whether Sabine or Tiburtine
(for those who have no desire to hurt Catullus call you
Tiburtine, while those who do want to hurt him argue
by any wager that you are Sabine)
but whether you are Sabine or (more truthfully) Tiburtine,   5
I was glad to be in your out of town
villa and got rid of a foul cough from my chest:
a cough which I deserved, as my stomach gave it me
while I was angling for luxurious dinners.
For while I was eager to be a dinner-guest of Sestius,   10
I read his speech against Antius' candidature,
a speech full of poison and disease.
At this a cold fever and a non-stop coughing
shook me to the point where I sought refuge in your bosom
and got myself better with inactivity and nettle.   15
So now, recovered, I give you the greatest of
thanks, for not taking revenge on my misdeed.
Nor do I make any objection, if ever I take up
the evil writings of Sestius, that their coldness might
bring a cold and cough not to me but to Sestius himself   20
who only invites me when I have read a bad book of his.

XLV

Acmen Septimius suos amores
tenens in gremio 'mea' inquit 'Acme,
ni te perdite amo atque amare porro
omnes sum assidue paratus annos,
quantum qui pote plurimum perire,   5
solus in Libya Indiaque tosta
caesio ueniam obuius leoni.'
hoc ut dixit, Amor sinistra ut ante
dextra sternuit approbationem.
  at Acme leuiter caput reflectens   10
et dulcis pueri ebrios ocellos
illo purpureo ore suauiata,
'sic' inquit 'mea uita Septimille,
huic uni domino usque seruiamus,
ut multo mihi maior acriorque   15
ignis mollibus ardet in medullis.'
hoc ut dixit, Amor sinistra ut ante
dextra sternuit approbationem.
  nunc ab auspicio bono profecti
mutuis animis amant amantur.   20
unam Septimius misellus Acmen
mauult quam Syrias Britanniasque:
uno in Septimio fidelis Acme
facit delicias libidinisque.
quis ullos homines beatiores   25
uidit, quis Venerem auspicatiorem?

XLVI

iam uer egelidos refert tepores,
iam caeli furor aequinoctialis
iucundis Zephyri silescit aureis.
linquantur Phrygii, Catulle, campi
Nicaeaeque ager uber aestuosae: 5

45

Septimius holding his love Acme
on his lap said 'my Acme,
if I do not love you desperately and am ready to love you
further continually through all my years
as much as one who loves most desperately,   5
may I be all alone in Libya and scorched India
and come face to face with a green-eyed lion.'
When he had said this, Love on the left as before
on the right sneezed approval.

But Acme, gently bending back her head   10
and kissing the swimming little eyes of her sweet boyfriend
with that crimson mouth of hers
said 'Thus, my life, my little Septimius,
let us be totally enslaved to this one lord
just as a much greater and fiercer fire   15
burns in the soft marrow of my bones.'
When she had said this, Love on the left as before
on the right sneezed approval.

Now starting out from favourable omens
with reciprocal feelings they love they are loved.   20
Love-sick little Septimius prefers Acme and her alone
to all your Syrias and Britains;
faithful Acme takes her delight and her pleasure
in Septimius alone.
Who has ever seen any people more fortunate?   25
Who has ever seen a more favoured love?

46

Now the spring brings back the ice-free warmths,
now the madness of the equinoctial heavens
grows silent with the pleasant breezes of the Zephyr.
Catullus, let the Phrygian plains be left behind
and the fertile field of sweltering Nicaea: 5

ad claras Asiae uolemus urbes.
iam mens praetrepidans auet uagari,
iam laeti studio pedes uigescunt.
o dulces comitum ualete coetus,
longe quos simul a domo profectos   10
diuersae uarie uiae reportant.

XLVII

Porci et Socration, duae sinistrae
Pisonis, scabies famesque mundi,
uos Veraniolo meo et Fabullo
uerpus praeposuit Priapus ille?
uos conuiuia lauta sumptuose   5
de die facitis, mei sodales
quaerunt in triuio uocationes?

XLVIII

mellitos oculos tuos, Iuuenti,
si quis me sinat usque basiare,
usque ad milia basiem trecenta
nec numquam uidear satur futurus,
non si densior aridis aristis   5
sit nostrae seges osculationis.

IL

disertissime Romuli nepotum,
quot sunt quotque fuere, Marce Tulli,
quotque post aliis erunt in annis,
gratias tibi maximas Catullus
agit pessimus omnium poeta,   5
tanto pessimus omnium poeta,
quanto tu optimus omnium patronus.

let us fly to the famous cities of Asia.
Already the mind is eager to wander, trembling in anticipation,
already the feet grow strong, happy in eagerness.
Farewell o sweet bands of companions,
who set out far away from home all together   10
but whom different roads are bringing back home on different routes.

47

Porcius and Socration, two left hands of Piso,
plague and famine of the world,
is it you that that shagged-out Priapus preferred
to my little Veranius and Fabullus?
Are you having rich banquets while it is still daylight   5
with no expense spared, while my friends
look out for invitations on the street-corner?

48

Juventius, if someone allowed me to carry on kissing
those honeyed eyes of yours,
I would kiss them right on to three hundred thousand
nor would I ever think that I was going to be sated
not even if the crop of our kissing   5
were denser than the dry ears of corn.

49

Most eloquent of the descendants of Romulus,
all that are, all that have been, Marcus Tullius,
and all that will be in other years;
Catullus the worst poet of them all
pays you the greatest thanks;   5
he is as much the worst poet of all
as you are the best patron of all.

L

hesterno, Licini, die otiosi
multum lusimus in meis tabellis,
ut conuenerat esse delicatos:
scribens uersiculos uterque nostrum
ludebat numero modo hoc modo illoc,   5
reddens mutua per iocum atque uinum.
atque illinc abii tuo lepore
incensus, Licini, facetiisque,
ut nec me miserum cibus iuuaret
nec somnus tegeret quiete ocellos,   10
sed toto indomitus furore lecto
uersarer, cupiens uidere lucem,
ut tecum loquerer, simulque ut essem.
at defessa labore membra postquam
semimortua lectulo iacebant,   15
hoc, iucunde, tibi poema feci,
ex quo perspiceres meum dolorem.
nunc audax caue sis, precesque nostras,
oramus, caue despuas, ocelle,
ne poenas Nemesis reposcat a te.   20
est uehemens dea: laedere hanc caueto.

LI

ille mi par esse deo uidetur,
ille, si fas est, superare diuos,
qui sedens aduersus identidem te
        spectat et audit
dulce ridentem, misero quod omnis   5
eripit sensus mihi: nam simul te,
Lesbia, aspexi, nihil est super mi
<vocis in ore>
lingua sed torpet, tenuis sub artus
flamma demanat, sonitu suopte   10
tintinant aures, gemina et teguntur

50

Yesterday, Licinius, with time on our hands,
we sported on my writing-tablets a lot
as we had agreed to be naughty,
each of us writing little verses
sported now in this metre now in that,   5
answering each other's ideas over jokes and wine.
I came away from there on fire with your
elegance, Licinius, and your humour,
so that neither food was any use to me in my wretched state
nor would sleep cover my little eyes with rest,   10
but wild with frenzy I tossed all over the bed
longing to see the dawn,
to speak with you and be with you.
But after my limbs were lying half-dead
exhausted with toil on the little bed,   15
I made this poem for you, my dear man,
to let you see my agony.
Now do not be rash and I beg you
do not spit back our prayers, dear thing,
in case Nemesis demands punishment from you.   20
She is a powerful goddess; beware of injuring her.

51

That man seems to be to be equal to a god,
that man, if it is right, seems to outdo the gods;
the one who, sitting opposite you again and again
sees you and hears you
laughing sweetly – a thing which steals   5
all sense from love-sick me. For as soon as
I caught sight of you, Lesbia, I have nothing left
of voice in my mouth
but my tongue is sluggish, a slender flame
steals under my limbs, my ears ring   10
with their own sound, my twin eyes

lumina nocte.

otium, Catulle, tibi molestum est:
otio exsultas nimiumque gestis:
otium et reges prius et beatas   15
    perdidit urbes.

8. uocis in ore : *supplevit Doering*

LII

quid est, Catulle? quid moraris emori?
sella in curuli struma Nonius sedet,
per consulatum peierat Vatinius:
quid est, Catulle? quid moraris emori?

LIII

risi nescio quem modo e corona,
qui, cum mirifice Vatiniana
meus crimina Caluos explicasset
admirans ait haec manusque tollens,
'di magni, salaputium disertum!'   5

LIV

Othonis caput oppido est pusillum,
et, trirustice, semilauta crura,
subtile et leue peditum Libonis,
si non omnia, displicere uellem
tibi et Sufficio seni recocto.   5
irascere iterum meis iambis
inmerentibus, unice imperator.

2 trirustice *Munro*: et eri rustice *V*.

are covered with night.
Idleness, Catullus, is a nuisance to you:
you exult and get too excited in idleness;
idleness has destroyed kings in the past   15
and prosperous cities.

52

What is it, Catullus? Why do you put off dying?
Nonius the wart sits in the curule chair,
Vatinius swears falsely by his consulship;
what is it, Catullus? Why put off dying?

53

I laughed just now at someone in the crowd,
who, when my friend Calvus had laid out
his charges against Vatinius in fine style,
in wonder raised his hands and said:
'great gods, a clever little prick!'

54

Otho's head is totally tiny,
and his legs half-washed, you bumpkin,
and the inconspicuous gentle farting of Libo –
if not all these things, then I wish some of them
would displease you and Sufficius the warmed up geriatric.   5
You will get angry again at my lampoons
innocent though they are, o commander without equal.

LV

oramus, si forte non molestum est,
demonstres ubi sint tuae tenebrae.
te Campo quaesiuimus minore,
te in Circo, te in omnibus libellis,
te in templo summi Iouis sacrato.   5
in Magni simul ambulatione
femellas omnes, amice, prendi,
quas uultu uidi tamen sereno.
a cette huc, sic usque flagitabam,
Camerium mihi pessimae puellae.   10
'en' inquit quaedam sinum reducens,
'en hic in roseis latet papillis.'
sed te iam ferre Herculi labos est;
tanto te in fastu negas, amice.
dic nobis ubi sis futurus, ede   15
audacter, committe, crede luci.
nunc te lacteolae tenent puellae?
si linguam clauso tenes in ore,
fructus proicies amoris omnes.
uerbosa gaudet Venus loquella.   20
uel, si uis, licet obseres palatum,
dum uestri sim particeps amoris.

9 cette huc *Camps* avelte *V*: usque *Munro* ipse *V*
10 en inquit quaedam *Goold*: q̄uaedam inquit *V*: sinum reducens *Avantius*: nudum reduc *V*.

LVI

o rem ridiculam, Cato, et iocosam,
dignamque auribus et tuo cachinno!
ride quidquid amas, Cato, Catullum:
res est ridicula et nimis iocosa.
deprendi modo pupulum puellae   5
trusantem; hunc ego, si placet Dionae,
protelo rigida mea cecidi.

55

We ask you, if perhaps it is not troublesome,
to show us where your hideaway is.
We looked for you in the smaller Campus,
in the Circus, in all the booksellers',
in the holy temple of highest Jove.   5
At the same time in the walkway of Pompey
I grabbed hold of all the tarts, my friend,
who I saw to have untroubled gaze.
'Give him here!' I kept demanding,
'worst of girls, give me my Camerius.'   10
One of them, drawing back her dress, said
'look he's here hiding in my rosy breasts!'
But to put up with you is a labour of Hercules;
you refuse your company, friend, with such pride.
Tell us where you are going to be, utter   15
it boldly, share it, publish the information.
Are the milky-white girls holding on to you?
If you keep your tongue locked up in a closed mouth
you will throw away all the fruits of love.
Venus is pleased with the talkative speech.   20
Or else, if you want, you may fasten up your mouth
so long as I am a partaker in your love.

56

O what an absurd thing, Cato, and what a laugh
worthy of your ears and your laughter!
Laugh as much, Cato, as you love Catullus:
the thing is funny and all too much of a laugh.
I just caught the girl's little pet   5
wanking: and so – if it please Dione! –
I banged him with my own stiffy in tandem.

LVII

pulcre conuenit improbis cinaedis,
Mamurrae pathicoque Caesarique.
nec mirum: maculae pares utrisque,
urbana altera et illa Formiana,
impressae resident nec eluentur: 5
morbosi pariter, gemelli utrique,
uno in lecticulo erudituli ambo,
non hic quam ille magis uorax adulter,
riuales socii puellularum.
pulcre conuenit improbis cinaedis.   10

LVIII

Caeli, Lesbia nostra, Lesbia illa.
illa Lesbia, quam Catullus unam
plus quam se atque suos amauit omnes,
nunc in quadriuiis et angiportis   → can also mean
glubit magnanimi Remi nepotes.   someone who   5
                                            is financially
  → obscene connotation   wasteful

LVIIIb

non custos si fingar ille Cretum,
non Ladas ego pinnipesue Perseus,
non si Pegaseo ferar uolatu,
non Rhesi niueae citaeque bigae;
adde huc plumipedas uolatilesque,   5
uentorumque simul require cursum,
quos iunctos, Cameri, mihi dicares:
defessus tamen omnibus medullis
et multis languoribus peresus
essem te mihi, amice, quaeritando.   10

versus 3,2 hoc ordine Muretus

57

They make a good pair, the shameless perverts
Mamurra and bumboy Caesar.
And no wonder – both of them has the same black marks
one from the city, the other from Formiae,
stamped on them for good and will not be washed away   5
equally diseased, a pair of identical twins,
both of them little scholars on the one same couch,
neither of them more greedy for sex than the other,
rival mates of the little girlies.
They make a good pair, the shameless perverts.   10

58

Caelius, my Lesbia, that Lesbia,
that Lesbia whom alone Catullus
loved more than himself and all his own people,
now in the crossroads and back alleys
she peels the grandsons of great-hearted Remus.   5

58b

Not if I were made that famous guard of the Cretans,
or Ladas or Perseus the wing-footed:
not if I moved with Pegasus' flight
of I were the snow-white swift chariots of Rhesus:
add to this the feather-footed and the flying   5
go look for the running of the winds at the same time,
you could hand me all those bound together
and I would still be tired out to the marrow of all my bones
and eaten away with many exhaustions
in looking for you, my friend.   10

LIX

Bononiensis Rufa Rufulum fellat,
uxor Meneni, saepe quam in sepulcretis
uidistis ipso rapere de rogo cenam,
cum deuolutum ex igne prosequens panem
ab semiraso tunderetur ustore.   5

LX

num te leaena montibus Libystinis
aut Scylla latrans infima inguinum parte
tam mente dura procreauit ac taetra,
ut supplicis uocem in nouissimo casu
contemptam haberes, a nimis fero corde?   5

LXIX

noli admirari, quare tibi femina nulla,
   Rufe, uelit tenerum supposuisse femur,
non si illam rarae labefactes munere uestis
   aut perluciduli deliciis lapidis.
laedit te quaedam mala fabula, qua tibi fertur   5
   ualle sub alarum trux habitare caper.
hunc metuunt omnes, neque mirum: nam mala ualde est
   bestia, nec quicum bella puella cubet.
quare aut crudelem nasorum interfice pestem,
   aut admirari desine cur fugiunt.   10

LXX

nulli se dicit mulier mea nubere malle
   quam mihi, non si se Iuppiter ipse petat.
dicit: sed mulier cupido quod dicit amanti,
   in uento et rapida scribere oportet aqua.

59

Bononian Rufa sucks Rufulus off,
the wife of Menenius, whom you have often seen
in graveyards snatching her dinner right off the funeral pyre,
running after a loaf that has rolled out of the fire
and getting banged by the stubbly cremator.   5

60

Could not even a lioness in the Libystine mountains
or Scylla barking from the lowest part of her groin
could give birth to you, one with so hard and foul a mind
as to hold in contempt the voice of a suppliant
in direst distress, o you of a heart all too savage?   5

69

Do not wonder why no woman
Rufus, is keen to put her slender flank under you,
even if you shake her resolve with the gift of a fine garment
or the delight of a gleaming stone.
There is a nasty tale which harms you, in which you are said   5
to have a fierce goat living under the valley of your armpits.
They are all scared of this. And no wonder: for it is a really bad
beast and one that a pretty girl would not go to bed with.
So either kill the vicious affliction of noses
or stop being surprised that they run away.   10

70

My woman says that she would prefer to marry nobody else
but me, not even if Jupiter himself asked her.
She says this: but what a woman says to her ardent lover
one ought to write on the wind and the fast-running water.

[handwritten annotations: "she hears what he wants to heal." / "don't trust what a hero says - women can't be trusted" / "Catullus finds ways to hint that his own responsibility for investing too much"]

LXXI.

si cui iure bono sacer alarum obstitit hircus,
    aut si quem merito tarda podagra secat.
aemulus iste tuus, qui uestrem exercet amorem,
    mirifice est apte nactus utrumque malum.
nam quotiens futuit, totiens ulciscitur ambos: 5
    illam affligit odore, ipse perit podagra.

5 apte *Kaster* a te *V.*

LXII.

dicebas quondam solum te nosse Catullum,
    Lesbia, nec prae me uelle tenere Iouem.
dilexi tum te non tantum ut uulgus amicam,
    sed pater ut gnatos diligit et generos.
nunc te cognoui: quare etsi impensius uror,   5
    multo mi tamen es uilior et leuior.
qui potis est, inquis? quod amantem iniuria talis
    cogit amare magis, sed bene uelle minus.

LXIII.

desine de quoquam quicquam bene uelle mereri
    aut aliquem fieri posse putare pium.
omnia sunt ingrata, nihil fecisse benigne
    <prodest> immo etiam taedet obestque magis;
ut mihi, quem nemo grauius nec acerbius urget,   5
    quam modo qui me unum atque unicum amicum habuit.

4 prodest *addidit Avantius*

71

If ever the accursed goat of the armpits rightly got in anyone's way,
or if limping gout torments anyone deservedly,
then that rival of yours, who is giving your love some training,
has caught both evils wonderfully and suitably.
For whenever he fucks he wreaks vengeance on them both: 5
he pains her with the smell while he dies himself with the gout.

[handwritten margin notes: comparing her to importance of political + dynastic ambition.]

72

You once said that you knew only Catullus,
Lesbia, and that you would not want to embrace Jupiter instead of me.
At that time I loved you, not so much as the mob loves a girlfriend
but as a father loves his sons and daughters' husbands.
Now I have got to know you: and so although I burn all the more
                                                          passionately
you are nonetheless much more cheap and fickle in my eyes.   6
How is that possible, you say? Because hurt like that forces the lover
to love more but to like less.

[handwritten: link to idea of like and love being different]

73

Stop wanting to earn any thanks from anyone
or thinking that someone can be made true.
All is thankless, there is no benefit in having acted kindly:
in fact it is even boring and more of a hindrance.
As in my case. Nobody besets me more heavily or more cruelly   5
than the man who only recently regarded me as his one and only
                                                          friend.

[handwritten notes: cruelty makes a lover all the more keen. — hate can inspire love, just an love can inspire different depth. hmm. no benevolence toward that person. you can have no fondness for a person yet still love them]

LXXIV

Gellius audierat patruum obiurgare solere,
si quis delicias diceret aut faceret.
hoc ne ipsi accideret, patrui perdepsuit ipsam
uxorem, et patruum reddidit Arpocratem.
quod uoluit fecit: nam, quamuis irrumet ipsum   5
nunc patruum, uerbum non faciet patruus.

LXXV

huc est mens deducta tua mea, Lesbia, culpa
atque ita se officio perdidit ipsa suo,
ut iam nec bene uelle queat tibi, si optima fias,
nec desistere amare, omnia si facias.

LXXVI

siqua recordanti benefacta priora uoluptas
est homini, cum se cogitat esse pium,
nec sanctam uiolasse fidem, nec foedere nullo
diuum ad fallendos numine abusum homines,
multa parata manent in longa aetate, Catulle,   5
ex hoc ingrato gaudia amore tibi.
nam quaecumque homines bene cuiquam aut dicere possunt
aut facere, haec a te dictaque factaque sunt.
omnia quae ingratae perierunt credita menti.
quare iam te cur amplius excrucies?   10
quin tu animo offirmas atque istinc teque reducis,
et dis inuitis desinis esse miser?
difficile est longum subito deponere amorem,
difficile est, uerum hoc qua lubet efficias:
una salus haec est. hoc est tibi peruincendum,   15
hoc facias, siue id non pote siue pote.
o di, si uestrum est misereri, aut si quibus umquam
extremam iam ipsa in morte tulistis opem,

74

Gellius had heard that uncle liked to censure
anyone who spoke or acted in a naughty way.
To stop this happening to him, he knocked off uncle's own
wife and made uncle a Harpocrates.
He did what he wanted: for even if he were to fuck   5
uncle's mouth now, uncle will not say a word.

75

Lesbia, my mind has been led down this road by your misdeeds
and so has wrecked itself by its own sense of duty,
so that by now it could not wish good for you, even if you become a
model person,
nor could it stop loving you, no matter what you did.

76

If a man gains any pleasure out of recalling previous acts of kindness
when he reflects that he is true
and has not outraged a solemn promise and has not in any contract
misused the power of the gods to deceive people,
then many joys lie waiting for you in a long lifetime, Catullus,   5
arising out of this thankless love.
For whatever good words or deeds people can do for anyone,
these have been said and done by you.
They have all gone for nothing, invested in a thankless mind.
So why will you continue to torture yourself any further?   10
Why not harden up your heart and rescue yourself back from there
and stop being lovesick when the gods are against you?
It is hard to lay aside a long love-affair suddenly.
It is hard, but you are to achieve this somehow.
This is the one hope of safety, this is a battle you have to win.   15
You are to do this, whether it is possible or not.
O gods, if it is your function to take pity or if ever
you have brought final help to anyone on the point of death,

me miserum aspicite et, si uitam puriter egi,
  eripite hanc pestem perniciemque mihi, 20
quae mihi subrepens imos ut torpor in artus
  expulit ex omni pectore laetitias.
non iam illud quaero, contra me ut diligat illa,
  aut, quod non potis est, esse pudica uelit:
ipse ualere opto et taetrum hunc deponere morbum. 25
  o di, reddite mi hoc pro pietate mea.

LXXVII

Rufe mihi frustra ac nequiquam credite amice
  (frustra? immo magno cum pretio atque malo),
sicine subrepsti mi, atque intestina perurens
  ei misero eripuisti omnia nostra bona?
eripuisti, heu heu nostrae crudele uenenum 5
  uitae, heu heu nostrae pestis amicitiae.

LXXVIII

Gallus habet fratres, quorum est lepidissima coniunx
  alterius, lepidus filius alterius.
Gallus homo est bellus: nam dulces iungit amores,
  cum puero ut bello bella puella cubet.
Gallus homo est stultus, nec se uidet esse maritum, 5
  qui patruus patrui monstret adulterium.

LXXVIIIb.

* * * * * * *

sed nunc id doleo, quod purae pura puellae
  suauia comminxit spurca saliua tua.
uerum id non impune feres: nam te omnia saecla
  noscent et, qui sis, fama loquetur anus.

then look at lovesick me and – if I have lived my life decently -
remove from me this disease and ruin 20
which, creeping like paralysis through the bottom of my limbs
has totally driven out joy from my breast.
I am not asking for her to love me in return,
or for her to want to be faithful (which is impossible).
I wish to be healthy and to put aside this foul sickness.
O Gods, give me this for the sake of my honest goodness. 25

77

Rufus, believed to be my friend in vain and all for nothing
(nothing? it actually cost me a lot of money and suffering)
is this how you have crept up on me and, burning through my insides,
have stolen all that we count good from lovesick me?
You have stolen from me, alas, alas, you vicious poison of our 5
life, alas, alas, you disease of our friendship.

78

Gallus has brothers. One of them has a very charming
wife, another has a charming son.
Gallus is a nice man: for he unites sweet lovers,
so that pretty girl sleeps with pretty boy.
Gallus is a fool, and doesn't see that he has a wife, 5
and that he the uncle is showing how to cuckold an uncle.

78b

..but what pains me now is that your foul saliva
has pissed on the innocent kisses of an innocent girl.
But you will not get away with this scot-free: for every age will
know you and the old woman rumour will speak of who you are.

LXXIX

Lesbius est pulcer. quid ni? quem Lesbia malit
quam te cum tota gente, Catulle, tua.
sed tamen hic pulcer uendat cum gente Catullum,
si tria notorum suauia reppererit.

LXXX

quid dicam, Gelli, quare rosea ista labella
hiberna fiant candidiora niue,
mane domo cum exis et cum te octaua quiete
e molli longo suscitat hora die?
nescio quid certe est: an uere fama susurrat   5
grandia te medii tenta uorare uiri?
sic certe est: clamant Victoris rupta miselli
ilia, et emulso labra notata sero.

LXXXI

nemone in tanto potuit populo esse, Iuuenti,
bellus homo, quem tu diligere inciperes,
praeterquam iste tuus moribunda ab sede Pisauri
hospes inaurata palladior statua,
qui tibi nunc cordi est, quem tu praeponere nobis   5
audes, et nescis quod facinus facias?

LXXXII

Quinti, si tibi uis oculos debere Catullum
aut aliud si quid carius est oculis,
eripere ei noli, multo quod carius illi
est oculis seu quid carius est oculis.

79

Lesbius is pretty. How could one disagree? Lesbia would prefer
him to you and all your family, Catullus.
And yet this pretty boy is welcome to sell Catullus and his family
if he can find three people he knows to kiss him.

80

What am I to say, Gellius, to explain why those rosy lips
grow whiter than winter snow
when you leave the house in the morning and when the eighth
hour wakes you from your soft slumber in the long day?
Something is certainly going on. Or is the rumour true which
whispers
that you swallow the massive stretchings at a man's middle?   6
That must be how it is. Poor Victor's shattered groin shouts it
and your lips stained with the white liquid that you have milked.

81

Iuventius, could you have found nobody in so great a population,
no nice man for you to start on a love-affair with
apart from that man of yours from the death's-door abode of Pisaurum
a visitor paler than a gilded statue:
who is now your favourite, whom you dare to prefer to us
and are ignorant of what a crime you are committing?

82

Quintius, if you want Catullus to owe you his eyes
or anything else which is dearer than eyes,
then do not remove that which is much dearer to him ·
than eyes or anything dearer than eyes.

LXXXIII

Lesbia mi praesente uiro mala plurima dicit:
haec illi fatuo maxima laetitia est.
mule, nihil sentis? si nostri oblita taceret,
sana esset: nunc quod gannit et obloquitur,
non solum meminit, sed, quae multo acrior est res,
irata est. hoc est, uritur et loquitur.

LXXXIV

chommoda dicebat, si quando commoda uellet
dicere, et insidias Arrius hinsidias,
et tum mirifice sperabat se esse locutum,
cum quantum poterat dixerat hinsidias.
credo, sic mater, sic semper auunculus eius.   5
sic maternus auus dixerat atque auia.
hoc misso in Syriam requierant omnibus aures
audibant eadem haec leniter et leuiter,
nec sibi postilla metuebant talia uerba,
cum subito affertur nuntius horribilis,   10
Ionios fluctus, postquam illuc Arrius isset,
iam non Ionios esse sed Hionios.

5 semper *Nisbet:* liber V

LXXXV

odi et amo. quare id faciam, fortasse requiris.
nescio, sed fieri sentio et excrucior.

LXXXVI

Quintia formosa est multis. mihi candida, longa,
recta est: haec ego sic singula confiteor.
totum illud formosa nego: nam nulla uenustas,
nulla in tam magno est corpore mica salis.

83

Lesbia abuses me a great deal when her husband is present:
this is the greatest joy to that blockhead.
You donkey, have you no sense? If she forgot me and kept quiet,
then she would be free of love: but as she snarls and nags,
she not only remembers but – much more to the point –   5
she is angry. That's it – she is burning and she speaks.

even her hateful comments are a form of love, as she cares enough to spend time talking about him.

anger is a form of love.

84

Arrius used to say 'hadvantages' if ever he wanted to say
advantages, and 'hambush' for 'ambush',
and then he hoped that he had spoken impressively
when he had said 'hambush' with all the force at his disposal.
I believe that is how his mother had always spoken, and his uncle too,
and his maternal grandfather and grandmother as well.   6
When this man was sent to Syria everybody's ears had a rest;
they heard these same things smoothly and softly,
and they did not fear such words afterwards,
when suddenly a dreadful messenger is brought in: 10
The Ionian waves, after Arrius had gone there,
were no longer 'Ionian' but 'Hionian'.

85

✗

I hate and I love. Why do I do that, you are perhaps asking?
I don't know, but I feel it happening and I am in torment.

86

Quintia is attractive to many. I grant she is fair, tall,   ✗
good posture – I admit these individual points.
I deny that whole 'attractive' business; for there is no charm,
no grain of salt in so large a body.

Lesbia formosa est, quae cum pulcerrima tota est,　　　　5
tum omnibus una omnis surripuit Veneres.

LXXXVII

nulla potest mulier tantum se dicere amatam
uere, quantum a me Lesbia amata mea est.
nulla fides ullo fuit umquam foedere tanta,
quanta in amore tuo ex parte reperta mea est.

LXXXVIII

quid facit is, Gelli, qui cum matre atque sorore
prurit, et abiectis peruigilat tunicis?
quid facit is, patruum qui non sinit esse maritum?
ecquid scis quantum suscipiat sceleris?
suscipit, o Gelli, quantum non ultima Tethys　　　　5
nec genitor Nympharum abluit Oceanus:
nam nihil est quicquam sceleris, quo prodeat ultra,
non si demisso se ipse uoret capite.

LXXXIX

Gellius est tenuis: quid ni? cui tam bona mater
tamque ualens uiuat tamque uenusta soror
tamque bonus patruus tamque omnia plena puellis
cognatis, quare is desinat esse macer?
qui ut nihil attingat, nisi quod fas tangere non est,　　　　5
quantumuis quare sit macer inuenies.

Lesbia is attractive; she is all most beautiful   5
and what's more she alone has stolen all the charms from everyone.

87

No woman can say she has been loved
truly as much as Lesbia has been loved by me.
No trust this great has ever existed in any bond
as much as has been found in my love for you – on my side.

88

Gellius, what is he doing, who lusts with mother and sister
and does it all night with clothes thrown off?
What is he doing, who does not let his uncle have a wife?
do you know how great a crime he is undertaking?
He is undertaking one so big that not even furthest Tethys   5
washes it away, nor Oceanus father of the Nymphs:
for there is no crime that he could move into beyond this one,
not even if he lowered his head and swallowed himself.

89

Gellius is thin: how could he not be? When he has an obliging
                                                                            mother
who is so hearty, and so charming a sister
so obliging an uncle and the whole place so full of girls
related to him, why should he stop being thin?
Even though he never laid a hand on anything except what is
                                                            forbidden to touch,
you will still find as much reason as you could want for him being
                                                                              thin.

XC

nascatur magus ex Gelli matrisque nefando
  coniugio et discat Persicum aruspicium:
nam magus ex matre et gnato gignatur oportet,
  si uera est Persarum impia religio,
gratus ut accepto ueneretur carmine diuos   5
  omentum in flamma pingue liquefaciens.

XCI

non ideo, Gelli, sperabam te mihi fidum
  in misero hoc nostro, hoc perdito amore fore,
quod te cognossem bene constantemue putarem
  aut posse a turpi mentem inhibere probro;
sed neque quod matrem nec germanam esse uidebam   5
  hanc tibi, cuius me magnus edebat amor.
et quamuis tecum multo coniungerer usu,
  non satis id causae credideram esse tibi.
tu satis id duxti: tantum tibi gaudium in omni
  culpa est, in quacumque est aliquid sceleris.   10

XCII

Lesbia mi dicit semper male nec tacet umquam
  de me: Lesbia me dispeream nisi amat.
quo signo? quia sunt totidem mea: deprecor illam
  assidue, uerum dispeream nisi amo.

XCIII

nil nimium studeo, Caesar, tibi uelle placere,
  nec scire utrum sis albus an ater homo.

90

Let there be born a magus from the unspeakable union of Gellius
and his mother, and let him learn Persian fortune-telling.
For it is right and proper that the magus be born from mother and son,
if the Persians' unholy religion be true,
so that he may be pleasing and venerate the gods with acceptable
singing
as he turns the fat caul to liquid in the flames.   6

91

The reason, Gellius, that I was hoping you would be loyal to me,
in this wretched, this ruined love-affair of ours
was not because I had got to know you well or thought you reliable,
and able to restrain your mind from scandalous disgrace,
but rather because I saw that this woman, for whom deep love was
eating me away,
was neither mother nor sister to you.   6
And although I was joined with you in a long intimacy,
I had not thought that that was enough reason for you:
and yet you thought it enough: that's how much joy you take
in all misdeeds, in anything in which there is some crime.   10

92

Lesbia is always criticising me and never stops talking
about me: may I perish if Lesbia does not love me.
On what evidence? Because my situation is much the same: I
criticise
her all the time, but may I perish if I do not love her.

93

Caesar, I am not overkeen to want to please you,
nor to know whether you are a white man or a black.

XCIV

Mentula moechatur. Moechatur mentula? Certe.
Hoc est quod dicunt: ipsa olera olla legit.

XCV

Zmyrna mei Cinnae nonam post denique messem
quam coepta est nonamque edita post hiemem,
milia cum interea quingenta Hortensius uno
. . . .
Zmyrna sacras Satrachi penitus mittetur ad undas,   5
Zmyrnam cana diu saecula peruoluent.
at Volusi annales Paduam morientur ad ipsam
et laxas scombris saepe dabunt tunicas.
parva mei mihi sint cordi monimenta sodalis,
at populus tumido gaudeat Antimacho.   10

5 sacras *Morgan:* canas *V:* cavas ζη
8 sodalis *addidit editio Aldina*

XCVI

si quicquam mutis gratum acceptumque sepulcris
accidere a nostro, Calue, dolore potest,
quo desiderio ueteres renouamus amores
atque olim missas flemus amicitias,
certe non tanto mors immatura dolori est   5
Quintiliae, quantum gaudet amore tuo.

XCVII

non (ita me di ament) quicquam referre putaui,
utrumne os an culum olfacerem Aemilio.
nilo mundius hoc, nihiloque immundius illud,
uerum etiam culus mundior et melior:

94

Prick is an adulterer. An adulterer, Prick? Yes, for sure.
This is what they say: 'the pot picks its own herbs'.

95

The Zmyrna of my friend Cinna has been published at last, after nine
harvests and after the ninth winter after it was begun,
while all the time Hortensius ... five hundred thousand in one...
. . . .
Zmyrna will be sent all the way to the holy waves of the Satrachus;   5
hoary ages will long read Zmyrna.
But the Annals of Volusius will die right at the Po
and will often provide loose wrapping for mackerel.
May my friend's small-scale monument be dear to my heart;
let the people rejoice at the inflated Antimachus.   10

96

If anything welcome or acceptable to the dumb tomb
can arise from our grief, Calvus,
from the desire with which we renew old loves
and weep over friendships which we once let slip,
then for sure Quintilia is not so much grieved at her untimely death   5
as happy at your love for her.

97

So help me gods – I thought it made no difference
whether it was Aemilius' mouth or his arsehole which I smelt.
The one no cleaner, the other no dirtier,
but in fact the arsehole is cleaner and better:

nam sine dentibus est. hic dentis sesquipedalis,   5
gingiuas uero ploxeni habet ueteris,
praeterea rictum qualem diffissus in aestu
meientis mulae cunnus habere solet.
hic futuit multas et se facit esse uenustum,
et non pistrino traditur atque asino?   10
quem siqua attingit, non illam posse putemus
aegroti culum lingere carnificis?

XCVIII

in te, si in quemquam, dici pote, putide Victi,
id quod uerbosis dicitur et fatuis.
ista cum lingua, si usus ueniat tibi, possis
culos et crepidas lingere carpatinas.
si nos omnino uis omnes perdere, Victi,   5
hiscas: omnino quod cupis efficies.

XCIX

surripui tibi, dum ludis, mellite Iuuenti,
suauiolum dulci dulcius ambrosia.
uerum id non impune tuli: namque amplius horam
suffixum in summa me memini esse cruce,
dum tibi me purgo nec possum fletibus ullis   5
tantillum uestrae demere saeuitiae.
nam simul id factum est, multis diluta labella
guttis abstersisti mollibus articulis,
ne quicquam nostro contractum ex ore maneret,
tamquam commictae spurca saliua lupae.   10
praeterea infesto miserum me tradere amori
non cessasti omnique excruciare modo,
ut mi ex ambrosia mutatum iam foret illud
suauiolum tristi tristius elleboro.
quam quoniam poenam misero proponis amori,   15
numquam iam posthac basia surripiam.

8. mollibus *Lee*; omnibus *V*

at least it has no teeth. The mouth has teeth a foot and a half long   5
and gums like those an old wagon-box might have,
and a grin besides like the split open cunt
of a mule pissing in the summer.
He fucks lots of girls and thinks he is charming
and is not handed on to the mill and the donkey?   10
Should we not think that any woman who touches him
could lick the arsehole of a hangman with diarrhoea?

98

Smelly Victius, of you, if of anybody, it can be said
(that which is said to gasbags and blockheads)
with that tongue, if the occasion arose for you,
you could lick arseholes and peasant boots.
If you want to destroy us all altogether, Victus,   5
just open your mouth: you will achieve all you desire.

99

Honeyed Juventius, while you were playing, I stole from you
a little kiss sweeter than sweet ambrosia.
But I did not get it for nothing, for then for more than an hour
I remember being nailed on the top of a cross
while I excused myself and could not with any amount of tears   5
take away even a tiny bit of your savagery.
For as soon as it was done, your lips were wet with many
tears and you wiped them off with soft knuckles
in case any infection remained from my mouth,
as if it were the disgusting spit of some pissed-on tart.   10
Nor did you wait to hand me over, lovesick, to angry Love
and to torture me in every way,
so that that little kiss was transformed from ambrosia now
to be more bitter than bitter hellebore.
As this is the punishment which you inflict on a sad lover,   15
I will never again steal kisses from now on.

C

Caelius Aufillenum et Quintius Aufillenam
flos Veronensum depereunt iuuenum,
hic fratrem, ille sororem. hoc est, quod dicitur, illud
fraternum uere dulce sodalicium.
cui faueam potius? Caeli, tibi: nam tua nobis   5
perspecta ex igni est unica amicitia,
cum uesana meas torreret flamma medullas.
sis felix, Caeli, sis in amore potens.

CI

multas per gentes et multa per aequora uectus
aduenio has miseras, frater, ad inferias,
ut te postremo donarem munere mortis
et mutam nequiquam alloquerer cinerem.   *mihi = dative of*
quandoquidem fortuna mihi tete abstulit ipsum,   *disadvantage* 5
heu miser indigne frater adempte mihi,
nunc tamen interea haec, prisco quae more parentum
tradita sunt tristi munere ad inferias,
accipe fraterno multum manantia fletu,
atque in perpetuum, frater, aue atque uale.   10

CII

si quicquam tacito commissum est fido ab amico,
cuius sit penitus nota fides animi,
me aeque esse inuenies illorum iure sacratum,
Corneli, et factum me esse puta Harpocratem.

3 aeque *Vossius:* que *V*

100

Caelius and Quintius, the flower of the young of Verona,
are madly in love with Aufillenus and Aufillena,
the one for the brother, the other the sister. This is,
as they say, that real fraternal unity.
Whom should I favour more? You, Caelius; for your   5
singular friendship for me was proved out of the fire
when the crazy flame was scorching my bone-marrow.
Be happy, Caelius, be potent in love.

101

Through many peoples and carried across many seas
I come to these sad burial-rites, brother,
so that I might endow you with the final gift of death
and address your silent ashes to no purpose.
Since fortune has robbed me of you yourself,   5
alas, sad brother unworthily stolen from me,
but at any rate now receive these rites, which in the ancestral custom
of our parents have been handed down as a bitter gift at funerals,
rites flowing much with brotherly weeping,
and, brother, for all time, hail and farewell.   10

102

If anything was ever entrusted by a trusty friend to a silent one
whose loyalty of spirit was fully known,
then you will find me just as bound by their rule,
Cornelius, and turned into – let's say – Harpocrates.

CIII

aut sodes mihi redde decem sestertia, Silo,
  deinde esto quamuis saeuus et indomitus:
aut, si te nummi delectant, desine quaeso
  leno esse atque idem saeuus et indomitus.

CIV

credis me potuisse meae maledicere uitae,
  ambobus mihi quae carior est oculis?
non potui, nec, si possem, tam perdite amarem:
  sed tu cum Tappone omnia monstra facis.

CV

mentula conatur Pipleium scandere montem:
  Musae furcillis praecipitem eiciunt.

CVI.

cum puero bello praeconem qui uidet esse,
  quid credat, nisi se uendere discupere?

CVII

si quicquam cupido optantique optigit umquam
  insperanti, hoc est gratum animo proprie.
quare hoc est gratum nobisque est carius auro
  quod te restituis, Lesbia, mi cupido.
restituis cupido atque insperanti, ipsa refers te   5
  nobis. o lucem candidiore nota!
quis me uno uiuit felicior aut magis hac res
  optandas uita dicere quis poterit?

---

3 nobisque est *Haupt:* quoque *V*
7-8 res optandas *Lachmann:* est optandus *V*

103

Please, Silo, either give me back the ten sestertia
and then be as brutal and wild as you like;
or else, if the cash pleases you, then please stop
being a pimp if you can't stop being brutal and wild.

104

Do you think that I could have slandered the love of my life
who is dearer to me than both my eyes?
I could not have: if I could, then I would not love her so desperately.
But you and the clown are up to all sorts of things.

105

Prick is trying to climb the Mount of Pipla:
the Muses chuck him head over heels down again with pitchforks.

106

What would anyone who sees that an auctioneer is with a pretty boy
think but that he wants to sell himself?

107

If anything ever fell to the lot of one who desired and prayed for it
but dared not hope – then this is really pleasing to the mind.
That is why this is pleasing and dearer to me than gold,
the fact that you give yourself back to me who longs for you.
You give yourself back to the desiring one who dares not hope, you
come back
to us. O Day with a whiter mark!   6
Who lives luckier than me, or who will be able to speak of things
more to be wished for than this life?

CVIII

si, Comini, populi arbitrio tua cana senectus
    spurcata impuris moribus intereat,
non equidem dubito quin primum inimica bonorum
    lingua exsecta auido sit data uulturio,
effossos oculos uoret atro gutture coruus,   5
    intestina canes, cetera membra lupi.

CIX

iucundum, mea uita, mihi proponis amorem
    hunc nostrum inter nos perpetuumque fore.
di magni, facite ut uere promittere possit,
    atque id sincere dicat et ex animo,
ut liceat nobis tota perducere uita   5
    aeternum hoc sanctae foedus amicitiae.

CX

Aufilena, bonae semper laudantur amicae:
    accipiunt pretium, quae facere instituunt.
tu, quod promisti, mihi quod mentita inimica es,
    quod nec das et fers saepe, facis facinus.
aut facere ingenuae est, aut non promisse pudicae,   5
    Aufillena, fuit: sed data corripere
fraudando est furis, plus quam meretricis auarae
    quae sese toto corpore prostituit.

7 est furis *Munro:* efficit *V:* officiis *Bergk*

CXI

Aufilena, uiro contentam uiuere solo,
    nuptarum laus ex laudibus eximiis:

108
Cominius, if by the will of the people your white-haired old age,
polluted with filthy habits, were to die,
then I at any rate have no doubt that first of all your tongue
enemy of the good, would be cut out and given to a greedy vulture,
a black-throated raven would peck out and eat your eyes,   5
dogs attack your guts, wolves the rest of your limbs.

109
My life, you propose that this love of ours will be pleasant
and everlasting between us.
Great gods, make her able to promise truly,
and let her say that with feeling and from the heart,
so that we may be allowed through all our life to carry on   5
this everlasting bond of holy friendship.

110
Aufillena, obliging girlfriends are always praised:
they get the reward for what they undertake to do.
But you are no friend: you lied about what you promised,
you often take but do not give and so commit a crime.
An honest girl does it, a chaste one does not promise,   5
Aufillena; but to snatch what is offered
in deceit is the behaviour of a thief, more than that of a greedy whore
who prostitutes herself totally.

111
Aufillena, to live content with one man only
is the highest praise of all praise for wives:

sed cuiuis quamuis potius succumbere par est,
quam matrem fratres ex patruo parere.

4 *lacunam exhibuit V:* parere *supplevit Doering*

CXII

multus homo es, Naso, neque tecum multus homost quin
te scindat: Naso, multus es et pathicus.

1 est quin *supplevit Schwabe*

CXIII

consule Pompeio primum duo, Cinna, solebant
Maeciliam: facto consule nunc iterum
manserunt duo, sed creuerunt milia in unum
singula. fecundum semen adulterio.

CXIV

Firmano saltu non falso Mentula diues
fertur, qui tot res in se habet egregias,
aucupium omne genus, piscis, prata, arua ferasque.
nequiquam: fructus sumptibus exsuperat.
quare concedo sit diues, dum omnia desint.   5
saltum laudemus, dum modio ipse egeat.

1 Firmano saltu *Aldinus* Firmanus salvis *V*
6 modio *Richmond:* modo *V*

CXV

mentula habet iuxta triginta iugera prati,
quadraginta arui: cetera sunt maria.
cur non diuitiis Croesum superare potis sit,
uno qui in saltu tot bona possideat,

but it is better to go to bed with anybody at all
than to be a mother giving birth to cousins from your uncle.

112

You're a great man, Naso, and there's not a great number of men who
                                                              don't
fuck you: Naso, you're a great guy and a poof.

113

When Pompey was consul for the first time, Cinna, two men used to
                                                              do
Maecilia. Now he has been made consul again
the two have stayed, but a thousand have grown up for each one.
Seed is fertile in adultery.

114

Prick is called rich in his estate at Firmum, and rightly so
as the estate has so many outstanding features in it,
fowl of all kinds, fish, meadows, ploughland, game.
All for nothing: he exceeds his income with his expenses.
So I don't mind him being 'rich' as long as he has nothing.   5
Let us praise his estate so long as he hasn't even a cup of corn.

115

Prick has about twenty acres of meadow
and twenty-seven of ploughland. The rest is swamp.
Why is he not able to outdo Croesus for his wealth,
as he has so many good things in his estate,

prata arua ingentes siluas vastasque paludesque   5
usque ad Hyperboreos et mare ad Oceanum?
omnia magna haec sunt, tamen ipsest maximus ultro,
non homo, sed uero mentula magna minax.

1 iuxta *Scaliger:* instar V
5 vastasque *Pleitner:* saltusque V

CXVI

saepe tibi studioso animo uenante requirens
  carmina uti possem mittere Battiadae,
qui te lenirem nobis, neu conarere
  tela infesta mittere in usque caput,
hunc uideo mihi nunc frustra sumptum esse laborem,   5
  Gelli, nec nostras hic ualuisse preces.
contra nos tela ista tua euitabimus acta
  at fixus nostris tu dabis supplicium.

7 acta *Baehrens;* amitha V

meadows, ploughlands, huge forests and vast marshes   5
right up to the Hyperboreans and Oceanus' sea?
These are all great, but the master is the greatest of all,
not a man but a big threatening prick.

116

Often searching with a diligent mind hunting out
how to be able to send you poems of Battiades
to soften you towards me and stop you trying
to fire hostile weapons right at my head,
I now see that this labour was undertaken in vain,   5
Gellius, and my prayers had no strength at all in this.
So in return we will evade those weapons which you have launched
but you will be pierced by ours and pay the penalty.

1

A dedicatory poem addressed to Cornelius Nepos (110–24 B.C.), a contemporary of the poet, of whose massive output only fragments and the brief biographical essays survive. Modern opinion is less kind than Catullus': Horsfall describes Nepos as an 'intellectual pygmy' (*CHCL* 2.116) and the latest *OCD* lists his faults as 'hasty and careless composition and lack of control of his material ... As historian his value is slight ... his style is plain.' (*OCD* s.v. 'Cornelius Nepos'). There is one reference to Catullus in the surviving works of Nepos (*Att.* 12.4). Poem 102 (q.v.) mentions a 'Cornelius' and there is a reference in 67.35 to a Cornelius 'with whom this woman committed shameful adultery' – but Cornelius was not a uncommon name in Rome and it would be unwise to identify such characters with too much certainty.

For the convention of dedicating a poem to a named individual, cf. Lucretius dedicating the *de rerum natura* to Memmius, the governor whom Catullus served in Bithynia (poems 10 and 28–9–10). The convention of addressing a named person in didactic poetry has the appearance of naming the person whose 'conversion' is sought by the text – from Hesiod's good advice to his brother Perses onwards. Catullus' poems have no such protreptic ambition and the dedication is a literary compliment, and one which the dedicatee returned when he named Catullus and Lucretius the most significant poets of the generation (*Att.* 12.4, cited Syndikus 71).

Metre: hendecasyllabics

1   **To whom ...?**: The indicative form of the verb introduce a catechism-like quality to the opening of the poem; 'to whom is the book dedicated? To Nepos'. It is surely not the 'deliberative' form of the indicative – since the dedication is presumably not imagined as being decided in the interstice between lines 2 and 3 but is fixed long before by great kindness on the part of the dedicatee (cf. 3–5).

The three final words of the line all describe the appearance of the book but are also all highly charged in late Republican poetry. *lepidum* has the basic sense of 'charming, elegant' and bears more than a trace of the Greek *leptos* familiar as a term of poetic approval since Callimachus. *nouum* of course connotes the *noui poetae* ('Neoterics') of whom Catullus was a leading voice, and the term was used by Virgil to refer to the 'new poetry' of Pollio (*Ecl.* 3.86) who wrote erotic *nugae* (Pliny *Ep.* 5.3.5); and the diminutive *libellus* also suggests the small-scale perfection of form to which the new poets aspired, as opposed to the verbose epics ridiculed in 95 as 'paper to wrap mackerel'.

2   **just polished**: The line refers again to the outward appearance of the book: pumice stone was used to smooth off the ends of the papyrus roll (*uolumen*) and such stone is notoriously dry. The term *expolitum* contains a metaphor also, however, in that the verse itself is also 'highly polished' but *aridus* is a term usually used of tedious and unadorned oratorical style (*OLD* s.v. *aridus* 9) and also harsh or grating vocal sound (*OLD* s.v. 5). This allows Catullus the quaint paradox that the *arida* stone can produce a book of poetry which is *lepidus* and a thing to last for ever (*perenne).*

3   **Cornelius**: For Cornelius Nepos see introductory note. Notice here the repeated *tibi ... tu* stressing the personal dedication and its motives, and also the reciprocity suggested in *meas* following after *tu.*

4   **trifling**: The poet dismisses his poetry as *nugas*; a term used of lighter verse-forms in later poetry (Martial 1.113 etc) and recalling the Greek term *paignia* (e.g. *A.P.* 6,322, 12.258.1; see *LSJ* for further reff.) but here used in less generic terms as simply a foil to the grandeur of the dedicatee's own literary output; cf. how later on the book is again lightly dismissed as *quidquid ... qualecumque.*

5-7   Nepos wrote a History (*Chronica*), now lost, in three volumes. This is not by any means a long piece of work – dwarfed by Nepos' own 16–book *de uiris illustribus* and minute compared to Livy's gigantic *ab urbe condita* in 150 books. The reference to Nepos' three volumes has led some editors to speculate that Catullus published *his* poetry in three volumes also (see Introduction: 'The Transmission of the Text').

6   **rolls**: *cartis* is 'hardly a grand synonym for *uolumina* (Quinn); the word is certainly not pejorative, however, as is clear from Lucretius 3. 10 ('O illustrious (Epicurus), from your *chartis* we ... feed on your golden words.'). The word *explicare* is the term for unrolling a scroll – Roman 'books' were in fact scrolls of papyrus – and also has the sense of 'explaining, giving an account of' (*OLD* s.v. 8). The joke here is that three pages would not need a lot of (literal) *explicatio* but might contain a great deal of metaphorical *explicatio*.

7   **learned**: *doctus* is a term of high praise in literature of the period; but *laboriosus* is a more elusive term, connoting hard work in the creation of the book (*OLD* s.v. 1) but also pain perhaps in the reading of the volume.

9   The ms reading is *qualecumque, quod patrona uirgo* which would introduce an address by the poet to his 'patroness virgin' the Muse and would leave the line a syllable short metrically – a gap which editors usually fill by adding *o* after *quod*. The reading is not impossible: for the poet's relationship to the Muse as one of Roman *clientela* Fordyce compares [Sulpicia] 11 ('descend to the prayers of your *cliens* ... ') and Lucretius (6.92–5) addresses Calliope as leading him to the conclusion of his poem where the poet's hopes of winning the 'crown with outstanding praise' depend on his divine patroness. It would also be hardly surprising to have the poet address the Muse at the beginning of his book of poems. A tempting reading is Bergk's *qualecumque quidem est patroni ut ergo* which supplies a verb for *quidquid* and *qualecumque* and also provides neat closure of the dedicatory poem with a reminder of the power of the dedicatee. After the self-deprecating tone of the description of the poem, this faith in the dedicatee is well-placed. The corruption can easily be explained as a failure on the part of the scribe to understand the comparatively unusual *ergo* and reading *virgo* instead. For the use of *ergo* cf. Lucretius 3.78 ('people die *statuarum et nominis ergo* – for the sake of statues and a name').

2

The first of the love poems and (possibly for that reason) the most famous poem in the collection. The poem and the succeeding one made the sparrow as famous as the poet, Catullus' mistress being referred to simply as 'the girl whose dead sparrow disturbed her bright eyes' in Juvenal *Sat.* 6. 7–8.

A playful poem about the pet bird of the poet's mistress conceals a lot of literary artistry and no less difficulty for the editor. The poem is in hymn-formula, with a named address to the bird followed by almost eight lines of description before a final two lines of prayer. It is in a tradition going back to the Greek Anthology; Meleager (*A.P.* 7.195–6) composed similar hymns to a locust and a cicada, and poems addressed to birds are also found (*A.P.* 7.199, 203). There is also a scholarly debate which has raged for hundreds of years about the meaning of *passer* which (some say) here is a pet name or slang term for the poet's phallus: the innuendo certainly works – see for instance the sexual language of lines 2–3 and 12–13 – but such coyness is not the poet's usual style and the matter cannot be regarded as certain either way.

Metre: hendecasyllabics

1 **Sparrow**: Note how the poem begins with the keyword, and the line is framed by the alliterative *passer ... puellae.* The line is strongly emphatic in that it contains four vital words – the bird, the darling, the girl – and she is 'mine'. *deliciae* is used frequently; cf. 3.4, 45.24

2–3 Note the tricolon crescendo of relative clauses: *quicum...quem...cui* and also the expressive and appropriately dental alliteration of p, d and t in line 3. The reciprocal movement of the bird and the mistress is well evoked by the juxtaposition of *dare appetenti.* Above all, note the sexual undertones of the girl's behaviour with the bird: *ludere* has the sense of 'sexual sport' (*OLD* s.v. 'ludo' 4), the *sinus* is the bosom and the closeness of intimacy (cf. 37.11), the sharp bites recall 8.18 and Lucretius 4.1109. The girl is seen as a sexual being even when she is only playing with the *passer;* and cf. the way in which the behaviour of lovers is compared with that of doves in 68. 125–7: sparrows are presented pulling the chariot of Aphrodite in Sappho frag. 1.9–12. The association of birds and sex is thus hardly novel.

5 **gleaming with longing**: *desiderio* has attracted controversy: Nisbet (1978) has argued convincingly that the word cannot be dative agreeing with *nitenti* but rather ablative after it ('gleaming with longing'), which clearly makes linguistic sense and helps the theme of the poem to be expressed: when she is ardent with desire she can play with the sparrow and thus help her *grauis ardor* to abate.

7 **little solace**: Note the diminutive *solaciolum* to express the tiny bird. The mss reading is difficult here:

   et solaciolum sui doloris/ credo, ut cum grauis acquiescet ardor

et does not make sense and has usually been replaced with *ut* meaning 'as'; likewise *cum* is suspect and is better emended to *tum* ('so that her heavy passion might then rest') as by for instance Fordyce and Quinn. Munro (followed by Goold) transposes the two lines and reads:

   credo, ut cum grauis acquiscet ardor
   sit solaciolum sui doloris

which places a very different interpretation on the lines: far from the bird being a means to assuage her passion, it is now a consolation for her when her passion does not burn. The decision must rest at least partly on the meaning of *dolor*: the primary meaning 'pain' is here either the mental anguish of feeling no desire (Goold translates: 'so that, I fancy, when her fierce passion subsides/ it may prove a diversion for her pain') or else the anguish of desire (where *dolor* would have to be *ardor* unsatisfied). *ardor* is properly 'burning' and can mean both passion and also anger (e.g. Lucretius 3.289, Livy 5.41.4). The phrasing *grauis acquiescat* is medical in tone and suggests that *ardor* may even carry the sense of 'fever' (*OLD* s.v. 3b) or perhaps more aptly sexual excitement and passion (cf. Lucretius 4.1086). Transposing the lines would give a more natural sense to the lines: when her passion/fever abates, she always has the bird to cheer her up. The sparrow is hardly adequate to dispel the fever, but is there to provide entertainment once the *ardor* is past.

9–10 The usual reading of the lines urges that the poet is contrasting the *grauis ardor* of the mistress which can be relieved by a bird and the *tristes curas* of the poet which this simple remedy not help. One expects the poet to say that he wishes he were enjoying the same closeness to the mistress as the bird; *tecum ludere* picks up *quicum ludere* of line 2. *ipsa* here means the 'mistress'.

11–13 There is no certainty about the placing of these lines. They can be made to follow on from line 10 by emending *possem* to *posse* and making the whole sentence in apposition to the infinitive: 'to be able to play with you ... is as welcome as ... ' (so Goold). The 'swift girl' was Atalanta who agreed to marry the suitor who could beat her in a running race and was duly beaten by Hippomenes/Milanion who had been given a golden apple by Venus which he threw down in front of Atalanta and thus distracted her. The tale is referred to in Propertius 1.1 and told in detail in Ovid *Met.* 10.560–680

3

A lament for the death of the bird addressed in poem 2. The poem follows the conventions of the dirge: the Greek Anthology has a fair number of such Animal Threnodies (*A.P.* 7. 189–213). The tone of the poem is open to conjecture in interpretation: what appears to be a dirge for a bird ends with the poet's sorrowing gaze fixed firmly on the girl who owned it, an ending prefigured in the opening line with its grief (*lugete*) outweighed by love (*ueneres cupidinesque*): and the very use of the dirge form is bathetic in the context of the dead bird – much as Ovid was later to compose a burlesque dirge for Corinna's dead parrot (*Am.* 2.6).

Metre: hendecasyllabics

1–2   The opening invocation appears to invoke the plural goddesses of love as described by Pausanias in Plato's *Symp.* (180d–182a) – a heavenly Aphrodite Uranios and the 'ordinary' Aphrodite Pandemos, each with her attendant Cupid. The mock solemnity of this opening is quickly called into question with the word *uenustiorum* which means both 'men of Venus' and also 'men of *venus* (i.e. charm)', the term placed for emphasis on the end of the second line after what we thought was going to be simply a 'gods and men' phrase.

3–4   **sparrow ... sparrow**: Note the obvious repetition of words here: *passer...meae puellae* occur in both lines, and line 4 is an exact repetition of 2.1. The repetition has a fittingly incantatory, dirge-like effect.

5ff.   The bird is described in terms often used of the human beloved: *deliciae* is often used to mean 'mistress' (cf. 6.1); for the beloved as 'dearer than eyes' see 82.3, 104.2; this bird is 'honey sweet' as is the beloved in 48.1, 99.1, Plautus *Cas.* 135, Cicero *Att.*1.18.1.

7   **mistress**: For the use of *ipsa* as mistress cf. 2.9. For the love as filial cf. the poet's own love expressed at 72.3–4 as 'not so much as the mob loves a girlfriend but as a father loves his sons and daughters' husbands'.

9–10   The sounds and movements of the bird are well evoked in the Latin: *modo huc modo illuc* of the jumping bird, *pipiabat* nicely onomatopeiac of the chirping sound.

11–12   **Now**: After the cheerful reminiscence of the past the poem suddenly jumps to the present: *nunc*. Note here the obvious *it–er–it–er* sound-effects of *it per iter*, the long adjective *tenebricosum*, and the *topos* of *unde negant redire quemquam* on which Fordyce cites Theocritus 17.120 and Philetas fr. 6 (Powell). These lines sound parodistic in the case of a dead bird: and yet Syndikus believes them to be sincere expression of the poet's love which allows him to share her grief and thus indulge their un-Roman sentimentality without embarrassment. The verb *it* is however unfortunate in that case: for grief to be heartfelt we do not expect to be presented with a picture of the little bird hopping down the road to death. The lines are more easily read as burlesque of the dirge tradition in literature, and the fact that many earlier Greek poets had addressed animals in similar terms does not of course prove anything either way.

13   **you**: The poet turns to address the shades of Orcus (the king of the Underworld), with obvious repetition in *male ... malae* and *tenebrae* picking up *tenebricosum* from line 11.

14–15   **pretty**: Note the repetition of *bella...bellum* and the parallel verbs concluding each of the two lines.

16 The ms reading leaves a hiatus in the middle of the line which modern use of punctuation can conceal but which needs Goold's conjecture *quod* to remove: there is a parallel for such a hiatus after an exclamation in 38.2, and the reading is otherwise secure; but Roman texts did not use punctuation.

17–18 **my girl's**: The real reason for the poet's grief is at last revealed; it is not the suffering of the bird but the grief of his girlfriend which upsets him. Notable here are the use of diminutives (*turgiduli...ocelli*) and also the repetition of the *l* sound. The ending of the poem explains what has gone before and settles the issues of the poet's tone. His sentimentality over the bird is now seen as both genuine and also insincere at the same time: he is 'genuinely' moved with grief, but not for the bird.

4

After a burlesque of grief over a dead bird, the poet turns to personify a boat in a burlesque of the 'retirement' or even 'obituary' speech. The poem belongs in a group with 46 and 31, all of which refer to Bithynia, which also happens to be the region where this boat originated. Chronologically the order appears to be reversed, in that poem 4 looks back on a journey which poem 46 looked forward to. I have translated *phaselus* as 'yacht'; the sea-faring boat referred to was originally from Egypt, its Greek name meaning the 'bean-pod' which it resembled; later on it came to be a pleasure-craft for rich Romans. A *phaselus* carried Atticus to Epirus (Cicero *Att.*1.13.1, and Propertius (3.21.20) imagines a *phaselus* carrying him to Greece.

The Greek Anthology contains epigrams purporting to be spoken by objects being dedicated in gratitude at the end of their working life, and some of these (vi. 69, 70) feature a ship. Elsewhere (ix. 34, 36) ships tell their own story, but in 'obituary' rather than dedicatory style. This poem is unusual in the way in which the ship's story is reported at second hand by the narrator. It is also a highly impressive piece of imaginative writing, in which the world of nature comes to life. Not only does the yacht speak (*ait ... negat ... sibilum edidit ... ait ... dicit*) but it personally dedicates itself to the Dioscuri having not made any *uota* before; but then also the places are brought to life both with personifying adjectives (*minacis ... nobilem ... trucem*) and by direct apostrophe from the narrator (line 13); these places 'know' the yacht, their peaks and waters having had the yacht on them as the poet reminds them pointedly (*tuo ... tuo*): the leaves talk (*loquente ... coma*), the wind 'calls' from one side or the other (*uocaret*); the poem thus creates a world of magic realism in which a talking boat suddenly ceases to surprise us. This boat was, according to its own account, faster and more successful than all others, the seas all *impotentia* in comparison. The poem has divided critics, some of whom have seen it as 'proof' that Catullus had a boat on Lake Garda, others (such as Copley) who have rejected such 'biographical' interpretation and seen the poem as totally free of all historicity, in the manner of the New Criticism (see Introduction on 'Interpretative Strategies'). A more fruitful critical stance is afforded if one keeps in mind the fact that there is a voice intermediate between that of the poet and the yacht, and that the yacht's 'story' is being reported (and possibly sent up) by this intermediate voice; the phraseology of epic language (rare compounds such as *buxifer* for instance) is arguably pointing up the distance between the tale and the truth, between the remote narrator (the yacht), the intermediary narrator – and the poet who orchestrates it all into a single whole.

Metre: iambic trimeters, the metre of Greek tragedy, used here (suggests Syndikus) to give the movement of the poem a swift impetus appropriate to the movement of the yacht.

1–5 The narrator addresses *hospites* which might recall the 'o stranger' motif on Greek sepulchral epigrams or may suggest the group of friends whom the narrator is showing around the estate. The narrator claims to be able to quote the words of the yacht (*ait*) with the Greek nominative and infinitive construction in place of the Latin accusative and infinitive. The *oratio obliqua* here is rhetorical and forceful: the double negative *neque ... nequisse* (there was no ship that he could not overtake), followed by the neat disjunction of *siue ... siue*. The metaphor *natantis* is hardly striking, but the combined effect of 'the force of no swimming beam' certainly is, as is the sudden movement from swimming to flying (*uolare*) in line 5 and the more specific 'canvas' (*linteo*) for 'sails'.

6ff. The yacht name-drops shamelessly, as proof that he has been to all these places and knows them all by name. For the poet revelling in geographical travelogue of this sort cf. Aeschylus *Ag.* 281–316. The yacht here unravels his journey: returning down the Adriatic Sea, past the Cyclades and Rhodes up into the Propontis (Dardanelles) and thus into the Black Sea to Amastris, its 'birthplace'. The places are neatly depicted with thumbnail sketches: the Adriatic is 'menacing', Rhodes is 'famous', the Propontis is rough and breezy. Note the double negative *negat ... negare*.

7 note here the juxtaposition of *litus insulasue* as the boat surveys the different coastlines. The Cyclades are islands surrounding Delos in the Aegean, notorious for their winds: see Horace *Odes* 1.14.20 with Nisbet and Hubbard *ad loc.*

8 **honourable Rhodes**: cf. Horace's *claram Rhodon* at *Odes* 1.7.1. The ms reading *Thraciam* as an accusative adjective agreeing with *Propontida* is possible: Thomson's ingenious reading *Thracia* referring to the North North West wind the *Thracias* in the ablative case (giving the sense 'Propontis breezy with the *Thracias*') is tempting.

9 The jingle of *Propontida ... Ponticum* is striking, as is the use of *trux* to describe the inhospitable waters of the Pontic Gulf.

10 **later ... earlier**: The poet draws up an effective contrast between what was later to be a yacht and used to be forest, with the key words *post..antea* placed around the thing being described, the *phaselus,* and the surprising term *comata silua* kept back in effective enjambement.

11 **haired**: The metaphor of foliage being like hair is as old as Homer (*Od.* 23.195) and continued in many Roman poets (e.g. Horace *Odes* 4.7.2): note here how *comata silua* is picked up again at the end of the following line (reversed) in *sibilum.. coma.*
Amastris ... Cytorus: The hills behind Cytorus and the whole Southern coast of the Black Sea were heavily forested and useful in providing timber for ship-building (Horace *Odes* 1.14.11) and smelting (Fordyce).

12 Note the onomatopeia of repeated sibilants suggesting the whispering leaves. For the metaphor of leaves/trees whispering cf. Virgil *Ecl.* 8. 22, Theocritus 1.1, Aristophanes *Clouds* 1008.

13f. **box-bearing**: for the famous boxwood of Cytorus cf. Virgil *G.* 2. 437. This line is notable for being almost entirely proper names: the places are addressed in epic apostrophe and high-sounding rhetoric. Note for instance the rhetorical *fuisse et esse* and the variation of vocabulary in *ait ... dicit,* the striking anaphora of the initial words *tibi ... tuo ... tuo* and the neat symmetry of lines 16–17, *tuo stetisse..in cacumine* followed by *tuo imbuisse.. in aequore.*

17 **little palms** recalls line 4.

18 **powerful**: *impotentia* is a clever usage: its surface meaning 'powerless' is maintained even though the secondary meaning 'uncontrolled, raging' is uppermost, with the effect of suggesting that the seas were powerless to thwart the little boat for all their savagery.

19–20 **master**: *erus* is the slave's word for his master; this yacht acts out of service for the master, not seeking glory for itself. The yacht might tack to left or right, unless the wind was favourably behind it and hit both sheets (*pedes*) at once. Note how the wind is here named *Iuppiter* the weather-god; thus *secundus* is to be taken both as simply meaning 'favourable wind' and also as a hint of the kindliness of Jove. The repeated sibilants in this line well evoke the foaming waves as the boat sails happily on.

22   **vows**: Mention of Jupiter brings in the theme of votive offerings to the gods. When in distress on the sea, sailors were in the habit of making vows to the gods of the sea that they would make lavish offerings in their temples if the gods brought them home safe and sound: for this see e.g. Nisbet and Hubbard on Horace *Odes* 1.5.13, Virgil *Aen.* 12. 768–9. This yacht can now safely boast that it did not ever need the help of the gods to reach home.

24   **nearest**: the 'final sea' is the Adriatic, the 'limpid lake' is usually presumed to be Lake Garda into which Sirmio (poem 31) projects.

25–7 In contrast to the old days of danger and independence of divine help, the yacht is now put away in peace, growing old and dedicated to the Dioscuri.

      Castor and Pollux, the so-called Dioscuri or sons of Zeus, were a useful constellation in the sky and therefore also the patron gods of sailors: see 68.65, and *OCD* s.v. 'Dioscuri'. The phrasing of line 27 is perhaps unusual in that Pollux is not named except as the 'twin of Castor'.

5

The first poem in which the name 'Lesbia' is used, and a text of deceptive sophistication. The first word is 'let us live' the last word is 'kisses'; the first line suggests that 'living' is equivalent to 'loving', the two verbs framing the name Lesbia. The theme of life leads on to the poet's discussion of eternal death, while the theme of loving brings on the opposing theme of contempt– both of the *senum seueriorum* for the poet and his mistress, and also vice versa of the poet for the old men. The second half of the poem is a repetitive sequence of imperatives telling Lesbia to give the poet kisses: the repeated numbers suggest a mathematical sum being aimed at – only to find the poet ending with the deliberate confusing of the figures. The second half of the poem thus builds up an attitude of exactitude which it then confounds. The text thus sets up polarities of life vs death, light vs night, young vs old, good vs bad, counting vs muddling the accounts which allows the expression of love to be set against a dark background of threats. The love is shown not least in the frequent use of the first person plural ('we', 'us') for the poet and Lesbia, suggesting a reciprocity which the poet does not elsewhere endorse (cf. e.g. poems 75–6).

Metre: hendecasyllabics.

1   **Let us ... :** The line is framed by the two verbs, which together amount to an assertion that life is love. For discussion of the identity of the woman addressed here as Lesbia see Introduction.

2–3 **old men**: The poet immediately assumes a stance of rebellion against the older generation; note the effective juxtaposition of *omnes unius* and the hissing sibilants. The *as* was the smallest Roman coin, weighing a pound in early times but by the time of Catullus being the equivalent of a 'penny' in English. For the phrase cf. 42.13.

4   **sun**: The sun can die and rise again every day, but humans cannot; this picks up the motif of life announced in *uiuamus* and develops it into an argument for making the most of the time available.

5–6 **light ... night**: The contrast is well brought out by the juxtaposition over the line-break of *lux/nox*, words similar in appearance but as different as the living and the dead. Line 5 sees a series of short words ending with a monosyllable: line 6 begins with two monosyllables and then broadens out into a long sonorous phrase evocative of the eternity of death – note the elision of *perpetua una*.

7-9 **kisses**: The poet asks for kisses, listing the numbers of kisses at such length to show verbally the long sequence of such kissing in fact, with repetition of *dein(de)*. Each of the three lines asks for a thousand and then a hundred (convenient round numbers), leading the reader towards a putative calculation – which line 11 rebuts decisively.

11 **do not know**: the poet does not specify why it is important for them not to know the total: Quinn suggests that there may be an element of not wanting to 'count their chickens' as well as the more obvious need to hide from the grim elderly auditors of line 2 just how much 'business' has gone on,

12 **evil eye**: *inuidere* means primarily 'cast the evil eye upon'.

14 the poem ends with the striking word *basiorum*: the poet leaves the reader with this image of physical affection in his mind as the net result of the argument and then the 'calculation' which has produced it.

6

Flavius, the addressee is unknown to us. The poem is a light-hearted piece of verse purporting to remonstrate with Flavius about his secrecy concering his girlfriend's identity: the ending of the poem assures the addressee about the glory which poetry can confer and turns the personal topical poem into a text of more general poetic significance.

Metre: hendecasyllabics

1 **Flavius**: The name is signposted at the beginning of the poem, as that of the poet is signposted at the end of the line, the two names framing the central *delicias tuas* – neatly encapsulating the poem's theme in verbal form as the two men are divided by the identity of this anonymous *delicias*. The gender of the *deliciae* is left vague at this point.

2 **unsophisticated**: For the meaning of *lepidus* and its opposite cf. 1.1 etc.

3 **not be able**: Flavius would want to speak of his love – in fact he would not be able *not* to speak of it: for this strong affirmation cf. Juvenal's assertion *difficile est saturam non scribere* (*Sat.* 1.30). Notice again how the line is chiastically framed with the two subjunctives *uelles ... posses* on the outside, the two infinitives inside them, and *nec* in the middle.

4 **hot little**: *febriculosi* properly means 'feverish'; translated by Goold as 'pasty-faced', as 'Some scabrous little slut' in Michie's version. *scortum* can only mean 'prostitute', and it is unlikely that the word *febriculosus* can mean ardent for sex, as suggested by Garrison. Why, one would ask, would Flavius be ashamed of a girl who was so ardently desirous? He would however be ashamed of a girl who looked ill and weak.

5 **tart**; the pejorative word *scorti* is emphasised by the enjambement from the previous line; note also the derogatory use of the partitive genitive *nescio quid scorti* somewhat akin to Ovid's use of *puella* in the singular as the object of the amatory hunter in *Ars am.* 1.45–50.

6 **celibate**: *uiduas* ('bereft of a husband or wife') can properly only apply to people but here is applied to the nights which the celibate endures: for this transference cf. the 'unmarried bed' (*lectus caelebs*) of 68.6, the 'married door' of 67.6, the 'happy bed' of Propertius 2.15.2.

7 **shouted ... silent**: a paradoxical line: how can a 'silent' bed 'shout out'? The bed is in fact 'silent' in that it is incapable of human speech – but its movements are noisy enough to convey the message at full volume – note the alliteration of *c*.

8-11 The evidence of the love-life is gathered sense by sense: the fragrant Syrian olive perfume tells the nose, the pillow dented on both sides tells the eyes, and the noise of the bed tells the ears. For the lover's expenditure on garlands and perfumes cf. Lucretius 4.1132. Note here the use of legalistic terms *argutatio inambulatioque* and note especially how the term *argutatio* ('creaking') suggests *argutari* (to speak) thus continuing the idea of the bed as telling the truth when its owner refuses.

12 The ms read *nam inista praeualet*, variously emended. Quinn reads Scaliger's *nam nil stupra ualet* but this is hardly convincing as sex with a *scortum* was never *stuprum*. Goold prints Skutch's *nil perstare ualet* ('it's no use standing fast in denial'). The strengthening of an initial *nil* with a subsequent *nihil* is attractive, and Lachmann's simple *nam nil ista ualet* is probably the simplest emendation which is both palaeographicaly plausible and makes easy sense.

13 **shagged out:** After the elegant phrasing of the circumstantial evidence summarised in lines 8–11, the poet produces a sudden vulgarity in *latera ecfututa*, delivering a decisive blow to any defence which Flavius might have. For the pale appearance of the energetic lover cf. Horace *Odes* 3.10.14, Propertius 1.1.22, 1.5.21–2. For compounds of the vulgar word *futuo* used to denote exhaustion through excessive sex, cf. 29.13, 41.1.

14 **fooling about:** *ineptiarum* is interesting: the word has a dismissive sense of 'fooling about' but here clearly also has a sexual sense: cf. *ineptire* in 8.1, where see note.

15 **good or bad:** So far the poem has assumed that Flavius has reason to hide his beloved: here the poet turns to the possibility of good as well as bad, leading to his offer to use poetry to transform her.

16–17 The ms reading *uocare* has been suspected by Nisbet (1978, 93) on the grounds that Catullus cannot 'call anybody to the sky unless he is already there himself': the word can also mean 'to address by name' (e.g. Propertius 2.13.28) but this then makes *ad caelum* sound odd and we would then prefer to read Baehrens' *ad cenam uocare*; the point of the ending being that the poet wishes to invite Flavius and his girlfriend to dinner and wants to know her name to put on the invitation. Nisbet's suggestion *levare* (cf. Propertius 3.1.9) maintains the poetic conferring of immortality without the jarring incongruity of *uocare*. The phrase *ad caelum* is not as grandiose as it may sound: see *OLD* s.v. 'caelum' 3d.

The ending of the poem recalls the opening in a neat closure: *amores* recalls *delicias,* as *lepido* recalls *illepidae*. The *deliciae* which are *illepidae* at the beginning of the text can become *amores* through the transforming power of *lepidus uersus*, a neat piece of self-referential writing as (presumably) the text which is this poem has already made the anonymous beloved of Flavius both famous (*ad caelum uocare*) and also *lepidae* by the grace of the poetry itself. No further poem is promised or necessary – poem 6 is both promise and fulfilment.

7

This poem picks up where 5 left off: the poet begins with a picture of Lesbia asking him (*quaeris*) exactly how many kisses would be enough for him. The poem avoids easy categorisation, however, as the text manages to use poetic *topoi* with the sort of variation which transforms the (otherwise) unoriginal into something original. The text ends up as a study of itself, a piece of poetry clearly nodding to literary predecessors in a self-conscious tradition but which ends up denying 'talk' (*lingua*) altogether; the initial questioning starting-point (*quaeris*) is answered – but that answer is then described as one which could stop the unwelcome talk about kisses which the poet's extravagant use of imagery would only encourage.

Metre: hendecasyllabics

1   **You ask**: the poet engages in second-person dialogue with his addressee, as at 72.7, 85.1. In poem 5 the poet spoke in the first person plural. *basiatio* is an unusual word, an abstract noun formed from the concrete noun *basium* – Syndikus sees it as parallel to *osculatio* in 48.6 and Cicero *Cael.* 49 and feels that the lengthened form expresses the incessant and exaggerated kissing. The poet notably puts *mihi...tuae* around the word to suggest the intimacy of their relationship.

2   **and more than enough**: Why add *superque*? The phrase is clearly colloquial cf. Horace *Epod.* 1.31, 17.19, Virgil *Aen.* 2. 642. The phrase also adds to the alliteration.

3–8   'as many as the sands on the shore ... as many as the stars in the sky' is something of a literary topos; for the sands cf. Homer *Il.* 2.800, 9.385, Pindar *O.* 2.98, Ovid *Met.* 11.615 etc., for the stars cf. Homer *Il.* 8.554–6, Callimachus *Hymn* 4.175; for both together cf. Plato *Euthyd.* 294b. Catullus injects originality into the phrasing by specifying the supremely literary sand of Callimachus' home complete with the Callimachean detail that this place produces silphium and that there is a tomb of Battus (who was not only the founder of Cyrene but also an ancestor of Callimachus) and a temple of Jupiter there – a nice example of the Alexandrian parade of learning and a clear signal to the reader to look beyond the superficially 'sincere' love of the poem towards the literary effects.

4   **silphium** (asafoetida) was an export of Cyrene mentioned by Strabo (2.4.37) and was imported into Rome for its medical uses; see Herodotus 4.169, Aristophanes *Plut.* 925 ('the silphium of Battus' used as proverbial expression comparable to our 'all the tea in China'). Paoli (210–211) gives a vivid account of the high value of the juice of the plant as an aid to digestion and as a panacea against bites, boils, gout, dropsy, asthma, epilepsy, dropsy and pleurisy (Pliny *HN* 22.101ff). It was even part of the famous recipe against baldness. Hardly surprising that the state imported thirty pounds of the stuff at public expense from 93 B.C. and that the notoriously bald Caesar acquired 1500 pounds of it at the start of his dictatorship.

5   **oracle**; The Egyptian god Ammon was associated with Zeus/Jupiter and had a temple in the Libyan desert which was the centre of the famous oracle (cf. Propertius 4.1.103).

7–8   The topos of the numerous stars is given a personal edge. What begins life as a simple simile (as many kisses as stars) leads into the image of the stars looking down at the illicit loves of men and women while the night 'enters into the conspiracy of silence' (Quinn); the poet's own affair is illicit – cf. how his mistress came to him in a *mira nox* bringing the *furtiua munuscula* (68. 145). The stars only come out at night – but then the night lends welcome darkness and silence to secret affairs, and the multiplicity of stars leads naturally to a multiplicity of lovers all like the poet. In this way the particular relationship of the poet is widened out into the common experience of mankind – only to be pulled back into the poet's individual and eccentric isolation again with *uesano...Catullo* in line 10.

9   **kisses ... to kiss**: the cognate accusative and infinitive *basia...basiare* is unusual in Latin but common in Greek. The phrase here serves to bring back the theme of *basiationes* in line 1 just as *satis et super* recalls line 2 – and thus introduces the closural device.

10   Note how *mihi* of line 1 is here rendered in the third person name *Catullo*. The adjective *uesano* is strong and puts the poet outside the normal parameters of human experience (*ue-sanus*); in Virgil the word usually denotes mad hunger (see e.g. Harrison on *Aen.* 10. 723–4) and transfers easily into the context of love which is both a desire and a form of madness (cf. 100.7, Propertius 2.15.29).

11 **nosy**: Note the concessive quality in *curiosi* – no matter how inquisitive they are they could not count out the kisses. Who are these 'nosy' people? Are they the 'over-strict old men' (*senum seueriorum*) of poem 5, the 'evil one' of that same poem who might 'give the evil eye' (*inuidere*)?

12 **bewitch**: The word *fascinum* usually means a phallic-shaped thing – the penis itself (Horace *Epod.* 8.18), a dildo (Petronius 138.1) or else a phallic amulet worn around the neck to avert the evil eye. The verb here means 'to bewitch' or 'cast a spell upon'. The placing of 'tongue' (*lingua*) at the end of the poem is perhaps significant in this poem about kisses.

8

A concise study in melancholia and repressed wishes. The poem varies its narrative stance and its addressee a great deal: it begins with the poet's apostrophe to himself in second person (lines 1–11) before passing to an address to the girl in the second person (12–18) before returning to addressing the poet in the final line. In this second section, however, where one would expect the poet to speak in the first person while addressing the girl in the second person, 'Catullus' is put into the third person in a sequence of three verbs (*obdurat ... . requiret ... rogabit*).

This poem is all too often seen as pure autobiography. Fordyce finds that the 'simplicity of the words ... is a guarantee of their sincerity'. Garrison 'explains' the context as being that 'Lesbia has broken off her affair with Catullus, who considers his foolishness and urges himself to tough it out'. Quite apart from the fact that the poem never names the *puella*, this sort of biographical criticism does poor service to the poem. Syndikus well compares the inner dialogue here with those in Greek Tragedy (e.g. Euripides' *Med.* 1040–59) and with the indecisive lover in (e.g.) Apollonius Rhodius *Argon.* 3.466–70, 636–664 and even comedy. This text is part of a literary tradition of which it is clearly aware, and the poem contains within it the tensions which make it a fine piece of work: the tensions between the love expressed and the love denied, between the hardness aimed at and the wistful longing which so quickly succeeds it, the tension between the tone of the poet when addressing himself and that used to rebuke the *puella*. The question of whether this poem was inspired by a biographical event is neither important nor answerable; far more important is the issue of how the narrator ('Catullus') distances himself both from the *puella* and also from his *persona* as lover-poet ('"Catullus"'). The text is obviously an artefact with its own dynamic which is not reducible to an event in the poet's life but is a masterpiece of the poetic craft with all the shifting uncertainties and slippages which a poetic text can produce.

Metre Choliambics (otherwise known as Scazons or 'limping iambics')

1 **Love-sick Catullus**: The poem starts as it means to go on: *miser* sets the tone for the whole text. The word connotes 'lovesick' as at 64.140, Lucretius 4.1076, Ovid *Rem. am.* 658 (other exx. in *OLD* s.v. 'miser' 3a) in all cases suggesting that the lover is sick rather than healthy (*sanus*). For the poet's self-apostrophe cf. 46, 51, 52, 68.27, 76, 79; the device sets up a dialogue between the narrator and his *persona* which will produce the tension later on. For *ineptire* cf. Terence *Phorm.* 419–420 – Phormio uses *ineptire* of Demipho because he thinks he can dissolve his son Antipho's marriage to an 'unsuitable' woman. Terence *Ad.* 934, Plautus *Trin.* 1149, and Cicero *Orat.* 2.17; cf. also 6.14n.

2 **regard ... died**: An almost proverbial expression: Fordyce and Quinn compares Plautus *Trin.* 1026. The word *ducas* in the sense 'think' is well-attested (*OLD* s.v. 'duco' 30); it is used here to lead to *ducebat* in line 4.

3   **beautiful**: *candidus* is a charged word, used 15 times by the poet. Its primary meaning 'white' (as in e.g. *toga candida*) came to mean 'beautiful' in a sunny climate where the well-to-do could avoid the sun and keep their complexion pale, and also 'happy' – which is the dominant sense of the word here. The past nature of this happiness is well stressed by the perfect tense *fulsere* immediately followed by the adverb *quondam* as also by the use of the word *soles* (used to refer to the brevity of happy life contrasted with eternal death in 5.4–6). The line has a pleasing vocalic symmetry – note the assonance of *dam can– didi tibi* – as the poet reminisces about the pleasures of the past.

4   **when you...**: *uentitabas* and *ducebat* are imperfect tenses connoting the regularly repeated actions. The (past and present) passivity of the poet is stressed throughout this first part of the poem.

5   **loved ... loved**: *amor* is stressed by being repeated in two verbal forms, both of them applied to the poet and not to the girlfriend, and which refer to past and future time which leaves the poet looking both back and forward in the 'present' tense of the text.

6   **entertaining**: *iocosa* suggests 'fun' – 'the plaintive whimsy of understatement' (Quinn) – which the rest of the poem undermines as much as it recalls it here. For the phrase cf. Ovid *Ars am.* 3.580

7   **you wanted ... no**: the male 'wanted' and the girl 'did not say no', a nice example of the difference of the sexes and their attitude towards sex.

8   the repetition of line 3 (with slight alteration) marks the closure of the first part of the poem.

9   **she does say no**: the girl, who did not refuse in line 7, now *non uult. impotens* has the senses of: 'powerless (to affect the situation)', 'undisciplined' and also 'uncontrolled', 'raging' as in poem 4.18.

10   **live**: for *uiue* meaning simply 'be' cf. 10.33, *OLD* s.v. 'uiuo' 2.

11–12   **endure, become firm**: the imperatives in line 11 are addressed to Catullus, before the poet suddenly turns to address the girl and refers to himself in the third person. Note the repeated *ob–* in *obstinata ... obdura*.

12–18   A sequence of questions: 'The questions are rhetorical in the sense that they do not expect the answer "nobody" or "half of Rome"; still less a rival who could be named; their purpose is to challenge Lesbia to admit that the answer is "not Catullus"' (Quinn). The lover-poet is clearly thinking of the girl's present love-life with obsessive morbidity.

13   **asking**: *rogabit* is deliberately vague and given extra point by the juxtaposition with *inuitam* and the *r* alliteration after *requiret*. For the use of the word in an amatory sense cf. Ovid *Ars am.* 1.711

14   **asking ... asked**; *rogabit* in the previous line is repeated as *rogaberis. nulla* is a colloquial strong negative; cf. 17.20 with Fordyce *ad loc.* The virtue of *nulla* here is that it avoids the question 'asked by whom?'

15   **Poor fool**: *scelesta* ought to mean 'wicked' but that hardly makes sense in the context of the line and there is plenty of evidence that it can mean 'wretched' (e.g. Plautus *Cist.* 685). The sense of moral outrage is perhaps not totally forgotten, however, in this poem which laments the lack of reciprocity towards the poet's feelings for a girl who was 'loved by me more than any girl will ever be loved'. For the sense of *manet* ('is waiting for you') cf. 76.5

15–18   A sequence of seven sentences all beginning with the interrogative pronoun, with surprisingly little repetition of question words. The questions sketch the growth of a new love-affair: approach (*adibit*), finding her attractive, loving, having her name linked with his, sexual behaviour, biting the lips. At this point the poet breaks off, the memory of their own love and the thought of her loving another proving too painful and negating his decision to 'toughen up' with regard to her.

19 **resolved**: *destinatus* recalls *obstinata* in line 11 and forms a neat closure for the poem by which the passage from lines 12–18 is like a digression which ultimately proves unfruitful and which the poet discards with the ring-composition of verbal recollection, returning also from the apostrophe to the mistress to the initial apostrophe to himself.

9

After the wretched unhappiness of failed love in poem 8 there follows a celebration of male friendship in poem 9, addressed to Veranius who is returning from Spain. The poem is a 'welcome' poem but one whose primary player is the poet himself rather than the man being welcomed: note the stress on *meis ... mihi... mihi ... me ...*, the first person verbs (*uisam ... audiam ... suauiabor*), the ecstatic declaration of the poet's own happiness at the end, and the telling use of *iucundum* in line 9.

Metre: hendecasyllabics.

1–2 The poem begins with the name, signposted as the key word in the poem. For Veranius cf. 12, 28, 47. The first two lines of the poem celebrate the worth of Veranius in hyperbolic terms: out of *all* his friends Veranius is the best one to the extent of *three hundred thousand*. The number is a puzzle: having said that Veranius stands out from all his friends, why does he then specify the number? It can hardly be suggesting that the poet has three hundred thousand friends (Baehrens) of whom Veranius is the best; the Cicero text usually adduced to parallel this line (*Att.* 2.5.1 'Cato ille noster qui mihi unus est pro centum milibus') means 'one worth a hundred thousand' rather than 'the best one of a hundred thousand'. The precise number is not important, as it stands for any vast amount: cf. 48.3: there is more sense to be gained however from the suggestion of Muretus and Kroll that *milibus* here means 'miles' and so the colloquial expression 'best by 300 miles' gives purpose to the number which is otherwise somewhat otiose. Its drawback is that there are no parallels in Latin – although its Greek usage is well attested (Aristopanes *Clouds* 430, *Frogs* 91).

3–4 The poet gives a list of the welcoming elements: the home, the household gods, the brothers and finally the aged mother: note the poet's use of appropriate adjectives to stress the welcoming aspect – brothers need not be close but these ones are *unanimi*, and the mother is 'old' and (presumably) widowed. The adjectives are juxtaposed in the middle of the line which is framed by the nouns.

5 **you have come**: The poet answers his own question. cf. 12.6, 77.3–5, 88.4–5. *nuntii beati* has been read as genitive of exclamation (rare in Latin but common in Greek) but is more likely to be nominative plural as in Propertius 2.15.1 *o nox mihi candida. beati* sets up the theme which *beatiorum ... beatius* in the final two lines will pick up.

6–7 **see ... hear**: The poet will both see and hear Veranius. The line is notable for having three elisions, giving the impression of haste and excitement, as is also conveyed by the enjambement and then the asyndeton of *loca facta nationes* in the next line.

8 **as is your custom**: *ut mos est tuus* after the list of *loca facta nationes* suggests that the poet has often heard Veranius speaking at some length and also a faint sense that Veranius might dilate at excessive length.

8–9 **kiss**; The kissing is strongly affectionate and the poet's way of stopping Veranius' speech: cf. Cicero's brother writing to Tiro 'I will kiss your eyes, even if I see you in the middle of the Forum' (*Fam.* 16.27.2) and for other examples of greeting-kisses cf. Homer *Od.* 16.15. The poet's use of terms such as *iucundum* is perhaps less common and fits well with the subjective tone of the poem as a whole and its enthusiastic hedonism, especially with the suggestion of *suauis* in *suauiabor*. Note here also the jingle of *os oculosque* and the way in which the poet's kiss on Veranius' mouth will stop him from speaking. The poem ends with the key word *beatius* – but it is the poet's happiness which is being celebrated rather than that of the returning friend.

10

A piece of elegant social satire and gentle self-mockery. The girlfriend of Varus is transformed during the course of the poem from a 'little tart, but not without charm' to 'more brazen than she ought to be' to 'a nuisance' at the end; the poem thus recounts not only the events but also the manner in which the poet's perception alters as the events take place. Needless to say, the girl emerges victorious in the altercation and the butt of the mockery is the poet himself.

Metre: hendecasyllabics.

1   **Varus** is also mentioned in 22.1. This may be the Alfenus (Varus) of 30. The poem begins with the name of the interlocutor, as do many of the poems here (cf. 9, 11).

1–2   Varus is presented (unlike the Flavius of poem 6) as obviously proud of his (new?) girlfriend and takes the poet for no other purpose than to 'see' her: line 2 neatly begins with *uisum* ('just to have a look') and ends with *otiosum* ('I had nothing else to do anyway').

3   **a little tart**: *scortillum* may well not be pejorative here: the jocular context, the jocularity increased by the diminutive (only found here). *repente* is something of a surprise but means simply 'at once' here and qualifies the poet's initial opinion as a quick judgement which his later experience of the girl will certainly change.

4   **not without**: The poet's 'praise' of the girl is seriously understated. For the value-terms *lepidus* and *uenustus* cf. 1.1, 36.17, 3.2, 13.6, etc.

7–8   The question of how the province is naturally leads to the question of how the poet had profited from it, as the staff of provincial governors usually did. Note here how the key words *profuisset aere* are left to the end.

11   **head better oiled**: for the colloquialism *caput unctius referre* cf. Cicero *Verrines* 2.2.54. The oiling of the head marked out a holiday celebration and so the line comes to mean 'to have something to celebrate' as well as meaning 'to come back richer'.

12   **bastard**: The literal meaning of *irrumator* (one who forces others to perform oral sex upon him) is no more important in the derogatory usage than the literal meaning of (e.g.) the word 'bastard' is in English. The term is however interesting in that it denotes an attitude of domineering power over others which is highly relevant in the case of the governor. See Wiseman (1985) 10–14. The governor in this case is usually assumed (from being named in poem 28) to have been C. Memmius, Lucretius' patron and governor of Bithynia–Pontus in 57–56 B.C., a paradoxical figure in many ways but clearly of some note in literary circles (cf. Ovid *Tr.* 2.433 for his own poetic composition). As governor he is said here to have stopped his staff lining their pockets – which makes him unusually benevolent towards the provincials themselves.

13   **give a fig for**: *pili facere* is again colloquial: cf. 17.17. The phrasing *praetor ... cohortem* picks up *praetoribus ... cohorti* from line 10.

14   The question is put not by the girl alone but by both of them.

15   **litter-chair**: The Roman luxury transport, the *lectica* carried by slaves whose number depended on the wealth of the owner. The rich in their litters are a frequent butt of

satire; see e.g. Juvenal 1.32–3, 158–9, 3.239–42. In Juvenal 1.64–5 the rich man can afford six litter-bearers; Catullus here boasts of eight (cf. Martial 6.84).

16–7 The poet is candid about his behaviour; he seeks to impress the girl even though he knows that she is Varus' *amores*. *unum* is emphatic: cf. 31.11, 58.2, 107.7.

18–20   The poet piles on the self-praise: just because his province was *mala* did not mean that he did *maligne*: he could get eight men – and (furthermore) ones capable of holding themselves (and therefore the litter-chair) upright. Line 19 picks up the earlier conversation about the poverty of the province (lines 8–13) and answers the unspoken question: 'so you could not get litter-bearers, then?'

21–3 After the poet's 'public' statement comes the 'private' reality in what is in effect an aside to the reader. The grim reality is vividly put: he has nobody – not just not one who could carry a litter but not one who could carry the broken leg of an old bed. *ueteris* suggests flimsy old wood, *fractum* tells us that the leg is separate from the rest of the bed, *grabatus* being the word for 'the truckle-bed of the poor' (Fordyce). Garrison and Quinn are surely wrong to see this sentence as Catullus 'assuming the role of the penniless poet'; the point is that the cheap bed is light to carry and the argument *a fortiori*: if the (non-existent) litter-bearer could not carry the leg of a *grabatus* then all the more would he be unable to carry a proper litter-chair. The aside, coming after the grandiose lines 18–20 and before the pretentious ambition of the girl in lines 26–7, sets up a comic atmosphere and dramatic irony between the poet and the audience. Note here also the jingle of *collo collocare*: something of a traditional play on words (cf. Platutus *Asin.* 657, *Epid.* 360).

24   **tart**: *cinaediorem* properly refers to male passive homosexuals and here carries a distinct edge of disapproval.

25   Note the repetition of *mihi mi* and the familiar tone the girl adopts towards somebody who was until very recently a stranger.

26   **Serapis**: The oriental cult of Serapis was popular in Rome of the late Republic as a source of healing; the sick would 'incubate' (i.e. sleep) in the temple and the god would send them advice and/or cures in dreams, rather as in the cult of Asclepius in Greece. The girl is therefore seeking a cure for some ailment and wishes to travel there in style.

27–32   The poet stammers out a feeble excuse for not lending what he does not have. Note the inversion of *Cinna est Gaius* and the untidiness of the structure as the relative clause *istud quod ... habere* leads inconsequentially onto *fugit me ratio*. The Cinna referred to perhaps the poet whose *Zmyrna* is praised in poem 95.

33–4 **nuisance**: The girl who was *non sane illepidum atque inuenustum* in line 4 is now *insulsa*. Note the colloquial use of *uiuis* to mean simply 'you are' and the term *insulsus* coming from *sal* ('salt') meaning 'wit' as in the pun at 13.5. The poet means that the girl is tedious for taking literally his conversational boast: he tries to turn his embarrassment round by declaring that the girl is boringly pedantic and picks up on detail unnecessarily.

11

One of the most famous poems in the collection and one which continues to elude interpretation; many scholars link it with the only other poem in Sapphics (51) and see the two as a pair of contrasting attitudes towards love. The text is apparently in two halves, the first three stanzas addressed to Furius and Aurelius describing the extent of their loyalty/friendship, the final three stanzas giving the friends instructions for the message to convey to the poet's faithless girlfriend. Commentators are virtually unanimous in seeing this poem as a repudiation of the poet's girlfriend Lesbia, despite the problems associated with this sort of biographical interpretation and the fact that Lesbia is not 'named'. The places named date the poem to the period soon after 55 B.C.: it was in that year that Caesar crossed the Rhine and went to Britain, Gabinius went to Egypt to restore Ptolemy Auletes to his throne, and Crassus set out eastwards to fight the Parthians (unsuccessfully). For the poet to mention these places suggests that he is hinting that Furius and Aurelius would accompany him on any of the military ventures being launched that year.

The 'meaning' of the poem cannot be reduced to an event in the poet's life. For one thing, his relationship with Furius and Aurelius is elsewhere described in far less honourable terms (see poems 15, 16, 21, 23–24, 26) and his sudden description of them as inseparable companions to the ends of the earth is possibly ironic in the extreme, as Wilamovitz pointed out long ago (Wilamovitz 2.307). What is the purpose served by them in this poem? They are male friend-figures ready to be loyal and steadfast to the poet in any adventure he cares to name, in contrast to the faithless woman to whom he has been faithful but from whom he has received no loyalty in return. The exotic adventures in the first three stanzas are described in exaggeratedly epic terms (note e.g. the compound adjectives *sagittiferos ... septemgeminus*, the Homeric-sounding *longe resonante ... caelitum* and the glorious monuments of 'great Caesar', although the poet harbours little respect elsewhere (93) for the great man), in order to evoke a mood of shared masculine self-assertion (note the way he describes the 'effeminate' Arabs) with which he can dismiss his girl; the first three stanzas thus build up the voice without which he could not utter the following two stanzas, as he uses the bluntest of prose language to put the girl in her place in an attitude of curt dismissal. The final stanza – like the ending of poem 8 – gives the lie to all this bluster, as the text ends on a note of pathetic sadness; after the self-assertion comes the true vulnerability, after the affected indifference comes the affection which can still express itself in the highly emotional language of the lover. The male who could stride across the Alps is shown at the end as a lover whose love can be destroyed simply by a touch, the callous brutality of the fourth and fifth stanzas is seen through in the deep sensitivity both of the content and of the style of the final stanza. This slippage between the two halves of the poem is brought out by the *a fortiori* incongruity of the geographical reference: Furius and Aurelius are prepared to walk all over the world with Catullus – but all he needs is for them to walk across Rome with a message. This point is accentuated by the repetition of *ultimus* which refers in lines 11–12 to the Britons, in line 23 to the furthest edge of the field where the flower of the poet's love lies dying.

Metre: Sapphic stanzas (as 51)

1   **companions**: *comites* has the verbal force of *comitantes* (men who accompany me). The opening sentence of the poem refers to Catullus in the third person; in line 15 he changes to the first person (*meae*) and describes the girl in the third person.

2   **furthest**: the catalogue of places begins appropriately with *extremos* as the poet will emphasise the lengths to which his friends will accompany him. The name *Indos* is at once embellished by the descriptive phrase which occupies lines 3–4.

3–4 Note the assonant vowels and alliterative *n*'s of *longe resonante Eoa*, and also the jingle of *tunditur unda*. The whole phrase succeeds in evoking a distant seashore at the end of a long sea-voyage.

5   **Hyrcania** is on the southern shore of the Caspian Sea. The Arabs are often termed *molles* – a word indicating luxury and effeminacy, the assumption being that luxury is an enervating and effeminate thing (cf. e.g. Juvenal 6. 292–300).

6   **arrow-bearing**: Note the obvious jingle of *Sagas sag-*. For the famous archery of the Parthians cf. Virgil G. 4.313, Horace *Odes* 2. 13.17; these people were very much in the news in Rome in the 50's B.C. leading up to Crassus' defeat by them at the battle of Carrhae in 53 B.C., a tale often retold (cf. e.g. Cicero *Div.* 2.84).

7–8 **seven-fold Nile**: For the term *septemgeminus* cf. Virgil *Aen.* 6.800. The river Nile was much discussed in the ancient world: cf e.g. Herodotus 2. 15ff, Lucretius 6.712–37.

9–12 **Caesar**: The reference to Caesar in these lines dates this poem to a time after 55 B.C., which was the year in which he crossed the Rhine and moved to Britain. For Britain as the furthest place in the west cf. 29.4, Horace *Odes* 1. 35.29.

10 **seeing ... Caesar**: The line is grandiose and may be ironic: note the *m* alliteration and the framing of the line with *Caesaris ... magni*. For the poet's attitude towards Caesar cf. 93.

13 **all this**: The preceding travels are summed up as *omnia haec*, further qualified by the epic phrasing 'whatever the will of the gods will bring'. The term *caelitum* ('heavenly ones') of the gods is presumably modelled on Homer's *ouraniones* (*Il.* 1.570).

15–16 **announce ... words**: After the epic language of what has gone before, the poet now becomes alarmingly direct and prosaic.

17–20 **lovers**: The behaviour of the girl is described with lurid hyperbole and repetition of *u* and *t*. Her lovers are *moechis* (properly denoting adulterous men) of whom she holds three hundred (the indefinitely large number of 9.2) all at once, loving none of them truly (any more than she loved the poet truly) but repeatedly reducing them to sexual exhaustion.

17 **live and thrive**: The phrase *uiuat ualeatque* suggests final farewell: cf. Horace *Epod.* 1.6.67, *Sat.* 2.5.110.

18 **embrace**: *simul complexa* at first suggests multiple sexual partners in an orgy.

20 **breaking the balls**: *ilia rumpens* is left to the end of the sentence for maximum effect. The precise meaning is difficult to ascertain: Adams ((1982) 50–1) plausibly supposes that it means that the men find their groins bursting with frenetic sexual activity ('rupturing their loins' or 'breaking their manhood'; cf. 80.7–8). For the invective against the sexually insatiable woman cf. Juvenal 6.114–135.

21–4 After the supreme vulgarity of *ilia rumpens* the poet finishes with a sublime poetic simile reminiscent of Sappho's simile of the hyacinth trampled by herdsmen (Fr. 105c), appropriate to end this poem in Sapphics. *mea puella* is not to look for *meum amorem*: the *culpa* is all hers (cf. 75.1). Note how the poet leaves the image of the flower to the very end of the poem, and how fragile the flower (and the love) is if it can fall simply from being 'touched' by the passing plough. The simile brings out the force of the girl and the vulnerability of the poet; it is also instructive to note that the plough does not intend to damage the flower but does so without noticing, whereas the girl has inflicted her damage on the poet deliberately or at least by culpable negligence (*culpa*); finally, the flower depicted as fallen remains beautiful, just as the expression of the poet's love also remains beautiful in its artistic depiction here. The poet chooses to end the poem with this image as it is the heart of the poem: his friendship with Furius and Aurelius is a temporary distraction and a consolation, his show of arrogant dismissal of the girl is empty as it merges into this pathetic depiction of the painful love behind the 'masculine' feelings which the first five stanzas attempt to disguise. The poem, like poem 8, ends up a study in complex emotion and self-delusion.

12

After the serious tones of poem 11, a piece of light verse to tease Asinius for removing a napkin. The addressee is usually taken to be the brother of C. Asinius Pollio the historian. *Marrucinus* means 'belonging to the Marrucini' who lived far away on the Adriatic coast – such people were perhaps unused to the urban life and less likely to observe the social graces, as Quinn suggests.

The unsociable behaviour of Asinius is not judged by the poet on moral grounds; even though the napkin is expensive (implied in line 12), it is a lack of taste and judgement which appals him, as is clear from the terms of criticism used (*non belle ... sordida ... inuenusta*) and the contrast with the thief's brother who though younger (*puer*) has a lot more style. What does contain style and wit, of course, is the poem itself: and the poet threatens a lot more of the same *hendecasyllabos* if the object is not returned at once. There is thus a neat closure here: the poem takes Asinius to task for his lack of taste and does so in a poem of wit and taste; the text thus becomes proof of its own message as it shows Asinius in words what he so clearly lacks in behaviour.

Metre: hendecasyllabics

1–3 The first two lines deliberately keep back the essential point in order to set the reader's mind racing: 'you do not use your left hand nicely at dinner ... ' may suggest any of a number of misuses before the poet sets the record straight in line 3. The hendiadys of *in ioco atque uino* well evokes the drinking party: cf. 50.6. *lintea* were linen napkins used for wiping the hands and face at dinners, in an age where people ate with their fingers.

4 **smart**: *salsum* means 'smart' or 'witty' here (cf. *insulsa* in 10.33): the word *sal* ('salt') lies behind it, appropriate to a dinner-party, as at 13.5. *fugit te* is colloquial – cf. *fugit me ratio* in 10.29. *inepte* reminds us of 8.1.

5 **uncouth**: for *inuenusta* cf. 10.4.

6 **Pollio your brother**: C. Asinius Pollio (76 B.C. – A.D. 4) was a famous orator, historian and friend of Virgil and Horace; his work on the Civil Wars was famous (cf. Horace *Odes* 2.1) as was the Pollio Library which he had built.

7 **a talent** was a vast amount of Greek money: the Greek term has to be used here since there was no equivalent term in Latin for a single huge sum. Note here the alliterative jingle of *fratri ... furta* and the enjambement of lines 6–9.

8–9 **stuffed full of wit**: *leporum differtus* is a nice metaphor: the point here is that one can be a lot of fun (as the brother is) without stealing napkins. The difference between the brothers is that the one is a man of real wit and grace – even at a young age (*puer*) – while the other behaves in a manner which is *insulsus*.

10 **three hundred**: For the indefinitely large number 300 see 9.2, 11.18. The poet uses 'hendecasyllables' to mean 'this sort of verse' as at 42.1. Other metrical terms come to stand for the type of poetry which was composed in them: see e.g. *iambos* in 54.4 and *OLD* s.v. 'iambus' 2b; but, while this metre lends itself well to abusive verse, not all the poet's work in that metre is invective (see e.g. poems 5, 7, 9).

12 **not ... price**: It is not the financial loss which bothers the poet: cf. Petronius *Sat.* 30.10.

13 **memento**: Note the Greek word *mnemosynum* which only occurs here in Latin but which seems to have been the *mot juste* for a souvenir of the distant beloved in the *Greek Anthology* (*A.P.* 12,68,7).

14 **Saetaban** linen was the finest in Europe (Pliny *N.H.* 19.9). Note here how the two names are juxtaposed. Notice here the *s* alliteration.

15 Note the alliteration of *m*. For the giving of napkins as presents cf. Martial 4.88.4 etc. Fabullus and Veranius are mentioned together also in poems 28 and 47 and the affection for the pair of them (note the affectionate diminutive *Veraniolum*) is the closing note of the poem.

13

An invitation to dinner – with a difference. Fabullus is often presumed to be the same person referred to in the previous poem. The poem observes almost total ring-composition: *Fabulle* is in both the first and last lines, the gods in lines 2 and 13, lines 3 and 12 refer to gifts, lines 4 and 11 to the girl, lines 5 and 10 to the entertainment, line 6 asks Fabullus to bring things while line 9 tells him what he will receive, while line 7 repeats the opening phrase and contains the central paradox of the poem. The text thus neatly unwinds and rewinds itself in the manner of many a Homeric speech (see e.g. Homer *Il.* 7. 129–160, 9. 529–549).

Metre; hendecsayllabics

1 Notice how the poet stresses his giving of the dinner with repetition of *mi..apud me* which is leading up to the surprise in line 3.

2 **if the gods**: The poet's invitation observes the usual qualification 'if the gods are on your side' (i.e. if you are still alive) but there is also a note of the divine felicity of the proposed meal: this is picked up at the end in line 13. The vagueness of *paucis diebus* hints to us that the dinner-invitation is less than serious.

3–4 You will have a good dinner ... if *you* bring all the food and wine. For *candida* ('pretty') see note on 8.3.

5 **salt**: *sal* is here a pun: the word means both the salt on the table and the 'wit' which the guests will display: cf. 86.4, and the adjective *insulsus* at 10.33.

6 **my dear friend**: for *uenustus* cf. *Veneres* in line 12 and 12.5.

7–8 The repetition of *cenabis bene* from the same position in line 1 provides closure to this section as the poet finishes his explanation of the good dinner with a good joke: Catullus has a purse and it is full – but only of spiders/cobwebs. The surprise word *aranearum* is deliberately left to the end of the sentence.

9 **undiluted love**: the theme of poverty continues as Fabullus will get unmixed *amores* instead of the expected unmixed wine. Having just told Fabullus to bring his own *candida puella* this is something of a surprise, as *amores* usually means 'girlfriend' as at 10.1, 6.16. The word here may mean 'something to arouse your passion'.

11–14 The poet promises to give Fabullus the scent which the divine forces of love gave to his girlfriend. Is this a real scent or the 'fragrance of her person' (Quinn)? The Romans did spend a good deal on perfumes and such things were important elements in the dinner-party – but this may be to miss the point. If Catullus cannot afford food, then he will hardly be spending vast sums on perfume. The scent is anyway not one bought in the shops but given to the girl by 'Venuses and Cupids' (cf. 3.1.) and so more likely to be a metaphor for her sexual attractiveness in general. The addressee is being invited to a dinner with no food or wine – but it will be worth it when he gets a whiff of the poet's girlfriend. The poem ends with a cartoon-like picture of Fabullus as 'all nose' thus neatly bringing the reader to the point of the poem which is praise of his girlfriend. Notice how the final line is framed by the phrase *totum ... nasum*.

14

A poem addressed (presumably) to C. Licinius Macer Calvus (82–47 B.C.) the poet (of the *Io* among other things), orator and politician. The poem is a highly rhetorical piece about poetry. Note here the expressions of love for the subject (1–2) contrasted with the hatred inspired by the book (3): the protestations of innocence (3–4) and the mention of the *cliens* (a term especially used in the lawcourts); the speaker's suspicions (*suspicor*), his invocation of the gods and rhetorical exclamation (12), his imputation of base motives to the sender (14–15) exaggerated by the goodness of the day on which the book was received (15); the repetition *non non* and the assurance that the criminal will not get away with it (16) followed by the details of the punishment (*suppliciis*) threatened (17–20). The poem ends with the sort of rhetorical flourish which orators loved. There are several poems in the collection which express delight in composing poetry (50) and praise of 'good' poetry (35) or else violent disgust at 'bad' poetry (cf. 22, 36). The poets whom Catullus regards as like-minded (the so-called 'New Poets') tended to define themselves in opposition to other poets such as the ones named here in lines 18–19 (see Introduction).

Metre: hendecasyllabics

1   **more than ... eyes**: For the notion of loving 'more than the eyes' cf. 3.5, 82.2, 104.2

3   **Vatinian hate**: Calvus left 21 speeches, of which the most famous were those delivered in 54 against Vatinius on a charge of bribery during his election to the praetorship. Vatinius was defended on this occasion by Cicero and Calvus failed to secure the conviction. The mention of Vatinius helps the reader to see the forensic nature of the style of this poem.

5   Only now is Calvus' offence revealed: for the deliberate holding back of the offence cf. 12.1–3. Note here the alliteration of *m* and *p*.

6   **client**: The poet assumes that the offending book was sent to Calvus by a *cliens*, who (knowing of Calvus' poetic interests) had sent him a book of poems unaware of their quality. A *cliens* was a person who supported a richer or more influential *patronus*: in return for protection (e.g. in court) the *cliens* would offer political support to the *patronus*.

7   **unholy**: *impiorum* properly means 'unholy' and is here clearly hyperbolic.

8   **new**: *nouum* is not pejorative: the poet calls his own book of poetry *nouum* in 1.1; *repertum* has the sense 'recherché' and is also hardly damning. The two terms may, of course, be used with sneering sarcasm here.

9   **schoolmaster**: Quinn rightly sees a pun here: *litterator* means both 'critic' and also 'schoolmaster' and *munus* means both 'gift' and 'task'; the line thus means both 'the critic has given this gift' but also 'the schoolteacher has set you this task'. Sulla is not known.

10–11 the poet is pleased that Calvus' efforts (for his *cliens*) are not wasted as they have resulted in the gift of this book: the sentence is obviously sarcastic.

12   **dreadful**: For *horribilem* cf. 84.10; it seems to have been the sort of term which orators enjoyed to enunciate. *sacrum* means here 'outlawed' from human society and so closer to 'cursed' than the normal rendering of 'holy'. The poet now launches into exactly the sort of rhetorical exclamation which (we imagine) Calvus went in for in his speeches.

13–5 **your Catullus**: *tuum Catullum* turns the knife by alleging a closeness between Calvus and the poet which the foul gift has abused, just as the imputation of murderous intent in the next line exaggerates it, and the indignity of it all being done at the Saturnalia is brought out by *optimo dierum*.

16   The culprit will not get away with it: note the direct address to the villain as *false* and the rhetorical repetition of *non non*.

17–20 The poet enjoys detailing the names of the poets which will most upset Calvus. The *librariorum scrinia* were the cases of the booksellers in which the scrolls were kept. The plural names merely mean 'poets like ... ': Caesius is unknown, Aquinius may be the poet mentioned by Cicero (*Tusc.* 5.63), Suffenus is the poet belaboured again in poem 22. After the specific names Catullus sums them all up as 'poisons' (*uenena*), on which cf. 44.12, 77.5. *remunerabor* picks up *munus* from line 9.

21   **farewell and go away**: Note the peremptory asyndeton *ualete abite*.

22   **evil foot**: There is a play on words here: *pedem* meaning both literally 'foot' (saying that the poetry has made an ill-omened journey) and also *pedem* meaning a metrical unit and suggesting that these poets were not skillful practioners of their poetry.

23   The poem ends with a rhetorical flourish: two two-word phrases, the first highly metaphorical, the second blunt and to the point, assisted by effective alliteration.

14b

These three lines are clearly fragments of a larger poem: editors have often taken them as part of a second preface announcing a sequence of more daring and obscene poetry to follow, speculation which may be right but which cannot be proved.

1   For *ineptiarum* see on 8.1 *ineptire.*

15

A warning to Aurelius to keep his hands off the poet's boyfriend. The gender of the beloved should cause little surprise as the Romans tolerated male desire of both women and boys: cf. Lucretius 4.1053 where the object of male fantasy is described as 'a boy with womanish limbs, or else a woman radiating love ... ' . The intense homosexual love which we find in Greece (see e.g. Plato's *Symp.* 183a) was comparatively rare in Rome, but casual pederasty was acceptable and was not regarded as effeminacy (see Griffin 1976, 100–102, *OCD* s.v. 'homosexuality'). Love of boys is recommended by Propertius (2.4.17–22) and Juvenal (6. 34–7) for its lack of emotional complication – much as Horace recommends sex without love in *Sat.* 1.2 – although Ovid regards boys as giving less pleasure than women (*Ars am.* 2.683–4, but see Sharrock 27). The figure of the catamite is reasonably common in Roman literature – cf. Croesus in Petronius' *Sat.* (64.5–6), Lyne 1980, 173–4. Something of a 'double standard' obtains here, however, in that it was acceptable for males to pursue and penetrate others of either sex but it was highly unacceptable for a male himself to be penetrated and Roman satire is scathing on the subject (see e.g. Ovid *Ars am* . 1.524, Juvenal 2 with Morton Braund 168–172).

Metre: hendecasyllabics

1.   **myself** ... **my love**: *me ac meos amores* suggests that the subject of the poem is the trust which the poet places in Aurelius: this looks as if it is a conventional poem asking a third party to look after a minor, but the inclusion of *me* suggests otherwise. For *amores* meaning 'beloved' cf. 6.16, 10.1; Quinn proposes that the boy in question is Juventius of poems 24, 48, 81, 99.

2   Aurelius is presumably the same Aurelius as appears in poem 11 and 16.

      a modest favour: the word *pudentem* is ironic in this poem which explores the total lack of modesty exhibited by Aurelius. Note also the alliteration of *p.*

3   The poet appeals to Aurelius' own experience of wanting to preserve the innocence of anybody: but the sentence begins unpromisingly 'if you have ever desired anything with your heart ... ', suggesting the carnal lust of the addressee which the poet fears and describes later on.

4   **pure:** *castum* suggests 'freedom from stain' while *integellum* suggests 'whole, undamaged': the diminutive stresses the affection in which the poet holds the *puerum.*

5   **modestly:** *pudice* picks up *pudentem* from line 2 and completes the sense-block neatly with ring-composition.

6–10 The reader might assume so far that (a) Aurelius is a man of modesty and (b) he will be expected to act as a bodyguard to protect the minor from assault by strangers. Both of these points are now countered by the poet.

7–8   The people are too busy with their own concerns to notice the boy.

9–10 **penis:** The obscene word ends the line with great force and the following line endows the member with personality and danger. 'Bad boys' are presumably boy-prostitutes.

11-12 *quem* is Aurelius' penis: note the rhetorical force of the repetition of *lubet* and *qua* ...
quantum with the imperative *moueto*, finishing off with the rude caricature *foris
paratum* – Aurelius with his penis at the ready out of doors.

13   **modest**: *pudenter* again: the poet's request is 'modest' – though we must doubt whether
his feelings towards the boy are modest.

14   **madness**; For sexual desire as madness cf. Lucretius 4.1069, Virgil *Aen.* 4. 101, Horace
Sat. 2.3.325. Aurelius is motivated by *mala mens* as well as 'madness' and so his
madness will not exculpate him, although the language of *impulerit* might suggest
otherwise.

15   **sin**: For *culpa* used of sexual misconduct cf. Virgil *Aen.* 4. 172. Note here the
juxtaposition of *sceleste culpam*: it will all be Aurelius' fault.

16   **my head**: the meaning is ambiguous; it may refer to the poet himself or else the
boyfriend.

17   Note the alliteration of *t* and then *m* and the sequence of short stabbing words *a tum te.*
miserum is doubly appropriate here: Aurelius will be *miser* in the sense of 'love-sick'
for the boy (cf. 8.1) and also *miser* in the sense of 'wretched' when he suffers his
punishment.

18-19 The punishment is recounted in cinematographic terms: first the feet are pulled up,
then the orifice is opened before the radishes and mullets rush through in a final line of
triumph. The euphemism *porta* is uncommon and used here both for the alliteration and
also the metaphor of *percurrent* ('run through') which rather assumes a wide passage.
The poet adopts the language of the outraged husband in envisaged outrage at the
seduction of his boyfriend: the hyperbolic language and the disproportionate level of
feeling expressed create an image of the poet's *persona* as one of assertion and
aggression. For the mullets cf. Juvenal 10.317, and for the radishes cf. Aristophanes
Clouds 1083. The legal position on the punishments meted out by husbands to their
wives' lovers are discussed in Treggiari (1991) 271–5.

16

A text of importance for the interpretation of Catullus' poetry and its relation to real life. The
irony is that this poem so eloquent on the perils of the biographical style of interpretation has
itself been subjected to exactly that sort of approach: Garrison confidently states that 'Furius
and Aurelius ... have accused him of living indecently because he writes erotic poetry'. There
is clearly no need to postulate a 'real' situation to provoke this poem: the text justifies itself as
a piece of rhetoric which positively demands that we stop arguing from the verse to the poet's
life and *vice versa.* Furius and Aurelius are convenient addressees who fulfil various
functions in these poems: they have been indomitable companions of the poet (11), stingy
and poor (23, 26) and Aurelius is seen as a promiscuous pederast (15, 21).

Metre: hendecasyllabics

1   **bugger ... fuck**: Both actions indicate the exercise of power and an assertion of
masculinity, justified in the lines which follow. *pedico* ('bugger') derives from the
Greek *paidikos* ('boyish').

2   **pansy**: *pathicus* is one who submits to anal intercourse, *cinaedus* is properly used of a
catamite, a boy kept for sexual purposes: both words are transliterations of Greek
words of the same meaning.

3   **little poems**: Note the diminutive *uersiculis* – small evidence on which to base such
large claims – and the repetition *me ... meis.*

4   **unmanly**: *mollis* means 'soft, luxurious' and comes then to mean 'effeminate'. In other
words, the poetic *persona* in the verses seems less robustly male and more engaged in

the indulgence of pleasure than Furius and Aurelius expected; this leads to the conclusion that the poet is himself 'insufficiently modest' – as understated as the opening of the poem is not.

5–6 The distinction is drawn between the text and its author with stark clarity and explicitness. There is no evidence for Quinn's assertion that he is here not talking of his 'serious love poetry, but about his *uersiculi*'; indeed if exceptions of this kind were admited by the poet he would destroy the point he is making. Ovid later on makes the same point about his own work (*Tr.* 2. 354: cf. Martial 1.4.8, Pliny *Ep.* 4.14.5).

pure: the Latin word *pius* is difficult to translate: see 76.2–4 and discussion there. The term primarily indicates being 'devoted' and 'loyal' (especially when this is difficult or unpleasant) rather than 'pious' in the sense of religious devotion. The term here suggests 'personal integrity', positing a contrast between the uninhibited creations of the imagination and the 'real life' which is bound by social and moral strictures.

7 **wit and charm**: the poet's work is not autobiography but exercises in *sal* and *lepos* – both key terms in his aesthetic: cf. 1.1

8 the phrase is repeated from line 4.

9 the poet phrases his point well: it is possible (*possunt*) that his verses might arouse sexual feelings, especially in those either too young or too old to be sexually active themselves, but that is not their object.

12 **thousands**: picking up the calculation of kisses in poems 5 and 7

13 **read**; Furius and Aurelius have 'read' these lines which suggests that this verse was circulated privately before being published and performed in public. Note here the alliteration of *m*.

14 The poem ends with a repetition of line 1 to conclude the text with ring-composition.

17

A poem set in the northern provinces – *colonia* may refer to Verona as often assumed by commentators, but need not do so and the poet's vagueness is surely deliberate. The poem well evokes the atmosphere of the *colonia* and moves from describing the bridge to the man whose young wife is misbehaving. The structure of the poem is parody of prayer-formula as the colony is addressed, described (*quae* ... lines 1–4) and then asked for a favour (lines 7–26) after an expression of sympathy from the poet (5–6).

Metre: Priapeans

1 **O Colony**: The Colony is addressed and personified in high poetic style: *ludere* presumably refers to a festival full of merrymaking here, but the word also carries the sense of sexual misconduct which the poem will later exploit in line 17.

2–4 the colony continues to be addressed in second-person verbs.

3 **recycled**: *rediuiuus* is a builder's term for materials salvaged from one use and used again elsewhere.

5 **to suit your desires**: *ex tua libidine* is ironic: its surface meaning ('as you wish') has the sexual term *libido* lurking behind it appropriate to the young wife.

6 **Salisubsalus**: the term only occurs here and may be a cult-title of the god Mars, whose priests were called *salii* or else a reference to a local god Salisubsalus of whom nothing is known. There is the word 'jump' (*salire*) lurking in the word and this gives the pleasing picture of the 'Leaping Priests' who could safely carry out their leaping rites on the good bridge.

7 **laughter**: The word *risus* is kept until the end of the line as a surprise after *munus maximi* ... . The repetition of the apostrophe *colonia* recalls the opening line and marks the end of the first section of the poem.

8   **a certain:** The speaker is vague about detail again: an unnamed man in an unnamed place, suggesting that the poem is as likely to be a literary *jeu d'esprit* as a topical piece of satire. Note here the juxtaposition of *meum..tuo.*

10-11 Notice the effective description of the muddy marsh: the variation of vocabulary in *lutum ... lacus.. paludis ... uorago,* the use of powerful adjectives (*putidae.. liuidissima ... profunda*) and the intensifying terms *totius ... maxime.*

12   **idiot;** *insulsus* was used of Varus' girlfried in 10.33.

13   Notice how the poet turns a simple insult ('he has no sense') into a vignette of a 'two-year-old child sleeping on its father's trembling elbow' which lifts the poem from mere invective into imaginative writing of a high order. *tremuli* suggests the rocking movement of the parent, rather than the trembling of old age.

14   The progression of thought is neat: he has not the sense of a *puer* in his father's arms, and he has a *puella* to look after. For the metaphor *uiridissimo flore* of sexual prime cf. 62.39-47, Lucretius 4.1105-6, *OLD* s.v. 'flos' 8b. What is interesting here is the sequence of imagery as the poet presents us first with a flower, then a kid, then grapes.

15   **girl ... girl:** the repetition is highly emphatic especially with the diminutive *tenellulo* (from *tener*). *delicatus* means 'capricious' (cf. 50.3) and the simile refers to the girl's naughty behaviour rather than her vulnerability: for the amorous nature of goats cf. Horace *Odes* 3.13.4-5 and the cult of Pan.

16   **grapes:** the image changes abruptly to that of grapes: the 4-word line is remarkable for its metrical dexterity. The point of the image here is to shift the blame from the girl to the husband who is not looking after her well enough: the image of the kid leaves open the interpretation that she is no better than she should be, but the imagery of tender grapes suggests her innocence.

17   **fool about;** *ludere* is picked up from line1: its erotic overtones are clear, as in 61.211, 68.17, 99.1, Ovid *Am.* 1.8.43, Cicero *Cael.* 42.

18-22 The simple statement that he does not care what his wife gets up to is elaborated into a series of descriptions of his physical and mental state: he is physically static and mentally dead.

19   **hamstrung:** *suppernata* is a double image: 'hamstrung' cannot apply to the log but only to an animal: and so the husband is like a log which is like a hamstrung animal. Liguria is a large highland area to the north of Rome and the west of Verona. As with the image of the young child, the poet dramatises the picture with detail such as the Ligurian axe and the ditch.

21   **dolt;** *meus stupor* here means 'that stupid man of whom I write'. For the use of the abstract noun 'stupidity' to mean 'a stupid man' cf. 29.13. Note here the repetitious catalogue of the man's ignorance: the repeated *nil.. nihil ... sit..sit ... sit* and the jingle of *sit.. nescit.* He is ignorant of his own ignorance, as at Lucretius 4.469-670 and Plautus *Aul.* 714-5.

22   *nunc* sums up the argument: and the poet now wishes to hurl the man off himself, whereas before he merely wished that he might *ire praecipitem* (line 9).

24-6 The poem ends with a fine poetic conceit: the man might leave his lethargy behind in the mud like a mule leaves its shoe. Note the hint of *uetus* (old) in *ueternum* and the continuation of the 'lying dead' theme in *supinum.*

26   **mule:** Roman mules and horses did not have metal shoes nailed into their hooves but wore leather shoes with metal soles which could well come off in mud. *uoragine* picks up *uorago* in line 11 and embellishes *in graui.. caeno* from the previous line.

21

Poem 15 warns the sexually voracious Aurelius off the poet's young boyfriend this poem repeats the message. 'Ostensibly a warning-off and ostensible obscene; in reality, like poem 15, a pasquinade and a further example of *uersiculi* that are *molliculi* and *parum pudici*: the *sal ac lepos* lies in the exploitations of a similar ambiguity.' (Quinn) The boy in question is assumed by most editors to be Juventius of poems 24, 48, 81, 99.

Metre: hendecasyllabics

1   **father of famines:** a mock title, deriving no doubt from Aurelius' permanent poverty and also from the hunger induced by his voracious sexual activity, as in the case of thin Gellius in poem 89. Aurelius is hungry – and not just for food.

2–3   **of all those ... :** Ironic embellishment of *esuritionum* which shows the reader that this poem is hardly to be taken at face value. He uses this formula also at 24.2–3 (a poem to Juventius) and 49.2–3 (an ironic poem to Cicero).

4   **bugger:** the word *pedicare* comes as a bathetic shock after the previous honorific lines. For *amores* of the beloved cf. 10.1 etc.

5   the asyndeton suggests the animation of the poet's concern about Aurelius' behaviour, although the behaviour he describes hardly amounts to being caught *in flagrante delicto*.

6   **trying everything:** *omnia experiris* is vague through either reticence or (more likely) lack of hard evidence. *latus* is of course highly suggestive, being often used to suggest the male genitals (see Adams, 49) especially when the phrase talks of 'joining' or 'sticking to' as here (cf. Lucilius 305M, Ovid *Her.* 2.58). Lack of evidence does not stop the poet using strong innuendo.

7–8   **fucking your mouth:** Bathos again as the poet ends the high-sounding sentence with the low word *irrumatione*. Presumably the point of the threat is that once Aurelius' oral rape by the poet has become widely known then the boy will not be interested in him any more. The purpose of the *irrumatio* is not to relieve sexual desire but to express power and dominance over Aurelius: see poem 16, Wiseman (1985) 10–14.

9–11   **starve:** Harking back with *esurire* to the initial apostrophe as *pater esuritionum* and also continuing the 'oral fulness' theme of *irrumatio* the poet elegantly combines the two ideas here. He complains that Aurelius is too poor to feed the boy properly – and threatens to fill Aurelius' mouth as a consequence. To add to the 'oral' theme, it can hardly be accidental that the poet uses the word *tacerem* (I would keep mouth closed) meaning 'I would not mind'.

12   **So...:** For *quare* to sum up the punishment cf. 12.10.

13   The poem ends on the suitably aggressive note of *irrumatus* after the harshly alliterative *finem facias*.

22

As often, a poem about poetry; firstly about the gap between the quality of poetry and the image it presents, in that Suffenus produces elegant-looking volumes of which he is conspicuously proud, but their superficial elegance is not matched in the text itself. Secondly there is the gap between the man himself who is described in terms of which we should approve but whose verse is the opposite. Thirdly there is the familiar neoteric point that quality and quantity are usually in inverse proportion to each other. What raises this poem above the level of simple invective against Suffenus is the final confession of sympathy by the poet who admits that all creative artists in some ways are a Suffenus. Notice here the stress on appearances (the details of the fine book-production in lines 5–8, the repetition of parts of *uidere* (lines 11, 13, 19, 21) and the use of *fallimur* in line 18) and the ironic way in which the poet applies labels of disapproval to Suffenus but also recognises features which they both share: both the pleasure which Suffenus takes in composition (cf. poem 50) and especially the self-criticism which this poem prompts (lines 18–21). The genuine paradox of all this is brought out in the repetition of *idem* (lines 3, 14, 15, 18).

Metre: scazons ('limping iambics')

1 **Suffenus ... Varus**: the poem opens with the relevant names of the subject and the addressee. For Suffenus cf. 14.19, for Varus cf. poem 10.

2 **charm, articulate ... civilised**: all words of approval: for *uenustus* cf. 3.2, 13.6; *urbanus* comes to mean 'civilised' by being 'citified' (Garrison) and its opposite is therefore *rusticus,* the countryman whose lack of wit and grace was long the subject of comedy (see *OLD* s.v. 'rusticus' 4b, 5,6,7 with numerous examples). The contrast about to be drawn is between the man's general nature (*homo*) which is *urbanus* and his published work which is *rusticus.*

3 **quantity**: Suspicion naturally attaches to excessive quantities of verse: cf. Hortensius' work in 95.3–4, Horace's criticism of Lucilius (*Sat.* 1.4.9–13) and Juvenal's suffering of interminable epic in *Sat.* 1.1–6: the Alexandrian aesthetic of 'small is beautiful' (as in Callimachus' famous *Aetia* prologue 1–16 (on the influence of Callimachus on Catullus see Hutchinson 296–325))

4 **ten thousand**: The phrasing gives the impression that Suffenus produces work in units of a thousand lines at a time.

5–8 No expense is spared in the production of Suffenus' poetry: the point here is both that the quality of the text does not live up to the glamour of the book and also the strong contrast between the richness of the book and the poverty of its contents, so that Suffenus comes over as both vain and foolish. Note here the anaphora of *noui ... noui* and the way line 8 is itself *aequata* by having the participles at either end with the *p*–alliterated words in the middle.

5 **re-used paper**: In an age where papyrus was prohibitively expensive, it was common practice to erase what was written on the papyrus or parchment and re-use it: cf. Cicero *Fam.* 7.18.2.

6 **imperial paper**: *cartae regiae* is a technical term in publishing for best-quality paper: the *carta* is the paper which went up to make the *liber*: Catullus and Lucretius use the word *carta* as a dignified term: cf.1.6, Lucretius 3.10, 4. 970. The term *regia* ('royal') adds to the grandeur.

7 **bosses**: The *umbilicus* was properly the stick of wood (or ivory) around which the parchment or papyrus was scrolled (cf. e.g. Martial 4.89.2): here the plural term refers to the 'bosses' or protruding knobs which could be painted (Martial 3.2.9). The *lora* were the leather thongs for tying the *membrana* which was the parchment jacket to protect the book.

8 The paper was marked with lines to keep the scribe's writing in straight lines: for this purpose a circular piece of lead was used. For the use of pumice-stone to smooth the ends of the paper cf. 1.2.

9–10 The poet delays the judgement on Suffenus for comic effect, so that the *bellus et urbanus* becomes *caprimulgus et fossor*. The generalised adjectives of approval become all too specific nouns of contempt, intensified by *unus* ('any old'). *caprimulgus* (only found here) literally means 'goat-milker', *fossor* is a ditchdigger (also found in Persius 5.122 with the meaning 'hillbilly').

11 **once again**: *rursus* is used here in the sense of 'back to what he was': Suffenus was a witless peasant who seemed elegant when one saw his book but who then went back to his real nature when one read the text, a process elaborated on in lines 12–14. There is also a suggestion here of *rusticus* and *rus.*

12 **we**: The poet and Varus make up the 'we' of the verb. *scurra* is a term of approval.

14   **bumpkin:** For the boorishness of the countryside cf. the very similar criticism of Volusius' *Annales* as *pleni ruris et infacetiarum* (36.19).

16   **happy...:** *beatus ... gaudet ... miratur;* For the pleasure of writing poetry see the poet's own admission in poem 50: the poet appears to be mocking (with a sneer) the self-satisfied smile of another poet unaware of his own mediocrity: until the last few lines of the text place himself under the same criticism.

18–19 The first four words are adequate to make the point that we all labour under this sort of delusion: the rest of the sentence brings Suffenus back as a type of behaviour: the first-person plural verb pitting the poet and Varus against Suffenus (*putemus* line 12) is now a first-person plural showing the common nature of the poet and Suffenus (*fallimur*) and Varus is invited to disprove the point in the second person *possis*, emphasised by its position at the end of the sentence but the beginning of the line.

20–21 **bag:** In Aesop's fable Zeus gave us two knapsacks, the one carried on the front which contains the faults of others, the other carried on the back and containing our own faults. We are much better at seeing the faults of others.

23

A neat exercise in satire. Furius is imagined as asking for a large amount of money and the poet refuses on the grounds that Furius does not need it. The money is not mentioned until the very end, after the poet has indulged in an increasingly bizarre account of the 'rich poverty' which Furius enjoys; he may have no property (lines 1–2) but he is still sufficiently *beatus* (15, 27) as he has no need of property – and hence no need of the poet's money. The poet goes through the *topoi* of the Stoic 'consolation' of poverty – the wise man will avoid wealth as it will only make him a target for crime and anxious about losing it all, good health is worth all the money in the world and is effected by austerity rather than luxury anyway; even his bowel-habits are free of the messiness which bothers everybody else. The parody of such philosophical arguments becomes pointed when it becomes obvious that the poet who is advancing these considerations is doing so simply to avoid having to part with his money; he thus is hardly practising what he preaches.

Metre: Hendesyllabics

1–2   **who has neither ...:** The catalogue of what Furius does *not* possess is comic. It begins in straightforward style (no slave or money-box) but then goes onto the comic conceit that Furius is so poor that even bedbugs and spiders avoid him in preference for someone richer. *ignis* is important as the poem proceeds and the Furius family is seen as lacking any need of fire in that their health is secured by the sun and cold.

3–6   **father and stepmother:** their ability to eat flint is presumably a sign of their inhuman hardiness, the description of the stepmother as *lignea* is anything but kind (cf. Lucretius 4. 1161). Notice how the poet makes every attempt to show the hardness of the pair: the mention of *dentes* eating *silicem* is explicit, and the use of *possunt* proves that it is their ability to eat flint which is being commented on rather than the (real or imaginary) poverty which compels them to do so.

8–11 The consolation of the poor is that they are not targets of crime or danger, a theme of ancient philosophy (cf. Juvenal 10. 18–22). Note here the anaphora of *non* and the manner in which the poet – having said that they fear 'nothing' goes on to itemise some of the things which they do not fear, four of them occupying a half-line each while the final summary one takes a whole line to itself.

11   **no other...dangers:** *casus alios periculorum* sums up all the dangers which the preceding list has omitted.

12-4 The sun, cold and fasting have given Furius' family dry bodies: note the variation of vocabulary in *sicciora ... magis aridum* and the familiar *siquid* + comparative figure as at 13.10, 22.13, 42.14, 82.2; note also the effective alliteration of *c* in line 12. For the idea that a healthy body is dry (and thus free of humours) see Cicero *Tusc.* 5.99, *Sen.* 34, Lucilius fr. 611.

15   After discussing Furius' family, the poet now turns to address Furius alone.

16-17 A neatly constructed couplet with anaphora of *abest* inside a chiasmus whose outer cola are alliterative, and in line 17 *m* alliteration joining the two similar phrases delineating nasal fluid. For the unwelcome sight of saliva cf. the girl's lack of a 'dry mouth' in poem 43: for catarrh cf. Horace *Epist.* 1.1.108, where Mayer (1994, *ad loc.*) comments that Horace 'directs a jibe at tiresome Stoic disquisitions about indifference to illness, in which a runny nose commonly figured (Arr. *Epict.* 1.6.30)'.

18   **cleanness...more clean**: Note the repetition *munditiem ... mundiorem.*

19   **cleaner**: *purior* is variation on *mundiorem*: for the *salillum* cf. Horace *Odes* 2.16.13–14, Persius 3.25.

20   **shit**: In a natural transition the poet moves from the *culus* to its products. The logic appears to be simply that if no food is eaten then no bowel-movements will occur, and if the body is dry then the stools will also be dry. For the vulgar word *cacas* cf. 36.1.

22-3 **you could**: The poet proposes that Furius test the truth of his words and describes the experiment in graphic detail: note the emphatic *tu*, the mention of *manibus* and then *digitum*, the pair of verbs *teras fricesque* prolonging the experiment and creating a vivid sensation for the reader. The paradox is that this activity which would normally render the hands most unclean has no such effect in the case of Furius.

23-7 The final sentence reveals the 'point' of the poem, with neat closure afforded by the repeated *beata ... beatus.* Notice also the repetition of the addressee's name from line 1 (ring composition), the chiastic pairing of the two infinitives *spernere nec putare* within line 25, the appropriately emphatic pause after the word *desine* ('stop').

26-7 **hundred sestertia**: 100,000 sestertii is a large amount of money, a year's income for middle-income men.

24

The poem is clearly paired (by the poet or the editor) with the preceding poem; this poem repeats three times the description of Furius *cui neque seruus est neque arca* from 23.1. It is possible that the sobriquet was invented and used by Furius himself in a poem of his own, so that the famous quotation was all that was needed to identify the man. The logic of the poem is less than perfect: the poet urges Juventius rather to give the poor man money than love (4–6), on the grounds that however smart he is he is poor (7–10) – but if Juventius did give him money then the poet would have no grounds for urging him to withhold his love.

Metre: Hendecasyllabics.

1   **flower**: For the image of the flower cf. 63.64, 100.2: here the diminutive shows the poet's appreciation and affection.

2-3 For this familiar figure cf. 21.2–3, 49.2–3

4   **Midas** was proverbially wealthy (Tyrtaeus 9.6, Plato *Resp.* 408b) as a result of the magic power by which all he touched turned to gold. Notice here the symmetrical alliteration of *m – d – m – d.*

5   **that man**: *isti* is contemptuous: the poet does not need to name the man but only to describe him.

6   Note the assonance and alliteration of *sic te sineres.*

7-8   **'What?'...**: Note the effective way in which the poet first imagines an objection from Juventius and then answers it by quoting the term *bellus* as if in inverted commas and then repeating the phrase *cui ... arca* from line 5. For *bellus* cf. 22.9.

9   **Discard and make little of**: *abicere* and *eleuare* are technical rhetorical terms, as the editors all remark. The reason for the poet using them here is perhaps to depict Juventius as steeped in the jargon of the rhetorical education which sees the world in high-flown language, only to have the grim reality of the man's poverty repeated bathetically.

25

Like poem 12, an appeal to return the poet's property. The appeal of the poem lies primarily in its choice of imagery and imaginative language: the poet insults and threatens Thallus with a rage and a controlled invective which reminds the reader of Archilochus and the Horace of the *Epodes*.

Metre: iambic tetrameters catalectic.

1   **pansy**: For *cinaedus* see 16.2, 10.24: a term often used to denote the effeminate (*mollior*), although it originally means one who submits to penetration from another male. The poem begins effectively with this insult.

1-3   The poet creates five images of 'softness' with which to build the picture of Thallus' effeminacy. Interestingly, *cuniculus* means 'rabbit' but also has a secondary meaning of 'diarrhoea' (see Adams 139). The images are chosen both for their sounds – note the strong preponderance of *ll* sounds here – and for their sense: the rabbit's hair leads on to the goose-liver (as *OLD* conjectures the meaning s.v. 'medulla' 1b): then the bottom of the ear-lobe (a common enough phrase to denote softness as at Cicero *Q. Fr.* 2.15a.4), then the old man's penis with its 'cobwebby decrepitude' (Garrison). The old man's penis is of course a symbol of passive impotence, the cobwebs the symbol of sloth and decay. This soft, old, decayed, slothful impotent of lines 1-3 is then suddenly described as *turbida rapacior procella* in the next line.

4   **the same man**: *idem* brings out the paradox of the extreme contrast in the man's nature. *rapacior* is highly appropriate of Thallus who 'snatches' all he can.

5   The ms read *cum diua mulier aries ostendit oscitantes* which makes no sense. The line seems to mean 'when people are off their guard' and Munro's suggestion *Murcia* (an obscure goddess, presumably one of sloth from the evidence of the adjective *murcidus)* is tempting. Goold prints Skutsch's conjecture *diues arca rimulas* ('when a well-stocked linen-chest has openings showing') but this is far from the ms and inexplicable on palaeographical grounds. The obscure *Murcia* would easily be 'corrected' by an ignorant scribe to *mulier*. That leaves *aries* to deal with: and MacKay's suggestion *arbitros* for 'onlooker' (i.e. dinner-guest) makes better sense than most suggestions. This text therefore, as Quinn's, reads: *cum diua Murcia arbitros ostendit oscitantes.*

6-7   **send me**: After the long descriptive build-up the poet finally gets round to the message of the poem. After the initial vague *pallium*, Thallus' thefts are itemised in detail with the impressive 'designer-labels' *Saetabum ... Thynos*. For the former cf. 12.14; the latter is clearly a Greek term and suggests something embroidered or at any rate marked. *Thynos* refers to the place of origin as Bithynia: cf. 31.5.

8   **you fool**: For *inepte* cf. 8.1. Thallus makes no attempt to hide his thefts but parades them as if they were his own family heirlooms.

9   **Unglue**: The poet imagines that Thallus has the napkins stuck to his fingernails; note the anaphora of *re– ... re–*.

10   Notice here the alliteration of *l* and *m* and the diminutives *latusculum* ... *mollicellas* as the poet stresses (again) the softness of Thallus about to be wounded, the notion of 'wool' in *laneum* reminding us of *capillo* in line 2.

11   **scribble on:** *conscribillent* is an excellent word to use here; the poet will 'write' upon Thallus' flesh, just as the napkins were written on with embroidery (*catagraphos*). The word *inusta* suggests that the marks will be burnt onto him, like the branding of slaves.

13   **sea...raging:** Thallus, the man who is more rapacious than the storm (line 4), will find himself in a storm of the poet's making; the threat is made all the stronger by the juxtaposition of *minuta magno* and the transference of the poet's anger into the *uesaniente uento*.

26

A poem playing on the two senses of *oppositus*, meaning both (1) 'facing' and also (2) 'pledged'. The house is notably *oppositus* not in sense (1) but certainly in sense (2)

Metre: hendecasyllabics

1   **Furius:** cf. 11, 23. The diminutive *uillula* is effective in emphasing both the vulnerable state of the house facing the assault of the winds and also the monstrous sum which the little house costs the poet. One ms reads *nostra* which would make the poem self-mocking: there is nothing *a priori* unlikely about that, but the reading *uestra* gives the address to Furius more point.

1–3   The four winds are named: Auster is South, Fauonus West, Boreas is North and Apheliotes the East, the last of these four being an unusual term for the more common Eurus and 'an appropriately learned touch to round off the first arm of the verbal ambiguity' (Quinn). The little house is well-placed, being sheltered from the winds: of the four the cold North is described as *saeuus*.

4   **15,200:** 15,200 sesterces is not a huge sum for a house – Caelius rented an apartment for 10,000 sesterces (Cicero *Cael.* 17) – but the point is the sudden shift in the meaning of *opposita* from 'facing' to 'mortgaged for'.

5   **plague-ridden:** A pun on the meaning of *pestilentem* as used generally it simply means 'unpleasant' and is applicable to both wind and mortgage, but when applied to a wind it carries its primary sense of 'bearing disease' and is more appropriate to winds than mortgages. For the belief that disease is carried on the wind cf. Lucretius 6. 1090–1124 and Horace *Odes* 3.23.5.

27

Ostensibly a drinking poem, reminiscent of two fragments of Anacreon:

'Come, boy, bring me a cup to drink deep, mixing ten ladles of water with five of wine, so that I may break out in Bacchic frenzy without disrespect' (43D)
'Bring water, bring wine, boy, bring us flowery garlands, so that I may box with Love' (27D).

In fact, there is a simple problem with this 'straight' interpretation in that 'bitter' wine is not 'better': it is possible that the poem is using the imagery of wine as a metaphor for poetry itself, as Wiseman (1969 7–8) suggested. The image of good poets and poor poets as wine and water-drinkers respectively is old (Fraenkel 1957, 340) (deriving perhaps from the fact that Dionysus is god both of wine and of the theatre): the idea is explored in Horace *Epist.* 1.19, taking as its starting-point the Greek comic poet Cratinus' remark that 'no water-drinker can produce anything clever' (*Poetae Comici Graeci* 203). The final word of the poem is thus nicely ambiguous: 'this man is neat Thyonianus' means that he is pure unmixed wine and also suggests the Greek *thuein* (to sacrifice, slaughter: Wiseman compares Horace *Odes* 1.17. 23). This still leaves the mystery of Postumia: but see note on line 3.

Metre: hendecasyllabics

1 **Slave, steward**: Note the repetition *minister ... puer* where the Greek simply says 'boy'. *uetuli* is affectionate diminutive: Falernian wine was better when old, which adds point to the adjective. There may be an allusion to Lucilius, 'whose home was Suessa Aurunca next to the *ager Falernus*' (Wiseman 1969, 8)

2 **bitterer**: *amariores* is hardly a term of approval for wine and should alert us that something odd is happening here. *calices* stands for their contents by metonyny.

3 **Mistress**: Roman drinking parties had a 'master of the drinking' (*magister bibendi*) who decided on the quality and pace of the drinking: 'Postumia' is a Roman name, its bearer no Greek girl but a Roman matron, causing surprise in modern readers: Wiseman 1985 (134) cites Cato (Gellius *N.A.* 10.23.4), Juvenal (6.300–319) and Pliny (*NH* 14.89f) on wine and women, and comments: 'drunkenness was traditionally second only to adultery (to which it was assumed to lead) in the catalogue of sins unforgivable in a Roman matron, yet Postumia is named, and her ancestry alluded to, in a poem which must have caused her staider relatives anger and shame.' This face-value reading of the text is less impressive than his earlier suggestion (1969, 7–8 that the 'wine' is standing here for poetry). The suggestion that Postumia is the wife of Cicero's correspondent Servius Sulpicius Rufus is more than a guess: at least her grand-daughter was Rome's only known female erotic poet (Treggiari, 121). If the 'wine' of which she is mistress is really poetry, then we may have the right family.

4 **drunker than the drunken**: For the polyptoton of *ebrioso ... ebriosioris* cf. 22.14, 99.2.

5–7 **You, water**: apostrophe to water, to be gone and leave the wine alone. The *seueri* are perhaps the same men referred to in 5.2, the word used of teetotallers in the Horace *Epistle* (1.19) which makes the link between wine and poetry. Notice the juxtaposition of *lymphae/ uini* and the emphasis on the strong imperative *migrate* at the end of the sentence and the beginning of the line.

7 **Thyonian**: Bacchus' mother was sometimes called Thyone (e.g. *Homeric Hymn* 1.21).

28

Veranius and Fabullus are having as bad a time on the staff of Piso as Catullus claims that he had under Memmius in Bithynia. For more information on Piso, see Nisbet 1961, 180–182.

Metre: hendecasyllabics

1 **Piso**: L. Calpurnius Piso Caesonius, consul 58 B.C. and father-in-law of Julius Caesar, was governor of Macedonia in 57–55 B.C. and prosecuted by Cicero. Poems 9 and 12 refer to Veranius and Fabullus being abroad in Spain: there is, however, no real difficulty with assuming that these two men went abroad more than once in their lives. *cohors* means 'company of soldiers' but also means the staff of the provincial governor, as in 10.10. The poet uses the term in the second sense in line 1, only to switch to the first sense in the following line. *inanis* here means 'empty-handed' (making the same point as at 10.9–11) but also implies 'useless'.

2 **knapsacks**: *sarcinae* are soldiers' packs, soldiers on the march being called *expediti*. This *cohors* of Piso's really deserved the name.

3 **Veranius...Fabullus**: The names frame the line, as in 16.1.

5 **scum**: *uappa* is flat wine, here used of Piso himself as a 'washout'.

6–8 **in the red**: The word *expensum* is a surprise, assisted by the enjambement, after *lucelli*. The language of finance is used repeatedly: the poet explains that he counts his expenditure (*datum*) as *lucello* (profit), presumably in the sense that he has learned by the experience even if he remains out of pocket.

9-10 **Memmius**: Picks up the term *irrumator* applied to Memmius in poem 10 and develops the idea further. Note here the comic exaggeration of 'well and long' (*bene ac diu*), with 'that whole beam' and 'slowly'. To complete the picture the poet imagines himself as *supinum*, and the decisive verb *irrumasti* is left until the end of the line and the sentence. For the metaphorical use of *irrumo* see 16.1.

11-13 The poet equates their experience with his by judicious similarity of expression combined with variation of vocabulary: *irrumasti* becomes 'you have been stuffed' (*farti estis* placed for emphasis at the end of the sentence), while the metaphorical 'beam' *trabe* becomes a more explicit *trpa* (penis).

13 **'Find good friends...'**: The kind of advice which was presumably given to young Romans and which the poet repeats ironically here.

15 **you**: *uobis* must refer to Piso and Memmius. Note here the effective alliteration of *m* and *d* and *r* all bringing out the force of the curse.

Romulus and Remus were the legendary founders of Rome and stand here for Rome itself and also for the tradition of historical greatness which they represent and which Piso and Memmius are impugning.

29

The first of several attacks on Caesar's favourite Mamurra in a poem addressed to Pompey and Caesar. The reference to these men as son-in-law and father-in-law dates the poem to before Julia's death in 54 B.C., while the mention of Britain places it in the early part of that year.

Metre: iambic trimeters.

1 **Who ... who:** the rhetorical repetition of *quis potest* displays indignation. In this case 'to see' comes to mean 'to see and do nothing about' i.e. 'to allow', a meaning familiar in Homeric Greek (Griffin 1980, 182)

2 Note how the terms accumulate and also set up themes which will be elaborated later: 'shameless' suggests general lack of inhibition, 'greedy' suggests that Mamurra keep on seeking more and more, while 'gambler' tells us that he is quite happy to risk losing all at once.

3 **Long-haired Gaul**: Transalpine Gaul was called *Gallia comata* because it was the fashion there to wear the hair long, unlike Cisalpine Gaul which was named *Gallia togata* as Roman customs of dress had been accepted there.

4 the ms reading *cum te* must be wrong; Mynors reads Faernus' *uncti* but much better and simpler sense is given by Statius' *ante*.

For the stock epithet *ultima* used of Britain cf. 11.12, Horace *Odes* 1.35.29, 4.14.47, Virgil *Ecl.* 1.66.

5 **Queer Romulus**: i.e. Caesar (Fordyce) or Pompey (Goold, Quinn). Caesar's sexual reputation was more questionable than that of Pompey and so he earns the title *cinaedus* more easily than his son-in-law, but the structure of the poem leads one to put Pompey here, since it is attractive to read lines 1-10 as being addressed to Pompey, lines 11-20 to Caesar, and the coda to them both. For the sarcastic use of the name Romulus applied to a politician cf. pseudo-Sallust *Cicero* 4.7. where Cicero is called 'Romulus from Arpinum'. *uidebis et feres* recalls *uidere ... pati* in line 1.

6 the Latin has a pleasing jingle of *super- ... super-*.

7 **walk round**: *perambulabit* suggests nonchalance, with the hyperbolic *omnium*.

8   **white dove:** the dove was the pet-bird of Venus and is used as a byword for amorousness at 68.125–8: cf. 2.1. Adonis was the lover of Aphrodite in Greek mythology (see *OCD* s.v. 'Adonis').

9   Line 9 repeats line 5 exactly, and line 10 recalls line 2, thus neatly affording closure to this section.

11   **general without peer:** *imperator unice* must refer to Caesar as Pompey did not travel to Britain. For the sarcastic title cf. 54.7.

13   **shagged-out prick:** a bathetic vulgarity after the grandiose phrasing relating the voyage of the peerless general to the farthest end of the world. Mamurra's sexual excess earned him the nickname of *mentula*: cf. 94, 105, 114–5. For *diffututa* cf. 6.13, 41.1. The metaphor becomes absurd as this 'prick' goes on to 'eat' a vast amount of money.

15   **If that ... then what is?:** for the usage see Nisbet 1961, 109, Powell 1988, 109–110.

16   **screwed:** the scholiast on Persius 1.18 sees *patratio* as having a sexual sense: see Adams 142–4. Note here the repetition of *parum*.

18   **Pontic loot:** i.e. the money won during Pompey's campaigns against King Mithridates of Pontus in 64–3 B.C.

19   **the Spanish stuff:** i.e. the money acquired during Caesar's campaigns in Lusitania (modern Portugal) in 61 B.C. when Mamurra was his chief engineer. The poet shows his knowledge of the country with the neat poetic phrase 'gold-bearing Tagus': Spain was Rome's chief source of gold: cf. Ovid *Am.* 1.15.34.

20   the ms reading *hunc timet* must be wrong for the simple reason that it does not scan. Attempts to keep *timet* as *timetur* ('fears are expressed for Gaul') with *hunc* emended to *nunc* are unsatisfactory: for one thing, *nunc* would produce an unacceptable spondee in the metre, for another, it hardly makes sense to say that fears are expressed for deeds already carried out in the past – line 2 made it quite clear that Mamurra now possesses whatever Gaul and Britain once had. Quinn suggests that Gaul and Britain 'have survived this first blow, but are likely to succumb, should Mamurra return to the attack' but this is hardly to be squared with the statement which opens the poem. Baehrens' emendation *eine ... optima* is attractive and palaeographically plausible: EINE become HUNC, and the scribe may have felt that the elision of *Galliae optima* was too strong and 'corrected' *optima* to *timet*.

21   **Why the hell:** *malum* does not agree with *hunc* but is rather a colloquial expletive: cf. Cicero *Phil.* 1.15, *Verr.* 2.2.43.

22   **gobble up fat inheritances:** in fact of the three 'fortunes' which Mamurra squandered in lines 17–19, only the first could be called an inheritance. Quinn's idea that *uncta* here means that the money acquired from military campaigns was the 'sauce' on Mamurra's inheritance is fanciful and ignores the manner (*prima ... secunda ... tertia*) in which the poet stresses that Mamurra got through his inheritance before turning to the fruits of conquest. The poet here more plausibly means simply that Mamurra squanders the sort of sums which other men would regard as a whole inheritance. The verb *deuorare* recalls the adjective *uorax* in lines 2 and 10.

23   **holiest men:** the ms reading *urbis opulentissime* is surely wrong and Haupt's suggestion *piissimi* fits the tone of sarcastic praise very well.

24   **son-in-law:** Pompey, to seal the political alliance, married Caesar's daughter Julia in 59 B.C., and their subsequent civil war was often summarised in these familial terms (cf. Virgil *Aen.* 6.830–1, Lucan 1.290, Martial 9.70.3).

30

An interesting poem whose surface meaning is conveyed in a style of almost parodistic melancholy which casts doubt on any attempt to posit a 'real-life' setting for it. We do not know who this Alfenus is (many scholars identify him with the lawyer Alfenus Varus of poems 10 and 22 but this cannot be more than conjecture) nor is there much point in speculating as to what incident is supposed to have provoked this anger and sorrow from the poet; the phrase *inducens in amorem* might mean simple homosexual seduction or else leading the poet into a heterosexual relationship. As with so many of these poems, there is a sense of bravura performance about it as Catullus demonstrates his mastery of the Great Asclepiad metre and composes a poem of suitable weight to do so, in language which he was to reuse later in Ariadne's lament in poem 64. The following extract in particular is remarkably close to the style of the present poem:

'sicine me patriis auectam, perfide, ab aris,
perfide, deserto liquisti in litore, Theseu?
sicine discedens neglecto numine divum,
immemor – a! – deuota domum periuria portas?
nullane res potuit crudelis flectere mentis
consilium? tibi nulla fuit clementia praesto,
immite ut nostri uellet miserescere pectus?
at non haec quondam blanda promissa dedisti
uoce: mihi non haec miserae sperare iubebas,
sed conubia laeta, sed optatos hymenaeos,
quae cuncta aerii discerpunt irrita uenti. (64.132–142)

('Is this the way you carried me off, traitor, from my father's altars, traitor, only to abandon me on this deserted shore, Theseus? Is this the way you ignore the power of the gods and depart, mindless – ah! – as you carry home your cursed broken oaths? Was nothing capable of turning the purpose of your unfeeling mind? Did you have no mercy in you, to make your cruel heart prepared to pity me? These were not the promises which you once gave me with your flattering voice, these were not the hopes you bade this love-sick woman to have, but rather joyful marriages, the wedding-songs I longed for – all of which the winds of the air scatter for nothing.)

One of the immediately striking features of the poem (and the translator's despair) is the way the poet constantly finds new words for the notion of 'treacherous': *immemor, false, prodere, fallere, perfide, fallacum* all in the first four lines. Note also the forceful second-person style of this text with its four questions and continuous use of second-person verbs (line 6 has the parenthetic *dic* to maintain this pressure).

Metre: Greater Asclepiad
1   **thoughtless:** cf. 64. 58, 123, 135.
2–3 Note the repetition of sounds in *te ... dure tui dulcis* and the sentimental use of the diminutive *amiculi* in line 2, and the repetition of *iam*. Note also the juxtaposition of *fallere perfide*.
4   **heaven-dwellers:** an epic compound word to denote the gods, used also at 64.386.
4–5 **now:** The ms reading *nec ... quae* is surely wrong, and the clear sense required in 4 is provided by either *num* of Schwabe or the indignant *nunc* of Baehrens (which better suits the sequence of *iam ... iam* in lines 2–3) with enjambement rather than a stop at the end of the line and the question mark at the end of 5. *quae* cannot refer to the *facta impia* and make sense – but then grammatically it cannot refer to anything else – and so should be emended to Guarinus' *quos* which picks up *caelicolis* and has the poet accuse Alfenus of ignoring the gods and deserting himself. The assumption that the gods safeguard the virtuous, so that neglect of them is synonymous with immoral behaviour,

is perhaps surprising in the context of Roman religious belief which was more concerned 'with success than sin' (Ogilvie 17) and which did not usually regard the gods as agents – or examples – of moral rectitude (see Ogilvie 17–19, Dodds 31–2). This 'moral' view of the gods finds expression however several times in Catullus: see e.g. 64, where the deserted Ariadne appeals to the Eumenides to avenge her plight and her prayer is heard by Jupiter himself (64.192–206) and where the poem's epilogue (64.384–408) describes the gods' absence from human society as being because of their revulsion at our moral standards; see also poem 76.19–20.

5   **misfortune**: The poet is vague about the circumstances of the *mala* and it is arguable that this deliberately forces the reader to focus on the style and the artistry of the 'lament' rather than seeing the poem as a document of real distress.

6   **trust**: *fidem* looks forward to personified *Fides* in line 11.

7   The line begins with a strong assertion *certe tute*. *animam tradere* has the sense of 'surrender my life' and (in that sense) is hyperbolic here as there was clearly no serious danger of death; the term *anima* also picks up *unanimis* from line 1.

8   **leading me into your love**: It is unclear (see introductory note) precisely what is meant by *inducens in amorem*: it may simply mean (as Quinn suggests) 'the affection of true friendship' or might designate a third party to whom Alfenus is supposed to have introduced the poet. Once again, the poem's vagueness is surely deliberate.

9   **despite that**: *idem* has clear force: the same man who seemed so reassuring now turns out to be faithless.

10   **winds**: for the *topos* of the winds blowing away the words of faithless people cf. 64.59, 64. 142, 70.4, Homer *Od.* 8.408, Virgil *Aen.* 9.312–3. Catullus reinforces his point by the reduplication of *uentos* in the adjective *aereas*.

11–12   The theme of remembering and forgetting with which the poem ends picks up *immemor* from the very first phrase and gives ring-composition to the whole. Note also the chiastic repetition of *di meminerunt meminit Fides* and also the suggestive juxtaposition of *facti faciet*. As Quinn states, *faciet* shows that this is a statement rather than a prayer.

31

The poem is built around the doublet figure, beginning with 'of all islands and peninsulas' and the text constantly brings out pairs of things (either complementary or contrasting) even where they are not really needed: lakes and seas (with one Neptune bestriding both), pleasure and happiness (*libenter ... laetus*), Thynia and Bithynia, the mind laying aside its burden and the body tired out, abroad vs home, the home and the bed.

Metre: scazons

1   Notice the way in which the name Sirmio is sandwiched between *paene insularum* and *insularumque*, perhaps creating an image of Sirmio standing out among the nameless islands.

2   **little eye**: *ocelle* is the diminutive of *oculus* ('eye'), often used as a term of affection for a person – cf. 50.19, Plautus *Asin.* 664, *Truc.* 579 and note how often Catullus speaks of loving somebody 'more than eyes' (e.g. 14.1, 82) – and also for a place (Fordyce compares Pindar *O.* 2.12 and Euripides *Phoen.* 802, Cicero *Att.* 16.6.2). The word is stressed by its position at the beginning of the line but the end of the phrase and imparts a highly emotional charge to the homecoming.

2–3   *liquentibus stagnis* must mean 'lakes' while *mari uasto* refers to the sea. 'Either Neptune' is difficult; does it mean 'the god of both seas' (i.e. the Adriatic and the Tyrrhenian, although Sirmio is found in neither of them) or is Neptune seen as god of

water both lakes and seas? The latter is clearly more plausible: and notice how the poet
builds up the picture of Sirmio as being the best not merely of the islands of Lake Garda
but of all islands in all still waters and then also of all islands in the 'vast ocean' – in all
the water governed by Neptune 'in either capacity'. The little word *fert* is apt,
suggesting that the god/sea 'carries' the islands as if on his back.

4   **how ... how**: Note the repetition of *quam* and also the variation of *libenter* and *laetus*:
        note also the continuing use of a personal verb *inuiso* (usually used of visiting a person)
        and the repeated apostrophe to the island (*te*).

5   It is possible that there is a slightly contemptuous edge to the phrase *Thuniam atque*
        Bithunos: certainly the poet expresses contentment to have left the dry plains for the
        liquid waves of his island and the unnecessary doublet corresponds to his style
        throughout the poem. The Thyni were a Thracian tribe who had settled in one part of
        Bithynia.

6   **left ... fields**: *liquisse campos* is an elegant play on word-sounds: the poet has left the
        dry plains of Bithynia for the liquid world of Sirmio: there is a possible play on
        liquentibus (line 2) in *liquisse* (although the quantity of the initial vowel is different),
        suggesting that by travelling home he has 'made liquid' the plains. Note also the
        alliteration and the continued apostrophe of *te in tuto*.

7   *o* expresses strong emotion (cf. Kenney 1971, 74) and is used three times in lines 7–13.
        Note also the ordering of the line allowing the oxymoron *beatius curis*.

8–9   **mind ...**: The *mens* drops its burden in a sequence of short words, before the poet
        describes the drawn-out toil of his previous experience with the suitably long adjective
        peregrino and the enjambement into line 9, followed by the forceful juxtaposition of
        labore fessi.
        The *lares* were the Roman gods of the hearth, here used to signify the house itself.

10   The poet luxuriates in the comfort of his own bed in a line made up of two long words
        followed by the metrically stressed *lecto*.

11   **toils**: *laboribus* picks up *labore* from line 9.

12   **Hail ...**: The poet continues the apostrophe of Sirmio and speaks of the place as a
        servant rejoicing in the return of its master, the polyptoton *gaude gaudente* split over the
        line-end. For servants rejoicing in the return of the master cf. Eumaeus in Homer's *Od.* ,
        the watchman in Aeschylus *Ag.* 32–5.

13   **Lydian**: The waves of the lake are 'Lydian' because the Etruscans of the region were
        said to have originally come from Lydia (Livy 5.33, Tacitus *Ann.* 4.55). The 'learned'
        allusion has caused the reading to be suspected by some editors and even emended.
        Fordyce well argues that 'Catullus had learned from Alexandria ... the romantic,
        associative value of the proper name' but fails to see the obvious point being made in
        that the waves of 'home' are just as much travellers as the poet himself; that he shares
        with them the journey from the east and so they should laugh as loudly as he himself.

14   **laugh ... guffaws**: notice how the line is sandwiched with 'laughing' words: for the
        idea of rippling water being like laughter cf. 64.273, Lucretius 2.559, 5.1395, Aeschylus
        P.V. 90 (where see Griffith *ad loc.*), W.H. Auden 'In Praise of Limestone' line 6. Costa
        ((1984)148–9) cites Hesiod *Theog.* 40 to show the parallel use of the Greek *gelan* to
        express pleasure or rejoicing. *domi* properly means 'at home' – Fordyce takes it more
        loosely to mean 'in stock' but the dominant theme of 'home' is clearly intended to be
        struck.

32

An invitation to a girl to give the poet an invitation. The language of the first two lines suggests undying affection (note the use of terms such as *dulcis, deliciae, lepores* which remind the reader of the language of the Lesbia poems) whereas the language of the last two lines suggests strong sexual lust. The opening apostrophe to Ipsitilla is clearly a parody of the sort of insincere affection which is designed to deliver the sex which the poem hopes for (cf. poem 70 for doubts about the sincerity of lovers' talk). After the opening two lines the poem becomes a list of requests conveyed in imperatives and iussive subjunctives (*iube ... adiuuato ... neu lubeat ... maneas ... pares ... iubeto*) and whose tone is as prosaic as the opening words are not: the poet uses colloquial phrasing such as *iube ueniam, si quid ages* and finishes the poem with a cartoon-like image of his priapic state, prepared for by the hyperbolic 'nine continuous fuckifications' he has envisaged.

Metre: hendecasyllabics
1 **Please**: the Latin word *amabo* is far more appropriate than the English translation, meaning (literally) 'I shall love' and thus representing the theme of the poem.
The name **Ipsitilla** is unknown to us: Garrison assumes that she was a courtesan, 'a hetaera with her own house where she entertains male visitors as she pleases'. Quinn speculates that she was the illegitimate daughter of Catiline. Neither of these have any evidence to substantiate them, and none of it is needed to appreciate this text for what it is – an ironical invitation poem in which the invitee invites himself to be invited. The name Ipsitilla may even be an obviously invented name as being the diminutive feminine form of *ipsa* ('mistress'; see *OLD* s.v. 'ipse' 12).
sweet: *dulcis* is the first of three words/phrases which butter up the beloved, leading on to *deliciae* and *lepores* in line 2.
2 **darling ... charming**: for *deliciae* cf. 2.1, 3.4, 6.1 etc. *lepores* is perhaps intended to convey the impression that the poet loves her not just for her body but for her wit and cleverness.
3 **tell me**: *iube* looks forward to *iusseris* in line 4. *meridiare* means 'to spend a siesta'.
5 **seeing that nobody**: *ne quis* is a quiet reminder not to bar the street door during the siesta.
6 **and that ...**: not urging her to stay at home during the siesta but rather tells Ipsitilla not to go out during the morning when she should be preparing for the poet's visit.
8 **fuckifications**: *fututiones* is a comic invented word (only found here and at Martial 1.106.6) which has the form of a technical term but with comically vulgar content – on the lines of *basiationes* in poem 7.1 but considerably cruder.
9–11 Quinn assumes that the poet is lying on his bed fantasising after breakfast about what might happen after lunch: it is more likely that *pransus* means 'having lunched' and that therefore *statim* really means what it says, as the poet lies with his outdoor clothes on waiting (and desperate) for the invitation. The poem ends with the superb comic touch that his ardour is beating through his several layers of clothing, neatly indicating his state of readiness in both senses. Notice also the effective alliteration of *p* and *t* suggestive of the action designated.

33

A piece of scathing invective against a father and son, the one accused of stealing from the baths while the latter is described as what we would now call a rent-boy. Both are told to go away as the father is now notorious and the son unsuccessful. What links the two is their greed for money – the father steals clothing in the baths, the son tries to sell his body for cash – and the poem appropriately begins with *furum* and ends with *uenditare*. Note also how the poem repeats the 'father – son' pair of words several times (2, 3–4, 6–8) to reinforce the idea that they are each as bad as the other.

Metre: hendecasyllabics.

1   **bath-house**: *balneariorum* is a grandiose long word: put with *optime* the line sounds like high praise indeed – except for the decisive opening word *furum*.

2   **poofter**: *cinaedus* cf. 16.2

3–4 the father is a thief, the son a rent-boy: the poet however chooses adjectives to describe them which seem misplaced, as the son is called 'greedy' (a term more properly applied to the thieving father) and the father 'dirty' (which one would expect to be said of the 'unclean' son). The couplet has a neat symmetry about it, with the relevant part of the body followed by the term father/son followed by the comparative adjective.

5   **go ... to Hell**: the idiomatic phrase *in malam rem abire* means 'to go to the devil' (Plautus *Capt.* 877) and the poet modifies it to fit in with *exilium*.

7   **hairy buttocks**: the unpleasant detail is appropriate in this piece of invective; the point of the hairiness is presumably that the son is by now too old to be passing himself off as a boy any more (cf. 16.10) and cannot sell his services even for the smallest Roman coin.

34

A hymn to Diana, in the mouth of a choir of boys and girls, rather as poems 61 and 62 are. The poem is thus 'public' rather than 'private' and a good example of the poet's skilful use of language and metre in a specific genre. There is no evidence that the poem was written to be performed on a specific public occasion.

Metre: three glyconics followed by a pherecratean: the same metre as poem 61.

1–4 The opening stanza employs a lot of hymnic repetition: the name Diana and the inverted repetition of *puellae et pueri integri* as *pueri integri puellaeque*.

5   **daughter of Lato**: *Latonia* denotes the daughter of Latona (the Greek goddess Leto) who slept with the god Jupiter (Zeus) and bore Artemis (Diana) and Apollo on Delos. Note the juxtaposition (over the line-end) of *maximi magna* and the blunt *deposiuit* ('dropped' for 'gave birth to').

8   **olive-tree**: the goddess was born under a tree according to the ancient texts, but they disagree about the place where it happened (Delos, as here, or Ephesus (Tacitus *Ann.* 3.61) and especially about the type of tree (olive, as here, or else a palm as in the *Homeric Hymn to Apollo* 117).

9–12 Diana as the goddess of the outdoors, evoked in four memorable phrases each in the genitive plural. Quinn's remark that 'the genitive plural is a little overworked in this stanza' is insensitive to the incantatory effects of the repetition appropriate in this hymn. Note also the poet's metrical skill in fitting the long words to the complex metre.

13–16 For Diana's involvement in childbirth see Ovid *Fast.* 3.269–70, Propertius 2.32.9–10.

      Lines 13–20 form a kind of tricolon crescendo as *tu ... tu ... tu* begins three phrases of two lines, two lines and then four lines in length. Note also the repetition of *dicta* in lines 14–16.

13–14 **Juno**: There is surprise here in that the goddess Diana is now being called the goddess Juno, but 'this syncretism is a distinctive feature of Greek and Roman piety' (Garrison). The overlap between different divine beings is well documented in the sources, which show that the Greek goddess of childbirth Ilythia and also Juno Lucina were associated with Artemis the Greek goddess of hunting (= Roman Diana): see e.g.

Horace *Carm. saec.* 14–15. The name Lucina suggests 'light' and leads neatly on to the image of the goddess as the Moon.

15 Yet more cross-association as Diana is now associated with the goddess of the crossroads Hecate, also goddess of the underworld and witchcraft who had long been associated with the Greek equivalent of Diana, Artemis (Euripides *Phoen.* 108). *potens* is a word often used of *magical* powers and especially of Hecate: Fordyce cites Ovid *Her.* 12.168, Virgil *Aen.* 6.247, Valerius Flaccus 6.440. *notho* is a transliteration of the Greek term for 'bastard' and is used by Lucretius (5.575–6) to describe the moon's 'borrowed' light. For the use of the word to mean 'fake, counterfeit' cf. 63.27.

16 **Moon ... light**: *lumine luna* is an effective juxtaposition, with *luna* recalling *Lucina* at the beginning of the stanza.

17–18 **monthly ... annual**: Note the pointed way in which the goddess measures out the *yearly* journey with her *monthly* course, the words *menstruo* and *annuum* falling emphatically at the end of the lines, and the *figura etymologica* of *menstruo metiens* as the word *mensis* (month) is derived from the root seen in *metior*.

19–20 **fill up**: Something of a surprise, perhaps, to find Diana credited with filling the barns with crops, but then the movement of the sun and moon could be seen as moving the seasons along and so delivering the crops: cf. Virgil *G.* 1.5–6, Horace *Odes* 4.6.37–40. Notice here the emphasis on *exples* at the end of the sentence and stanza.

21–4 The final stanza, after giving the goddess four different names (Diana, Latonia, Juno, Trivia) now covers all possibilities by allowing the goddess to be called by whatever name she chooses, just in case his first four attempts have not found the right name. Note here the archaic verb *sospitare* here used to recreate the flavour of archaic religious ritual, also evoked in the common prayer *topos* of 'as you have always helped us in the past ...'. The prayer is located both in the past and also in a specifically Roman setting by the use of the name Romulus, the ancient founder of the city.

35

A poem to a poet concerned with the effects of poetry. The text has the form of invitation – even edging close to the language of the 'invocatory hymn' (*kletikos hymnos* in Greek) in places – as the poet asks Caecilius to leave his home and come to Verona (lines 1–5): however most of the poem concerns itself with the effects of Caecilius' poetry on the girl whom he would be leaving behind if he came to Verona, and it is hard to believe that this is not the main effect and purpose of the poem, which begins with the words *poetae tenero* and ends with the title and author's name of the poem which enraptures the girl. We first see the girl's affection for the poet (lines 8–10) with a note of approval for the girl's beauty (*candida* line 8) before we see the reason for it in the form of the poem which she has read. The subject matter of Caecilius' poem is the Phrygian goddess Cybele, who induced ecstasy in her worshippers (see 14n) and it is again appropriate that the poem about the 'Mistress of Dindymus' should be given to the mistress of Caecilius.

Metre: hendecasyllabics

1 **love-poet**: The poem begins with *poetae* and that is clearly what the poem is going to be about. Editors state that *tener* here means a 'love-poet', comparing Ovid *Ars am.* 2.273: unfortunately, the only poem mentioned (on Cybele) does not sound like a love poem, and the *tener* thing about Caecilius is rather his love-affair with a nameless girl for which the poet teases him in lines 8–18. *tener* thus refers to the man rather than his poetry, in much the same way as Ovid's mention of *teneri carmen Properti* at *Ars am.* 3.333, and the sense of 'sensuous' and even 'effeminate' is prominent in Caecilius' inability to wrest himself away from the arms of his girlfriend. *sodali* may then have

further point in letting the poet admit that he too belongs to the same group of *teneri* (cf. 10.29, 12.13, 47.6).

2 **I would like ... tell**: The line is framed by the verbs *uelim ... dicas*. The poem is addressed to the papyrus upon which it is composed – a highly artificial form of address comparable to (e.g.) Horace's (*Epist.* 1.20) address to the book of poems itself.

3 **Verona** is thus the putative source of this poem. Novum Comum is about 100 miles west of Verona, on the south-west shore of the *lacus Larius* (now Lake Como).

4 **leaving ...**: The poet gives a thumbnail sketch of Caecilius' home with the unnecessary detail of 'walls' and 'Larian shore'; the whole phrase 'leaving behind the walls ... ' is (as Garrison remarks) most reminiscent of the prayer to a god: cf. 61.27–30, Homer, *Il.* 24.144–5, Horace *Odes* 1.30.2, Theocritus 1.125–6, 7.115. This is of course ironic here in the 'prayer' to a friend to come to see the poet and leads on to the bathetic lines 5–6.

5 **meditations**: *cogitatio* is deliberately vague and we never discover what these 'meditations' are.

6 **a friend of mine and his**: a joking way of referring to the poet himself, with *amici mei* picking up *meo sodali* from line 1.

7 **eat up the road**: the alliterative metaphor of *uiam uorabit* is not found elsewhere and may be colloquial.

8 **pretty**: For *candida* cf. 13.4. As Fordyce notes, the topos of the beautiful woman being blonde and white, however implausibly (cf. 66.62, 64.63) is indicative of Roman attitudes towards the 'fairer sex'.

9–10 The girl calls him back as he is leaving time and time again (*milies*) – and her subsequent embracing of his neck indicate that she always succeeds in bringing him back. Note the effective juxtaposition of *manus collo* showing verbally the action which the words signify. *morari* is also psychologically plausible: she does not ask him *never* to go, but just to wait a while.

11 **If what I am told**: This line suggests that the poet is in receipt of information from third parties about Caecilius and his girlfriend.

12 **helpless**: *impotente* means 'uncontrollable' here: juxtaposed with *deperit* it conveys the strong impression of desperate love to the point of death. For *deperit* cf. 100.2, 45.5

13–15 A surprise: the reason for the girl's helpless love is not sex but poetry, in the form of Caecilius' unfinished *Mistress of Dindymus*.

14 *Mistress of Dindymus*: Dindymus is a mountain in Phrygia, and the 'mistress' referred to is the goddess Cybele, the so-called 'Great Mother' (*magna mater*) whose worship came to Rome in the 3rd century B.C. and who was given her own temple on the Palatine in 204 B.C. The dancing of her priests was seen in the streets of Rome and prompted Lucretius (2.610–643) to produce a detailed description of it, and the ecstatic worship of this goddess causes Attis to castrate himself in Catullus 63. It is thus appropriate that a poem about ecstatic religious worship should cause ecstatic sexual love in its reader, as shown here. The phrase *Dindymi dominam* is possibly the opening words of the poem used as a title – but the phrase is not in hexameters (which is the metre one expects of an epyllion such as this (cf. poem 64)) and in the final line of this poem it is referred to as *Magna mater*.

14–15 **poor ... fires**: Note the assonance of *misellae/ ignes interiorem* and then *edunt medullam. misellae* – the diminutive of *miser* – adds pathos to the description of the girl (cf. 8.1 for its meaning 'lovesick'). For the topos of love burning like a fire in the marrow of the bones cf. 45.16, 64.93, 100.7, Virgil *Aen.* 4. 66, Plautus *Mostell.* 243. Notice how the phrase recalls Catullus' translation of Sappho (51.9–10) and thus leads neatly to the comparison of the girlfriend with Sappho herself.

16–17   **you**: Another surprise: the poet turns to address the unnamed girl – of whose existence he has only heard through rumour (line 11) – and say that he understands the girl's passion as the poem is worthy of it (with a nice jingle of *ignes ... ignosco*). *doctus* is a common term of approval for readers of poetry and also poets themselves: cf. 65.2 (of the Muses), Propertius 1.7.11 (of his girlfriend), Kenney (1970). Sappho was the most famous of ancient women poets and is thus appropriate for a woman of literary taste such as Caecilius' *puella*. The phrase 'Sapphic Muse' does not indicate any belief that Sappho was the tenth Muse as suggested in the *Greek Anthology* (7.14, 9.506), but is simply a periphrasis for 'Sappho the poet' as in Ovid *Ars am.* 3.329–330, *Ex Ponto* 4.16.29. The juxtaposition *puella/ musa* is also effective in pointing out the parallel between the feminine Muse and the female reader. *Uenuste* is then highly appropriate: the word denotes elegance and charm (cf. 3.2, 22.2 and the opposite *inuenustus* 10.4) but also suggests the goddess of love Venus whose agency is so visible in the girlfriend's reaction to the poem.

36

The 'story' behind the poem is firmly stated by the editors: the poet's girlfriend had vowed to burn the work of the 'worst poet' if her poet lover were restored to her and the stream of verse from him thus stopped. Her vow was vaguely phrased, however, and Catullus deliberately misinterprets her words to signify not his own verses but those of Volusius, thus neatly combining the themes of love on the one hand and literary criticism on the other in a witty and elegant poem – a poem in fact whose wit and elegance proves that its author was by no means 'worst of poets' and so would not have deserved the burning which the girl had promised.   Just as the previous poem was addressed to the papyrus sheet carrying the message, so this poem is addressed to a work of poetry itself. The poem divides into three sections: the first addressed to the *Annals* of Volusius, the second to the goddess Venus, and the final closure achieved by going back to Volusius.

Volusius is also ridiculed in poem 95, where his poetry is good – for wrapping fish.

Metre: hendecasyllabics.

1   **Annales** would be a historical epic poem, such as the *Annales* of Ennius, dealing with events in Roman history in a chronicle form. *cacata carta* has pleasing alliteration.

3   **Cupid and holy Venus**: cf. 3.1. The epithet *sanctae* stresses the divine power of this goddess: cf. 68.5, 64.95.

4   **she vowed**: *uouit* picks up *uotum* from the same position in line 2: note also the heavy alliteration of *s* in this line and the jingle of *essem desissemque*, as the restoration of the poet to favour would automatically bring about a cessation of hostile poetry.

5   **fierce verses**: *iambos* properly means 'iambic poetry', but here means the vitriolic sort of poetry traditionally composed in the iambic metre, of which poem 37 is a good example. *uibrare* is a metaphor from throwing a spear which would be brandished and then made to twist as it flew through the air (cf. Ovid *Met.* 8. 374).

6   **choicest ... worst**: There is a pleasing oxymoron in *electissima pessimi* which brings out the absurdity of choosing the choicest work of the worst poet, while also fulfilling the usual pattern of a vow of this sort (in which only the choicest victim is worthy of the sacrifice to the god). In this way, the *Annals* is the poet's 'finest' work – for the purpose of burning in sacrifice.

7–8   **slow-footed**: The compound adjective *tardipedi* refers to the fire-god Vulcan who was 'slow-footed' because he was lame: the allusive phrase here adds a note of mock-heroism and solemnity to the passage, further enhanced by the adjective *infelicibus* applied to the flames which are unlucky in having to deal with such awful work as

Volusius' *Annals.* (The word *infelix* also has a technical meaning in the context of ritual: *infelix* meaning 'cursed' came to mean 'sterile' and so the wood of sterile trees was used to burn things regarded as evil, as in Cicero's remark on the cremation of Clodius *infelicissimis lignis semiustulatum* (*Milo.* 33). The flames themselves were also aptly called by the same term here.

9   **worst**: *pessima* picks up *pessimi* from line 6: it is appropriate that the 'worst girl' should condemn the 'worst poet'– there is (after all) no other reason stated for calling the girl *pessima*.

10   **witty ... elegant**: Note the asyndeton of *iocose lepide*.

11–17   The poet here produces a fine model of prayer-formula (on which see Ogilvie 24– 40): he addresses Venus in a variety of ways, linking the catalogue of places with the anaphora of *quae*: there is the emotive use of the vocative *o* (line 11), the allusion to the birth of the goddess and the exhaustive list of her cult centres produced with the *doctrina* one expects of this sort of poet..

11   **goddess**: Venus traditionally emerged from the sea off the island of Cyprus, coming from out of the foam which issued from the testicles lopped off Cronos by his son Zeus. (Her Greek name *Aphrodite* is said to have derived from the Greek for 'foam' *aphros*). Catullus does not refer explicitly to the goddess' origin except in this allusive phrase.

12–15   A sequence of places of worship of the goddess, covering a broad expanse of the world. Idalium, Amathus and Golgi are in Cyprus (her 'birthplace'): but the poet also includes cult centres in Italy (Urii in Apulia – or possibly Tarentum – and Ancon in Picenum), Illyria (Dyrrachium was on the Adriatic coast of Illyria – modern Albania – directly facing the Italian port of Brundisium) and Caria (Cnidus). The poet conveys the wide spread of the worship by mixing up the different geographical locations.

12   Notice the chiasmus of the line as the two proper names are sandwiched between the adjectives. Note also the way the poet joins Cyprus and Italy together– places far apart and different in location and also in the sort of adjectives used to describe them (the one being 'holy' the other 'bleak') but united in their worship of Venus. Urii may refer to the coastal town of Urion in Apulia or else inland Uria between Tarentum and Brundisium. *apertos* ('open' – i.e. to the elements) suggests 'bleak'.

13   The proper names are again juxtaposed, a place on the Italian coast being put back to back with Cnidus in Caria. Cnidus was famous above all for its three temples of Venus, one of which contained the statue of Aphrodite by Praxiteles. Notice how the poet uses the learned adjective *harundinosam* ('reedy') of the place: Cnidus exported reeds (Pliny *HN* 16.157) and the unexpected reference here to its export reminds us of the poet's use of *lasarpiciferis* in 7.4.

14   The pace of the poem picks up with the repetition of *quaeque* and the hurried naming of two places without descriptive adjectives.

15   **Dyrrachium** was an important coastal town as it represented the favoured destination of sea traffic between Italy and Greece. It was not particularly famed for piety towards Venus, and its range of hospitality to mariners is coyly hinted at in the phrase 'inn of the Adriatic'. It may well be that the poet is suggesting that worship of the goddess of Love took more physical forms in this particular resting place for sailors: for which cf. the *taberna* of the next poem.

16   **receive ... paid out**: The language is technical and commercial. *acceptum facere* means 'enter as received' and *reddo* here means 'pay out'. After the hymnic style of lines 11–15 this jargon breaks the atmosphere suddenly, only to see the 'commercial' metaphor rewritten in the next line. For the sense in which the ancient *do ut des* attitude towards religious worship was 'commercial' see e.g. Plato *Euthyphro.* 14e6–8, Ogilvie (1981) 37–8.

17   **lacking ... elegance**: *lepidus* and *uenustus* are key terms of the poet's approval, both
       here used in litotes with *non* and the negative form of the adjectives.
19   **boorishness**: For the proverbial boorishness and inelegance of the countryman applied
       to poetry see also 22.10, 22.14.
20   The last line repeats the first line, the poem ending as it began (ring-composition) with
       apostrophe to the poems of Volusius.

37

A lampoon. Some editors like to think that the *taberna* is in fact Lesbia's house on the
Palatine, but there is clearly no evidence for this. The poem begins (1–8) with criticism of the
customers of the *taberna* as being deluded about their sexual prowess – a delusion which the
poet threatens to disabuse in a manner reminiscent of poem 16.1. He then threatens to scrawl
obscene graffiti on the wall (9–10) before explaining the source of his anger. Lines 11–14
explain that his girlfriend has left him and is now consorting with unfeasibly large numbers of
adulterers of all classes – chief among them being the caricatured figure of Egnatius. The
poem ranges widely in style and feeling: from the coarse (*mentulas ... confutuere,
sopionibus*) to the sentimental (line 12) and the mock-heroic (line 13), from harsh invective
(16) to brutal threats (7–8) to ironic mockery (17–20).

Metre: scazons (limping iambics)
1   **Randy tavern**: A strong opening with the strikingly pejorative word *salax*, a word
       deriving from *salire* ('to leap' used of males mounting their mates: see Adams 206).
       There is also a neat etymological point being made in *taberna ... contubernales*. Note
       also the personification of the inn as being as *salax* as its customers.
2   **hat-wearing**: Note the play on words in *pilleatis ... pila* which neatly sandwiches the
       rest of the line. The 'Brothers with Felt Hats' are Castor and Pollux who were often
       represented in art, coinage (etc.) wearing caps and whose temple was on the south side
       of the Forum.
3–5   The poet's indignation is expressed in the rhetorical anaphora of *solis* as well as in the
       repeated *–is* sounds in line 3 and the word *uobis* at the end of 3 agreeing with *solis* at
       the start of 4. For the slightly objectified phrase *quidquid est puellarum* cf. 31.14 and
       Ovid's similar use of the singular *puella* at *Ars am.* 1. 50. Line 5 begins strongly with
       the vulgar term *confutuere* stressed in enjambement from the previous line. The prefix
       con– suggests 'that the job is done properly' (Quinn). The word must be scanned as a
       dactyl (one long syllable followed by two short syllables) or else the second *u* is
       consonantal (pronounced *confutwere*).
5   **stinking**: *putare* is the reading of the ms and both picks up *putatis* from line 3 and looks
       forward to *putatis* in line 7: but more effective lampoon is created with Hermann's
       emendation *putere* ('to stink') which brings out the distinctive quality in the goats. For
       the foul smell of the *hircus* cf. 71.1, Horace *Sat.* 1.2.27.
6–8   The round numbers in line 7 are obviously not literal: the point being made is: 'no
       matter how many of you there are, I could punish the lot of you' in which the greater the
       number the greater the threat from the poet. This neatly reverses the situation of lines
       3–5 (where the *contubernales* think that they alone have sexual power) so that the randy
       lovers are themselves orally raped by the poet.
6   **sit**: The phrasing is interesting: *sedetis* (picked up in *sessores* (line 8) and *consedit* (line
       14)) implies 'just sitting there doing nothing' (*OLD* s.v. 'sedeo' 7) and thus suggests a
       passivity which the following lines will develop. *insulsi* means 'lacking in *sal*' (wit,
       brains: cf. 13.5n) and is placed for emphasis at the end of the line: *continenter* is

usually taken to mean 'all sitting in a row' but also has the strong sense of 'non-stop' and may thus rather suggest that their sedentary position is permanent.

7–8   The vowels of *centum ... ducenti* are mirrored in *me una ducentos*: notice the enjambement as the poet rushes over the line-end to surprise these *sessores. una ducentos* ('two hundred all at once') is a pleasing juxtaposition of numerical words.

8   **fuck ... mouths**: For *irrumare* see 16.1n *sessores* simply means 'men sitting' but in the context of *irrumatio* the word gives a visual idea of how the poet might carry out his revenge.

10   **scrawl**: the meaning seems to be that the poet will scrawl drawings of the human penis on the front of the tavern. *sopio* only occurs here and in graffiti.

11–14   The poet now explains the reason for his hostility to the place: his girl has fled and settled there. Notice how the girl's decisive actions *fugit* and *consedit* are separated by two lines of longer description of the poet's part in this: his love and struggle are developed in grandiose language, her actions are told in two simple verbs.

12   Repeated from 8.5 – which has led many to think that the girl referred to in poem 8 owns the 'tavern' described here.

13   **great wars**: The language is that of heroic epic used here metaphorically.

14   **there**: The pause after *istic* is strong: the two-word phrase *consedit istic* is all the more sharply effective after the two lines which preceded it. The phrase *boni beatique* denotes men of good family and wealth (cf. Cicero *Att.* 8.1.3 for *bonus* and see poem 10.17 for *beatus*).

15–16   Note the rhetorical repetition of *omnes* and the deliberate pause built into the lines by the parenthetic *quod indignum est* before the shocking phrase *pusilli et semitarii moechi. pusilli* ('weaklings' 'nonentities') are the opposite of the wealthy men of line 14: *semitarius* comes from *semita* ('street') and suggests 'back-street' low-life. The Greek term *moechus* was standard for the sexual profligate. The parenthesis is not a mere delaying tactic, however: and the poet does not mean solely that his girl deserves a better life but that *he* deserves to be cuckolded by a better class of person.

17–20   **Egnatius** was a poet who composed a *de rerum natura* and who kept his hair and beard long. It seems to have been the fashion among young men to wear their hair long (see e.g. Petronius *Satyricon* 27.1) and Egnatius is perhaps continuing to do so after his youth has long gone and so is 'unique' in this way. Note here the force of the juxtaposition *praeter omnes une.*

18   **Celtiberia** is in Spain, and the Spanish rabbit was famous for having long hair (cf. 25.1): the epithet *cuniculosae* is thus excellent in being both a 'learned' piece of background information about the place (like *harundinosam* in 36.13) and also a caricature of the long-haired Egnatius as being like one of his compatriot rabbits.

19   **beard**: Egnatius' thick beard makes him socially acceptable: young men cultivated a short beard (*barbatuli iuvenes* is Cicero's phrase for the young) while older men let the beard grow fuller. The term thus may suggest the older, grander look of the conservative senatorial man.

20   **teeth**: For Egnatius' dental hygiene cf. 39. 17–21: Diodorus (5.33.5) and Strabo (3.164) confirm Catullus' allegation that Spaniards kept their teeth white with urine. The poet saves the best until last: long hair is unusual, thick beards mark him out as a social climber, but his *teeth* ... Notice the singular *dens* for plural (cf. 64. 315) and the unnecessary adjective *Hibera*: if Egnatius is Spanish then so will his urine be Spanish, but the point here is also that this is the Spanish way of doing things.

A poem apparently *de profundis* purporting to ask for words of encouragement. The nature of the poet's 'bad state' is left deliberately vague, forcing the reader to focus on the literary artifice of the text: the contrast between the Herculean labours of the poet and the 'least and easiest' act of Cornificius, between the poet's love and his anger, the literary allusion to Simonides, the rhetorical repetition (of *male est*, of *magis*, of *allocutio*) and insistent questioning of the addressee, the elliptic final lines with verbs omitted culminating in a resonant concluding line of three long words. It might even be argued that a poet who can compose this sort of elegant 'lament' is clearly not so distraught as to need the consolation which it seems to request, and we are left with a text whose stylistic form belies the content.

Metre: hendecasyllabics

1   **Cornificius** was probably Quintus Cornificius, known to us as an orator and poet (his epyllion *Glaucus* is known to us but has not survived) and a friend of Cicero (cf. *Fam.* 12.17–30). He was an able and clearly ambitious military and political figure, fighting for Caesar as quaestor in 48 and in charge of Cilicia in 46 until he was transferred to Syria in 45. He was proscribed (i.e. condemned to death) by the second triumvirate of Mark Antony, Lepidus and Octavian (the future emperor Augustus) in 43 and killed at Utica in 41. As a poet he is bracketed with Catullus, Calvus and Cinna by Ovid (*Tr.* 2.435–6).
       Notice how the poet here puts the two proper names close to each other and how the second line does little more than intensify the first line.

2   **heavy going**: *laboriose* is used of illness at Cicero *Phil.* 11.8 (and cf. its use in poem 1.7) and is here highly effective after mention of Hercules in suggesting the hero's famous labours – cf. 55.13.

3   This line completes the three-line exposition of the opening phrase *male est* with the statement that the affliction is getting constantly worse. This is presumably to answer the objection that the poet's affliction will cure itself without any need for help from Cornificius.

5   **consolation**: *allocutio* means 'words of exhortation' (*OLD* s.v. 2) and 'encouragement' as if by a general before a battle. There is no parallel for it meaning 'a consolatory poem' as Quinn understands it: the element of 'consolation' is put in with the verb *solatus es*. When it recurs in line 7 it requires line 8 to determine the emotional colour.

6   A neat line, in which *irascor* and *amores* frame the line with contrary emotions, *tibi* and *meos* face each other around the little word *sic*. *sic meos amores* is obviously incomplete (a device known as aposiopesis) and may mean a variety of things: 'Is this how (you treat) my love?' seems to be the most obvious, but *amores* often means the 'object of affection' and this sets up the possibility that Cornificius has somehow misused the poet's beloved – or else that he is meaning Cornificius himself as his 'dear friend'. If it was vital for the reader to know the answer to this, then the poet would not have left it ambiguous: as often in Catullus, the literary effect is of anger contrasted with love.

7–8   **[Send]**: Another sentence in which the main verb ('send') has been omitted. Simonides of Ceos (556–467) was a skilled composer of a range of genres: noted for his pathos (Quintilian 10.1.64) but also for his victory odes, elegies and so on. There is quite probably a literary joke here referring to a famous poem of Simonides (why else refer to 'tears' as if it denoted a specific text?) which is appropriate to this poem but which we no longer have.

39

Egnatius, who was mentioned at the end of poem 37, now has a whole poem devoted to him and his eccentric dental hygiene. The poem breaks up into two sections: lines 1–8 in the third person describing Egnatius to the reader and then 9–21 addressed to Egnatius himself. The poem is a satirical picture of Egnatius first attacking his constant smiling and then (when the reader might have assumed the poem had ended) going on to satirize the man's methods of having the sort of teeth to show off. What begins as a comedy of manners in which inappropriate public behaviour is stigmatised ends up as a harsh attack on private habits.

Metre: scazons (limping iambics).

2 **beams**: *renidet* means 'shine, gleam' and only by transference 'to give a beaming smile'. Note how the word is repeated four times in lines 1–7 and how it depicts in verbal form the relentless repeated smiling of Egnatius.

2–3 Note the enjambement and the stress placed on *fletum* by its position at the end of the line and the metrical ictus. The point being made here is that the defendant (*reus*) would need sympathy from the court and a beaming smile is thus inappropriate. For the orator attempting to arouse grief and pity in the jury cf. Aristophanes *Wasps* 976–8, Plato *Ap.* 34c.

4–5 **mourning ... son**: Another case where a smile is out of place. The poet loads the case greatly by making the death that of an only son – and a 'devoted' one at that – whose bereaved mother weeps at the pyre. Again, the metrical ictus stresses *mater* and *fili*.

7–8 **disease**: *morbum* is a strong word to use: and the following line proves that it is metaphorical, as a real disease could never be imagined as *elegantem* or *urbanum*. The point of *urbanus* is that its meaning here is 'civilised' but that from line 10 onwards it is used in a more literal sense as 'born in the city' (i.e. Roman) and thus leads on the geographical catalogue which follows in lines 10–13.

11 **podgy Umbrian**: The Umbrians are not known for being 'stingy' which makes the ms reading *parcus* suspect: what is more, the other racial types are given adjectives describing their appearance rather than their character, which again makes this reading suspect. Lindsay's *pinguis* is thus printed here, as it is the quality which Persius (3.74) associates with the Umbrians and it mirrors neatly the obese Etruscan.

12 **Lanuvines** are chosen as their dark complexion makes their fine teeth look all the brighter by contrast. Notice here the jingle of *ater atque dentatus*.

13 **to get to my own people**: The poet himself came from Verona in Transpadane Gaul.

16 For the polyptoton of *inepto ... ineptior* and the deliberate jingle of *risu ... res* cf. e.g. 22.14, 27.4, 99.2, 99.14.

17–21 Having established that Egnatius has the 'disease' of inappropriate grinning, the poet now goes on the explain the pride he takes in his teeth by another reference to the Spanish custom of cleaning the teeth in urine, a custom mentioned by both Diodorus and Strabo (see 37.20n.).

19 **red gums**: *russam* proleptically indicates the state of the gum after protracted rubbing. The two nouns *dentem* and *gingiuam* frame the line.

21 **piss**: The poem ends with the obscene word *loti* for maximum effect: *bibisse* is an exaggeration, as brushing the teeth does not require drinking the water, and enhances the disgusting quality of the line.

40

The first four lines of the poem examine two different explanations of Ravidus' behaviour: either it is the result of *mala mens* or else some god is causing it: in both cases, Ravidus is seen as the passive victim of forces which he cannot control, both of which 'explain' his folly in crossing Catullus. The remainder of the poem takes a less charitable view, as his thirst for fame is considered as the motive behind his actions, which are only specified at the very end in a line of innuendo. The poem puts Catullus firmly in the tradition of Archilochus and other early Greek 'Iambic' poets: he uses the term *iambos* here to mean 'invective-poetry' (even though this poem is not in iambics), and the text is a threat that the power of the invective will cause Ravidus to rue the day he annoyed Catullus. The text is one of astonishing poetic pride: the poet cannot imagine that Ravidus would have crossed him unless he were compelled to do so by divine or psychological forces and then – as if conceding that perhaps no such forces were at work – ponders whether Rauidus' motive for his actions was simply to provoke this sort of poetic attack which would (such being the fame of the writer) guarantee him renown.

Metre: hendecasyllabics

1   **forlorn**: *miselle* is the diminutive of *miser* and suggests 'love-sick'. The address to Ravidus is made all the more striking by the alliteration of *m* and the strong verb *agit* stressed at the start of the next line with the effective adjective *praecipitem*. For *mala mens* cf. 15.14.

2   **lampoons**: *iambos* does not always mean simply 'iambic metre poetry' – for one thing this poem is not itself composed in that metre – but means rather 'abusive verses' which had been often composed in iambics (cf. the previous poem for one such poem in the iambic metre). The phrase here may mean simply that the poet is threatening to send 'iambics' later on.

3–4 **what god**: For the gods used as a reason for human misbehaviour cf. most famously Agamemnon's apology in Homer *Il*. 19. 86–90 and Helen's self-defense in Euripides *Tro*. 948–9, with Gorgias *Hel*. 6, 19. The quarrel is exaggerated into *uecordem ... rixam* which frame the line: *uecordem* ('lacking mind') picks up *mala mens* from line 1.

5   **public audience**: Ennius' epitaph boasted that his verses would allow him to 'fly living through the mouths of men' and Catullus is perhaps thinking of this here, except that *ora uulgi* ('mouths of the crowd') is hardly as flattering a destination as *ora uirum* ('mouths of men'). Ravidus is just after publicity at any cost.

7–8 The punchline comes with the revelation of Ravidus' offence (which will give him the fame he seeks) but the price he will pay (in the emphatic final word *poena*). There is also a joke at work here: 'you wanted to make love to my darling with a long *poena*' is innuendo, especially as the word *poena* ('penalty') may suggest *pene* ('penis').

41

A satirical poem attacking Mamurra's girlfriend who is allegedly overcharging for her favours. The poem is nicely held together by the repetition of *puella* in lines 1, 3,5, and 7 which keeps Ameaena at the centre of attention, and it builds up to the highly effective climax in the pun on *aes* at the very end. The poem is told as if addressed to the 'friends and family' of line 5 who are told of the girl's actions and then summoned to her assistance.

Metre: hendecasyllabics

1   For **Ameaena** cf. poem 43. The passive participle *defututa* means 'exhausted by sex' (cf. Adams 119) and is similar to *ecfututa* at 6.13 and *diffututa* at 29.13. Why is this an insult to Ameaena? Syndikus reads it as calling her 'an elderly tart', presumably feeling that the degree of her exhaustion reflects her years in service.

2   **cool ten thousand**: 10,000 sesterces was a fair sum of money – a year's rent according to Cicero (*Cael*. 17) – and may be a sum which the poet owed her rather than a fee for her favours.

3   **girl:** *puella* is repeated from line 1. The diminutive *turpiculo* is an affectation here, as the poet feigns 'detached assessment' (Quinn). The poet stops at the nose here, whereas in poem 43 he gives a more complete catalogue of her physical imperfections.

4   **bankrupt from Formiae:** i.e. Mamurra, a man close to Caesar and famously wealthy and ambitious, whom the poet attacks also in poems 29 and 57 and who is given the satirical nicknames of *mentula* ('the prick') in poems 94, 105, 114, 115. For the association of Mamurra with Formiae cf. Horace *Sat.* 1.5.37.

5   **not right:** The girl is mad, but (being mad) will not know that she is mad, and so the poet has to summon her family and friends to help her.

8   **mirroring brass:** The joke rests on the pun on *aes*: she asks for *aes* (money) but does not ask the *aes* (the bronze mirror) to tell her what she looks like. *imaginosum* only occurs here in Latin.

42

A mock *flagitatio* in which an aggrieved person seeks to have his property or rights restored by subjecting the culprit to public ridicule. The identity of the (real or imaginary) victim is neither revealed nor important: Syndikus nicely points out that while one could describe Lesbia as a 'tart', she could never be seen as ugly.

The poem builds up to the joke of the last line, with the choral invective of lines 11–12 repeated at 19–20 and then comically changed in the last line.

Metre: hendecasyllabics

1   **Hendecasyllables** are chosen not because this metre is always abusive (cf. e.g. 2, 3, 5, 7 for poems in this metre which are not), but simply because it is the metre of this poem and so that the poet can 'summon' his lines of verse as if they were street fighters prepared to humiliate the object of his attack. For the personification of a metrical form cf. 40.2)

1–2   Note the repetition of *quot estis … quotquot estis* and the way the second line is framed by a repeated *omnes*.

3   **tart:** *moecha* is the feminine of the more commonly used masculine *moechus* (cf. 37.16). Adams 133 points out that the poet addresses her with a sexual term which has nothing to do with the original accusation (i.e. of stealing his notebooks). It seems therefore that the term *moecha* here is not intended to be any more than a term of general vituperation.

5   Note the alliteration of *p* in this line. *pugillaria* were writing tablets with a wax surface (which could be scraped clear and rewritten repeatedly): such tablets were cased in wood and kept tied with laces in pairs so that the wax surfaces faced each other on the inside but were prevented from touching by a rim. Such things were more commonly called *codicilli* or *tabellae* and were used for the sketching out of poems or for quick letters which could be sent back with the message erased and the reply written in its place.

7   **you ask?:** the poet imagines the verses asking who the girl is: this both reminds us that the quarrel is between the poet and the girl with the verses used merely as hired thugs: and it also allows the poet to indulge in some personal abuse of her with the pretence of needing to describe her to strangers.

8   **disgusting … walking:** 'Her walk is *turpe*' must mean that she walks in a sexually provocative manner, as Cicero says of Clodia (*Cael.* 49). *mimice* is a touch of Roman snobbery; mime-actresses were popular performers and society ladies (Cytheris the mime-actress was mistress of Mark Antony) but were looked down on as not quite respectable: Augustus' social legislation, for instance, allowed Senators to marry non-

citizens but not actresses, and Roman law tended to put actresses in the same category as prostitutes (see Treggiari 61–2). So for Catullus to say that she laughs 'like a mime-actress' is clearly an insult to her respectability. Note also the alliteration of *m*.

9   **dog**: dogs (of course) do not laugh; the poet presumably means that her laugh makes her face look like that of a dog, and a Gallic puppy at that, a breed known for their ugliness (Arrian *Cyn.* 3.1–5).

10   The line is framed by the imperatives, the first of which is unnecessary but adds a touch of drama to the scene.

11–12   Repetition of the same words in a different order: the whole couplet is repeated below at lines 19–20. *putida* is a strong term of abuse ('rotting', 'stinking'). *codicillos* here means the same as *pugillaria* in line 5.

13–14   The poet describes the girl's reaction as if the scene were being enacted, and then addresses her with terms of even stronger invective. She who was 'rotten' is now 'mud', the 'tart' is now a whole brothel (*lupanar*), the phrase having a resonant sound of *lutum lupanar* with the alliteration of *l* and the assonance of *u* and *a*. *si quid* is broken up in line 14 by the alliterative *perditius potest*.

16–17   **blush ... brazen**: note the enjambement and the paradoxical juxtaposition of *ruborem/ferreo*: if her face is 'brazen' it is difficult to see how it might 'blush'. The girl is again (cf. line 9) described as being dog-like: for the tradition of canine shamelessness cf. Helen's self-accusation at Homer *Il.* 3.180 and Achilles' insult to Agamemnon as 'dog-eyed' (1.225).

21   **We**: the poet uses the first person plural to indicate that he is joining in with his 'hendecasyllables' in a chorus of abuse. Note the repetition of *nil ... nihil.*

22   **the plan and the method**: *ratio modusque* imparts a serious tone to the line: *ratio* indicates 'theory' while *modus* suggests 'technique': both words will raise the tone of the sentence to make the final line all the more bathetic.

23   **progress**: *proficere* picks up *proficimus* from line 21.

24   Fordyce quotes Afranius fr. 116 R which indicates that the phrase *proba et pudica* may have been something of a cliché. The poem ends with the third and final order to return the tablets.

43

A poem which appears to be addressed to the same girl as the addressee of poem 41 – at least both girls are girlfriends of a Formian bankrupt. This poem is a catalogue of female faults, all expressed in litotes, the force of which is to understate the criticism in a register of refined distaste. The poet's eye moves up and down her body – the nose and then the feet, followed by the eyes and then the fingers, then the mouth and finally the tongue: feet and fingers are each discussed at the beginning of consecutive lines, while nose, eyes and mouth all fall at the end of consecutive lines, the comment on the mouth being then expanded into a full line about her tongue. It is interesting to observe the features which the poet has *not* picked on – the girl might be an example of world-class beauty and still displease the fastidious poet for displaying these (minor) blemishes. The thrust of the poem is to suggest this and then to go on to declare that his own 'Lesbia' is free of even these minor imperfections. Quinn well points out that the first four lines are a reversal of the 'normal' lover's catalogue of the beauties of the beloved, as in Philodemus *A.P.* 5.132 – to which add Ovid *Am.* 1.5. 18–23: the poem is however more of an example of 'abuse poetry' (*aischrologia*) such as we find in (e.g.) 59, Archilochus fragments 35, 41–2, 196a.236–31, 205 (West) and later on in Horace *Epod.* 8 and 12 and Martial (e.g. 8.79).

Metre: Hendecasyllabics

1   **nose**: the poet begins with the nose, which is in this case unpleasantly large: in 41.3 the nose is described with the diminutive *turpiculo*. For the Roman distaste for large female noses cf. Horace *Sat.* 1.2.93, Juvenal 6.495.

2   **foot**: for the male taste for small feet cf. Ovid *Am.* 3.3.7; for black eyes cf. Propertius 2.12.23, Horace *Odes* 1.32.11–12.

3   **long fingers** were a mark of feminine refinement.

4   **tongue ... elegant**: the poet's vague expression allows for a variety of interpretations ranging from the girl's accent to her capacity to perform lewd oral acts.

5   The line is repeated from 41.4.

6–7 **Is it ...?**: Two indignant rhetorical questions, each occupying a whole line and beginning with a part of *te*. The *prouincia* is presumably Gallia Cisalpina, where the poet's birthplace Verona is situated: there may alternatively (as Quinn suggests) be the implication that her admirers are 'provincial' and that she would find less admiration in the metropolis. *bellam* is the more colloquial word for 'pretty'

8   For *infacetum* cf. 22.14, 36.19.

44

At face value the poet appears to be referring to his own country villa at which he recovered from a bout of ill-health. There is, of course, no need to postulate any such villa in fact: the point of the poem is partly the satire on Sestius, and in particular his speech against Antius. The ancients used 'frigid' as a term of literary disapproval: Aristophanes has the rivers freeze over when the 'frigid' poet Theognis had his plays performed (*Acharnians* 138–140: cf. *Thesmophoriazusae* 170) and Dover ((1993) 21) remarks that '[frigidity] is what alienates the hearer and fails of the effect for which the speaker or writer hopes; it includes jokes which fall flat and errors of taste (Aristotle *Rh.* 1405b35ff)'. For a full account of 'frigidity' see Demetrius *Eloc.* 114–127 (Russell and Winterbottom (1972) 194–6), a treatise which is probably contemporary with Catullus (Russell and Winterbottom 172). Demetrius is quite clear in his definition of 'frigidity' as 'akin to boastfulness ... the author who adorns a trivial subject with dignified language ... ' (*Eloc.* 119) and it is thus attractive to see this poem as itself a parody of precisely this sort of stylistic hyperbole. Sure enough, the minor ailment of a cough is adorned into *grauedo frigida et frequens tussis* and the style of the opening sentence with its elaborate qualifying clauses is clearly a satire of the oratorical pomposity of Sestius. The poet indulges in archaic terms (*autumant ... recepso*) and bathetic zeugma (*otio et urtica*) as well as couching the whole poem in the style of the prayer of gratitude (vocative *o* followed by alternative descriptive phrases, description of the ailment, thanks for the cure with acknowledgement of moral fault (line 17)). The joke therefore is a double one: that Sestius' 'frigid' speech produced a literal cold in the reader, and also the heavy irony that the frigid style has rubbed off on the reader who now couches his thanks for delivery from 'cold' in a 'cold' poem. Williams (1968) 137–140 elegantly unpacks the poem.

Publius Sestius was defended in 56 B.C. by Cicero on a charge of violence. cf. Cicero *Att.*7.17.2 for Sestius' literary abilities or lack of them.

Metre: scazons (limping iambics)

1   **O farm**: to address a farm in the vocative is itself hyperbolic: for the intense vocative address with *o* cf. 17.1, 33.1, Horace *Odes* 1.14.1, 1.35.1, Lucretius 3.1. It was customary to offer alternative (*seu... seu...*) invocations of a god in prayer-formula (cf. Horace *Odes* 3.21.2–4).

2–4 For the *nam* clause explaining why this matter is appropriate cf. Horace *Odes* 3.11.1–2, Virgil *Aen.* 1.65–9. The question of whether the farm is Sabine or Tiburtan is one of snobbery: Tibur was the sort of region where it was fashionable to own a farm,

Sabinum much less so. We are to imagine the farm in question lying on the further edge of Tibur and the near edge of Sabinum.

3   **desire ...**: the repetition of *cordi* is the sort of repetition found in prayers (cf. 34.2–4).

4   **argue ... wager**: the language is hyperbolic and oratorical: *contendo* is a forensic term (see *OLD* s.v. 'contendo' 4, 6, 7, 8) and the primary meaning of *pignus* is that of a legal mortgage or surety, although the significance here is clearly that of a 'wager'.

5   Note the repetition from line 1.

7   **got rid of**: the verb *expuli* suggests the act of coughing out and so is nicely appropriate for getting rid of a cough, as does the expressive alliteration of *p*.

8–9   The poet uses litotes to understate his culpability in catching the cold. There is a nice irony in that his stomach caused his cough and cold, in that his appetite for rich dinners caused him to read the 'cold' speech of Sestius. These two lines are a good example of hyperbaton with the verb *dedit* placed well out of its sentence in the following line. The effect is interesting: it throws emphasis on *cenas* at the end of the line, it throws the two verbs *appeto dedit* together in a striking manner ('I seek and it gave') underlining the poet's desire to be given food (only to be given sickness). The verb *dedit* can be understood in line 8: the effect here of the hyperbaton is one of discomfort.

10   **of Sestius**: the adjective *Sestianus* standing for the simple genitive (*Sestii*) sounds pretentious and thus appropriate for a guest of this pretentious man.

11   **candidature**: *petitor* was a candidate for public office: Antius is otherwise unknown. This line is striking for its metrical ingenuity in creating a whole line out of so few words, giving a (suitably parodistic) resonant and pompous effect.

12   **poison and disease**: the line first of all suggests that the speech is vitriolic and harmful to Antius (*OLD* s.v. 'venenum' 3b): but the second word leads to the meaning intended here that it was 'infectious' to the reader. The act of reading is left until the (stressed) end of the line and the sentence, showing the reader the simple act which was all that was needed.

13–14   Notice the expressive language as the cough 'shook' the sufferer and the sickness is described with suitably harsh alliteration of *f* and emphasised onomatopeic final word *tussis*.

15   For **nettle** as a remedy for cough cf. Celsus 4.10.4.

16–17   **give ... thanks**: Giving thanks to a god for a safe recovery or salvation from (e.g.) shipwreck was common enough: giving thanks to a villa for recovery in this way was not and the effect is one of parody of exactly the sort of 'frigid' hyperbole which (we assume) Sestius practised. In case we miss the parody, *grates* is archaic language for *gratias*.

17   **misdeed**: the poet's greed for dinners and consequent reading of the speech is now called a *peccatum*.

18–21   'Catullus could have ended his poem by saying: "Thank you for curing me this time. If I sin again, I offer no excuse why I should not pay the penalty." What he has said, however, is: "I offer no excuse why the penalty should not be paid by – not me but Sestius."' (Williams (1968)138–9). Note how the poet leads us to expect the former reading in lines 18–19, only to foil our expectation with the emphatic *non mi sed ipso Sestio*, rounding off the line with the harsh alliteration of *ferat frigus*.

21   The joke here is that if Sestius invites the poet when he has read a *malum librum* of his, then he can expect to catch the cold from the poet which reading the book will have given him.

45

A poem in three sections (1–9, 10–18, 19–25) depicting the love of a man and a woman: the man protests his undying love in the first section, the woman answers with her own declaration of love in the second, and the poet comments on their love in the shorter third section. The division of the first two sections is afforded by the use of the sneeze as a closural device, recalled with the word *auspicatiorem* which concludes the poem. The equality of the relationship depicted is described in the intimacy of their embrace (2, 10–12), in their protestations of love to each other, in the authorial comments on their mutual fidelity. This reciprocity is also evoked in the verbal patterning of the text (the verbal embracing of each other in lines 1 and 21, the asyndeton of line 19) and at face value the poem is an evocation of blissful love observed (*uidit* line 25) in others. The equality of the love is mirrored in the balance of the poem's structure and the frequent symmetries to be found (male vs. female, east vs. west) as well as in the relaxed sensuality of the love-making. The poem is a study in form as well as a delightful piece of sensuous poetry: the harmony of the relationship is evinced in the harmony of the literary form which has exactly balanced stanzas complete with refrain and delicate use of the couplet in the poet's last eight lines of comment. For the form of lovers conversation cf. Horace *Odes* 3.9 and Theocritus poem 8: the competitive 'amoebean' capping of one song by another is found in (e.g.) poem 62, Virgil *Ecl.* 3 and 7. The combination of immediate physical passion and lasting devotion depends on the use of words and concepts which derive their force from ideals of Roman marriage: so *omnes ... annos* with the phrase empasised by the type of hyperbaton which encloses the metrical unit, *huic uni domino usque seruiamus, ab auspicio bono, unam Acmen* (with the same type of hyperbaton) *uno in Septimio fidelis*. Mutual involvment and commitment find perfect expression in this poem. But ... the poem is not confessional; the poet is describing the feelings of another couple as a spectator.' (Williams (1968) 416). It is worth noticing that this is perhaps the one and only example of fulfilled love in the poems of Catullus.

Metre: hendecasyllabics

1   **Septimius ... Acme** the two names are juxtaposed to suggest the closeness of the two, with Septimius embracing Acme but his name being enveloped by her (*Acmen ... suos amores*). For *amores* used of 'beloved' cf. 10.1. Acme is a Greek name (meaning 'peak' or 'zenith') and the scene both suggests a love-affair between a Roman and a Greek freedwoman and also that she is 'the tops'.

3   **desperately**: *perdite* has the sense of 'to destruction' 'desperately'. Note the repetition of the key word 'love' in *amo ... amare*.

4   the line is framed by the phrase *omnes ... annos* in hyperbaton, with *sum ... paratus* enclosing the keyword *assidue*, giving the effect of a golden line.

5   The line notable for its sound (the alliteration of *q* and then *p*) and also the sense. *perire* here means 'to perish with love' so that the phrase means 'as much as he who can love to distraction the most' but the literal sense 'to die' lurks behind the words and suggests a secondary meaning of 'as much as a man who can die the most' which leads neatly on to the lethal situation which Septimius would face in lines 6–7.

6–7   **Libya and India** are the two places where a Roman might meet a lion: the fearful encounter is made the more fearful by the stressed *solus*. The primary sense of *tosta* is 'scorched by the sun' but this detail is strictly irrelevant here where the lion would be just as dangerous whatever the temperature; the poet may have chosen the word *tosta* because of the secondary meaning of *torreo* as 'to burn with love' (*OLD* s.v. 'torreo' 2b) as in Horace *Odes* 3.19.28, 4.1.12. Similarly the colour of the lion's eyes may be seen as strictly irrelevant except for the clear point that if the speaker is close enough to see the colour then he is too close; there is a reference to Homer *Il.* 20. 164–73 where a green-eyed lion attacks a hunter, but Lucretius also picks out the 'green-eyed girl' in his catalogue of lovers' euphemisms (4.1161). The juxtaposition of *ueniam ob uius* stresses the face-to-face encounter.

8–9 **Love:** *Amor* must mean Cupid, the child of Venus who was present at the lovemaking: *sternuit* means 'sneezed' and is seen as indicating an omen. *sinistra ut ante dextra* is best understood as meaning 'first on the right and then the left' which sidesteps the arguments about whose left and whose right is being referred to as the lovers are facing each other in different directions, and (besides) *approbationem* can only mean 'approval' and cuts out any possibility of the sneeze being ill-omened, whichever side is sneezed on. The couplet is repeated at lines 17–18 to mark the end of Acme' response to Septimius' declaration and thus the lines function as a closural device to indicate the structure of the poem.

10–12 The scene is one of sensuous closeness: she bends her head backwards (*reflectens*) lightly, her 'boy' is sweet, his eyes are drunk with love, her mouth is crimson (suffused with arousal, presumably). Notice the way the poet picks out the sequence of the girl's head, then the boy's eyes, then the girl's mouth: the boy's eyes are called *ocellos* (the affectionate diminutive as used at 3.18, 43.2) and described as *ebrios* which neatly suggests that they are 'swimming' with moisture (*OLD* s.v. 'ebrius' 3), that the boy is 'exhilarated' with the experience, and that the two of them are as if intoxicated. The connection of drink and sex needs no parallel: cf. Griffin 1985, 65–87. The girl's mouth is pointed out as 'that' mouth: *suauiata* sounds as if derived from *suauis* ('pleasurable').

13–16 Acme, unlike her male lover, does not offer to face a challenge to prove her love. Note her more affectionate use of the diminutive *Septimille* (he called her *mea Acme*) and her description of him as her 'life' as found in 104.1, 109.1.

14 **this one lord** is presumably Cupid. The concept of the 'slavery of love' has a distinguished history in later Latin elegy but is relatively unusual in Catullus (see Lyne 1979, 117–130) and denotes the subservience of the male to his 'mistress'. The lovers are here seen as both enslaved to the service of the god.

15–16 **burns:** for love as a fire in the marrow of the bones cf. 35.15, 64.93: *mollibus* means 'feminine' as often (see *OLD* s.v. 'mollis' 15) and also has the sense of 'voluptuous', and the line thus has a neat 'ABAB' symmetry of: fire – soft – burns – bones. Note also the striking alliteration of *m* in these lines.

19–20 **favourable omens:** the 'good omen' is the sneeze: notice the elegance with which the reciprocity of the love is brought out explicitly (*mutuis animis*) and then in the verbs in asyndeton *amant amantur* (for the device cf. Ovid *Ars am.* 1.99).

21 The chiastic structure of the line (ABBA) again shows the interlocking affection of the two. For *misellus* as meaning 'lovesick' cf. Lucretius 4.1076.

22 **Syrias and Britains** suggests the year 55 B.C. when Crassus was leading his (ill-fated) expedition to Syria and Caesar was about to invade Britain: but the names are also used as bywords for 'Eastern' (e.g. Seneca *Dial.* 3.11.4) and 'West' (Lucretius 6.1106) respectively, and the generalising plurals also cast doubt on how specific the places are.

23 After the plurals *Syrias Britanniasque* the poet goes straight onto *uno in Septimio*. He prefers Acme to all the countries of east and west, she prefers him to everybody else and is therefore *fidelis*.

24 **takes her delight:** *facit delicias* sounds flippant, but again expands *fidelis* from the line before, as Acme is satisfied with Septimius and does not seek pleasure with others.

25–6 **Who …?:** the poem ends with a rhetorical question addressed to the reader. *homines* includes both men and women, and the final word *auspicatiorem* recalls the good omen of the sneeze which concluded each of the first two sections of the poem.

46

A travel poem: the poet celebrates the arrival of spring as it signals the moment to leave Bithynia and return home by way of the tourist attractions of Asia. The generalised opening celebrating spring gives way to an explanatory section describing the desire to travel and ends with a farewell to his former companions. The link between the season and the travel is brought out in the verse: the spring 'brings back' the warmth in the first line, and the roads 'bring back' the travellers in the last; the sky has given up its passion and the poet picks up the passion to travel; the 'pleasant' breezes cause the poet to leave his 'sweet' companions as the open plains remarkable for nothing but heat and crops (5) give way to the 'famous cities of Asia'. *uer* induces *uagari*.

Metre: hendecasyllabics.

1   **Now**: note the repetition of *iam* ... *iam*.

2   **madness**: *furor* is usually used of human madness and passion: there is a nice irony in that the passion of the sky gives way to the poet's passion to return home. *aequinoctialis* refers to the spring equinox in March, notorious for stormy weather.

3   **grows silent**: the personification of meteorological phenomena continues with the 'passion' of the sky now 'growing silent': note how expressive the choice of vocabulary is here, as *auris* are 'breezes', lighter by definition than the winds referred to in line 2.

4   **Catullus**: the poet addresses himself, as in poem 8 (etc.), and produces neat alliteration of *c*.

5   **Nicaea** was the capital city of Bithynia. At face value this is a redundant line, in that it adds no substantial knowledge not already imparted. The poet may have added this line for the following reasons: the vague term *phrygii* is sharpened into the specific *Nicaea* and the general term *campi* becomes the more picturesque *ager uber aestuosae*. The lengthy adjective *aestuosus* refers to the summer heat which the poet is looking forward to avoiding if he travels quickly (*uolemus*) in the spring (*iam uer*).

6   **Asia** presumably refers to the Roman province of Asia, whose chief cities were Pergamum, Sardis and Ephesus. *claras* suggests that tourism was the object of the poet's visit.

7–8   The rational mind and then the more emotional feet are described as alike keen to travel. *uagari* suggests undirected travelling, *laeti studio* is an effective juxtaposition to reinforce the 'enthusiasm' idea.

9–11 **o sweet ... companions**: after addressing himself in line 4, the poet now addresses his companions: the lines assert that the group travelled together on the outward journey but will now make their separate ways home. Notice the pleonasm of *diuersae uarie* to bring out the variety of routes and the metaphor of *reportant*: note also the balanced phrasing of 'setting out' (*profectos*) and going back (*reportant*) and the irony that the 'companions' are no longer companions.

47

A piece of light verse deploring the unfair way in which the poet's friends Veranius and Fabullus have to angle for dinner invitations while others enjoy lavish banquets. Most editors work hard to establish an identity for the two men named in line 1: Goold tentatively asserts that Porcius is Gaius Porcius Cato (tribune 56 B.C.) and that Socration refers to the epicurean philosopher and poet Philodemus, but these identifications are uncertain and are surely unimportant. More to the point is that Porcius ('piggy') is an appropriate name for one who dines all evening: and 'little Socrates' reminds us that the real Socrates stayed at Agathon's symposium all night long (Plato *Symp.*). The terms suggest that the one is greedy, the other pretentious: their rapacity is evoked in the imaginative phrase *scabies famesque mundi* while the amorous Piso is memorably described as *uerpus Priapus ille*. Their crimes are not detailed beyond this rough invective: the point of the poem is better served if the poem solely draws the contrast between 'sweet little Veranius and Fabullus' hankering for invitations on the streets and the affluent pair of good-for-nothings.

Metre: hendecasyllabics

1   **left hands**: the left hand is the one used for thieving, as in poem 12.1, Ovid *Met.* 13.111.

2   **plague**: *scabies* is properly a skin disorder ('mange'), *fames* is 'starvation', both term here used metaphorically and imaginatively of the two addressees: Fordyce takes the genitive *mundi* as objective ('itching greed whose object is the *mundus*), but it is perhaps better to read it (as Lee has) as 'the world's Itch and Greed' or (as Syndikus takes it) 'causing disease and hunger in the world' (i.e. by plundering the province: for the phrase cf. Cicero *Rab. Post.* 2). 'Hunger' is of course highly relevant in a poem which bemoans the poverty of some and the lavish dinners of others, while *scabies* may suggest the 'itch' of sexual desire so prominent in Piso, just as it suggests financial greed in Horace *Epist.* 1.12.14., and just as with *prurire* at 16.9 and 88.2.

3   **my little**: for the use of the affectionate diminutive cf. 12.17

4   **shagged-out**: *uerpus* properly means ' having the foreskin drawn back' or 'circumcised' and generally denotes the effects of excessive sexual activity on the penis (Adams 12–14). The term is perhaps redundant here as the man is nicknamed Priapus, the god of fertility whose permanent state of arousal is well known (see e.g Horace *Sat.* 1.8.5, Martial 6.49, 73, Petronius 60). The line presumably refers to Piso himself, whose sexual activity is fair game for Cicero's invective in his speech *Pis.* of 55 B.C. Note here the contemptuous alliteration of *p*.

5   **rich ... no expense spared**: *lauta sumptuose* is something of a pleonasm. *lautus* has the primary sense 'washed' and then comes to mean 'well heeled' (Petronius 26.9) and then 'luxurious' by application: *sumptuosus* has the sense of 'extravagant' and reminds us that the Romans were given to passing 'sumptuary laws' limiting the amount of money which might be spent (e.g. the *lex Fannia* of 161 B.C. which limited expenditure on dinners).

6   **daylight**: *de die* means 'in the daytime': Roman dinners usually began at the ninth hour or later, and to begin dining or drinking earlier than that was a sign of conspicuous consumption as in Cicero *Att.* 9.1.3, Horace *Sat.* 2.8.3.

7   **invitations**: *uocatio* appears to be an invention of the poet's. For *uocare* meaning 'to invite to dinner' cf. 44.21: for the impecunious man's need to receive an invitation to dinner cf. the hangers-on at Trimalchio's table in Petronius *Satyricon*.

48

A neat poem of tender desire for the youthful Juventius, consisting of a single sentence and working on several metaphors ('honeyed', 'full of food', 'crop of kisses') in the course of its six lines. The first three lines convey the positive desire to kiss, the last three lines assert that this appetite cannot be limited: the enjoyment of Juventius is seen throughout in terms of eating (honey – full – corn) but the reciprocity of the pleasure is hinted at in *nostrae*. As often in Catullus, the surface erotic meaning of the poem is the vehicle of the style at least as much as the other way round: the text is a fine example of the poet's artistry.

Metre: hendecayllabics.

1 **honeyed** is applied to Juventius also at 99.1, just as Lesbia's sparrow was *mellitus* at 3.6. For the erotic overtones of honey see Plautus *Curc.* 164 (other exx. at *OLD* s.v. 'mel' 3), Lucretius 4. 1160 (the euphemistic use of 'honey-coloured' applied to a girl). For the kissing of the eyes cf. 9.9, 45.11–12.

2 The line implies that the youth is protected from such amorous advances by people who have the power to allow or refuse contact: this also allows the text to stay in the realms of fantasy. The line is notable for the alliteration of *s* and the assonance of *i*. *basiare* is picked up by *basiem* in line 3.

3 **three hundred thousand**: for the counting of kisses cf. poems 5 and 7.

4 The kissing is transformed into eating as the poet says that he will never be 'full' of them. Note here the strong double negative *nec numquam* (for *nec umquam*) and the assonance of *a* and then *u* in *–ar satur futurus*. *uidear* here means 'I would think' but the idea of sight is appropriate in the poem about Juventius' eyes.

5–6 **crop ... corn**: an intriguing metaphor: the 'crop' of kisses as 'thicker than dry ears of corn'. The term *osculatio* is another of Catullus' inventions (cf. *basiatio* at 7.1, *uocatio* at 47.6) and ends the poem on a note of 'high' poetry. The associations of the crop of corn are ones of fullness, ripeness, pleasure, sunshine: for *densas aristas* cf. 64.353, where the aggressive actions of Achilles are compared to those of the farmer: in this passage the negative image of 'dry' gives way to the richness of the 'crop', and the poetic jingle of *aridis aristis* with its assonance of *i* leads to the strong alliteration of *s* in the final line.

49

A poem of thanks to M. Tullius Cicero, the orator and politician. Cicero is described as 'most eloquent' in lines 1–3: he is then described as being as good a *patronus* as Catullus is as bad a poet, with a wry twist in the phrase 'advocate of all' at the end. Most editors see the poem as ironic, especially in view of the ironic self-deprecation with which the poet describes himself as the worst of poets, a term which he discusses in poem 36 as applied to himself and dismisses. If the poet is not in fact the worst poet, then (the reasoning goes) Cicero is not the best advocate either and what appears to be fulsome praise is anything but praise, the poem being in fact a parody of the hyperbolic oratory which Cicero practised for anybody who paid him (*omnium patronus*). Notice the five superlatives in seven lines and the extravagant 'past, present and future' expansion of *Romuli nepotum* in lines 2–3, the mock-humility of *pessimus omnium poeta*, the incantatory repet ition of this phrase and the balanced answer *optimus omnium patronus*. The alternative is to see the text as modest and self-deprecating praise of Cicero; the degree of irony in the poem is a matter of individual judgement in a text which is quizzical and teasing to the reader.

Metre: hendecasyllabics

1 **descendants of Romulus**: 'grandsons of Romulus' is a mock-heroic phrase for 'Romans', as at 58.5, and comparable to Lucretius' *Aeneadum* (1.1). The phrase may appear to be laudatory, but of course any real 'grandson of Romulus' would by now belong to a very old generation indeed and the term may conceal a hint of Cicero's old-fashioned ways.

2–3 The lines are a tricolon crescendo introduced by *quot*: for the 'past, present and future' idea cf. 21.2–3, 24. 2–3.
Marcus Tullius: a formal style of address used in senatorial sessions (cf. Cicero *Cat.* 1.27)

4 **Catullus**: The poet names himself, thus casting the poem into the third person as a more formal message.

5–7   Lines 5 and 6 are linked by the repetition of *pessimus omnium poeta*, while lines 6 and 7 are linked by the correlative *tanto* ... *quanto* and the balanced symmetry of *pessimus omnium poeta* giving way to *optimus omnium patronus*.

7   **patron**: *Patronus* usually indicates a man of power who grants help and protection to men of lower rank in society. The meaning of the term in legal circles is closer to our 'advocate' and for Catullus to call Cicero 'everyone's advocate' suggests that Cicero would plead anything for anybody if it helped their case. This use of *omnium* is paralleled in Cicero's own attack on Clodia (described as 'girlfriend of all' in *Cael.* 32) and turns the laudatory poem into an attack on the orator.

50

A poem about poets writing poetry, describing the process of playful composition and the after-effects on the excited poet who begs to repeat the experience. The poem affects to be a prayer to Calvus, and (in good prayer style) the poem reminds the addressee of what he has done in the past before going on to make the prayer. In case we miss this formal style, the poem ends with mock-religious mention of the goddess Nemesis.

The poem has attracted a good deal of attention for the light it casts on the sort of poetry it exemplifies. It is a self-consciously ironic text, asserting the sort of passion usually associated with sexual love in a message to a fellow poet, written in hyperbolic style and concluding with a dire religious warning: it comes over as a prayer-poem which the poet sends to Calvus to describe his feelings (as if Calvus needed reminding of what they had done the day before) and the view of Bacchic poetic frenzy which it conveys puts it in the tradition of Plato's *Ion* (533e3–534a5) and *Phaedrus* (245a) and the whole literary tradition in which the true poet is 'possessed' and even mad (Aristotle *Poet.* 1455a, Horace *Ars P.* 300, 453–76). The poem is of course a tightly controlled piece of writing, for all the uncontrolled frenzy it describes, and is clearly a 'display-piece' of exactly the sort of 'trivial' poem which he and Calvus are said to have composed the day before. It is thus a highly sophisticated poet writing a sophisticated poem which pretends to be anything but sophisticated: a poem which both seeks Calvus' continued friendship and also demonstrates that the poet deserves it for the quality of this poem: a poem describing 'play' which it itself a playful parody of a prayer to a god and which elevates the qualities of wit and style (*lepore ... facetiisque*) above all else in creating the poetic excitement which possesses him. The text elevates these qualities of literary skill and humour in Calvus while also displaying them in itself, thus encompassing its own aesthetic values of delight and artistic enjoyment in a text of playfulness and pleasure.

Metre: hendecasyllabics

1   **Licinius** is usually taken to be C. Licinius Calvus Macer (82–47 B.C.), also seen in poems 14, 53, 96 and the poet of the (lost) miniature epic *Io. otiosi* is important here in setting the scene: writing poetry is *otium* (leisure) rather than *negotium* (business) and this concept of poetry as *otium* is found also in (e.g.) Virgil *G.* 4. 563–5, Ovid *Tr.* 4.10.17–40.

2   **sported**: for *ludere* used of musical and poetic composition cf. Virgil *Ecl.* 1.10, 6.1, *G.* 4.565. The term also has a sexual connotation ('fooling about' i.e. indiscreet affairs, as in Cicero *Cael.* 28, which leads neatly onto *delicatos* in line 3. *tabellis* are the *pugillaria* of poem 42.5.

3   **naughty**: *delicatus* was used of the 'playful' wife in 17.15 and the concept of 'skittishness' well suits this context here of unserious poetry. There is also the extended sense of 'naughtiness' found in the uses of the word (and its cognate *deliciae*) but the primary sense of the word when applied to poetry is that this sort of writing is 'art for art's sake' rather than poetry with any serious didactic or moral purpose. The poets

'played' in different metres (line 5) and the result was excitement rather than any grave work of literature.

4   **little verses**: The diminutive *uersiculos* conveys the light nature of the poetry – a self-effacing touch such as we find in 1.4 (*nugas*) and 16.3.

5   **sported**; The repetition of *ludo* from line 2 (which 'hardly earns its keep' according to Quinn) is done so as to stress the vital word and keep the image of lightness uppermost in the reader's mind, as in the next line with *per iocum atque uinum*.

7–13 **on fire**: *incensus* ('ablaze with passion') is a common metaphor for sexual love (cf. 64.19, 91–3, 253; 68.73) but here is used of the poet's excitement at his companion's 'brilliance and humour' (Fordyce). *miserum* is used of the lovesick at 8.1, and it is well-evidenced that the lovesick will go off their food and be unable to sleep at night   (cf. Virgil *Aen.* 4.529–31) if the beloved be not with them. This sentence thus provocatively puts a sexual edge on the relationship of the two poets as a metaphor to convey the enormous excitement felt by the poet at the act of composing poetry.

11   **wild**: *indomitus* properly means 'untamed' of animals and here suggests the wild frenzy of the poet, especially in juxtaposition with *furore* ('madness') and the unnecessary descriptive adjective *toto* ('over the whole bed').

12   **longing**: *cupiens* is again suggestive of sexual desire, but the poet here desires the dawn.

13   The objects of the poet's desire are spelled out in plain speech. *simul esse* is colloquial (cf. 21.5, Horace *Epist.* 1.10.50).

14–17   The frenzy of lines 7–13 gives way to exhaustion (stressed both in the adjective *defessa* and also in the hyperbolic *semimortua*), rest (*iacebant*) and then more poetry – in this case a poetic message to Calvus.

15   **half-dead**: *semimortua* is apparently Catullus' own invention: *lectulo* adds pathos as the poet creates an image of a lonely small bed, on which the poet's limbs are 'lying' (as if dead).

16   **my dear man**: *iucunde* continues the note of close affection between the two poets, as before at 14.2: cf. 64. 215 (Aegeus to his son).

17   **agony**: *dolorem* is again often used of the pain of love and loss, but it also refers to literary pathos (Cicero *De or.* 2.73, 3. 96, *Orat.* 130) and it may well be that the poet is drawing attention here to the affecting manner in which this poem conveys the pain of literary longing. The poet thus has it both ways: he wants Calvus to see 'his pain' but also 'to appreciate his pathos'.

18–21   The poet has declared his feelings and expressed them in such a way that the addressee may see them (*perspiceres*). He now cautions him – note the tricolon repetition of *caue ... caue ... caueto* ending the poem on this note – in order to turn the tables on the addressee whose power over the poet this poem demonstrates but who will himself suffer if he rejects the literary overture. For the warning against rejecting prayers cf. the similar warning of Phoinix to Achilles in Homer *Il.* 9. 502–514.

19   **spit back**: *despuas* is a strong word and leaves the addressee the room to accept some measure of the poet's friendship so long as falls short of 'spitting it out' completely.

20   **Nemesis** ('righteous indignation') is an ancient goddess who avenges wrongdoing mercilessly (cf. Pindar *Pyth.* 10.44) and punishes *hubris* (Euripides *Phoen.* 183): she is paired with *Aidos* ('shame') in Hesiod *Op.* 200, the one being an inner deterrent against wrongdoing, the other being an external check on such behaviour.

21   **powerful god**: Nemesis is cast in the same guise as the 'jealous gods' of mythology who punished human arrogance with hideous torments (e.g. Arachne transformed into a spider for boasting that she could spin as well as Minerva). Unspecified punishment awaits Calvus if he too spurns the goddess.

51

This poem is clearly modelled on a famous poem of the Greek poetess Sappho. The original runs as follows in translation:

'That man seems to me to be equal to the gods, he who is sitting facing you and listens close by to your sweet speaking and your charming laughter; this has made the heart in my breast to flutter. For when I look at you even for a moment, then I no longer have the power to speak but my tongue is paralysed and at once a slender flame has run under my skin, I see nothing with my eyes, my ears sound, sweat pours down me, a trembling seizes my whole body, I am greener than grass and I seem to myself to be on the point of death. But all is to be endured, since? even a poor man? ... ' (fr. 31)

It is instantly noticed that Catullus has kept the metre (sapphic stanzas) of Sappho's original and also that the content of lines 1–12 follows the Greek lines 1–12, until his final stanza, which some editors believe to be from a different poem altogether.

Metre: Sapphics

1–2 The poet begins with a *makarismos* of the man who enjoys the company of his beloved, and repeats *ille* for emphasis and declares that the man is equal to 'a god' (Sappho had him equal 'to gods'). The line ends with the stressed *uidetur* emphasising that the poet is concerned with the way this man appears to him rather than with how things are in fact. The poem is one of a subjective internal state as the observer examines how things appear to him and then how his own internal state alters as a result.

2 **right:** *fas* is the law of god, and to claim that someone 'outdid' the gods in anything was a dangerous thing to boast, as the poet had claimed only just in the last line of the previous poem. To be more fortunate even than the 'blessed gods' would be felicity indeed, and the poet thus conveys the sense of a happiness greater than which cannot be conceived, with the qualifying *si fas est* covering himself from divine retribution.

3 **again and again:** *identidem* (not in the Greek) well conveys the poet's jealousy of the man being able to see and hear the girl over and over again: it contrasts with the *simul ... aspexi* whereby one glance was enough to drive the poet to distraction. Note also the understatement of *sedens* whereby it is enough just to sit opposite the beloved: closer contact is not required for bliss.

4 **sees ... hears:** the two verbs are well emphasised by their position in the short line: Sappho did not speak of 'seeing' but only of hearing, and Catullus has amplified this perhaps in keeping with his opening verb *uidetur* and also in accordance with the common ancient emphasis on the place of sight in love (e.g. 64.86, Euripides *Hipp.* 525–6, Lucretius 4.1101–2, Propertius 1.1.1).

5 **laughing sweetly:** *dulce ridentem* cf. 61.212. Quinn notes that the man in Sappho's poem hears her speak as well as laugh – Catullus' girl could as well be unable to speak his language – and it is Horace who later supplies the Sapphic *dulce loquentem* in *Odes* 1.22.23–4. More significant here is the oxymoron of *ridentem misero* with the implication that her laughter causes instant misery in the lovesick poet.

5–6 A general statement of sensual paralysis followed by concrete examples of this malaise. The notion of love as a disease has a long and distinguished history: cf. 76.20, Euripides *Hipp.* 476–7, Sophocles *Trach.* 445.

7 **as soon as ...:** Sappho said that she only had to look for a moment to be struck with love: Catullus slightly alters this to a statement that he was in love 'as soon as he caught sight of her'. His use of the vocative Lesbia is highly appropriate in this adaptation of a poem by the great Lesbian poetess.

7–9 For the inability of the love-struck to speak cf. Virgil *Aen.* 4.76. *uocis in ore* is Doering's suggestion to fill the stanza, adopted by most editors.

9 A pleasing line, beginning with *lingua* and ending with *artus,* with the alliterative pair of words *torpet tenuis* in the middle and another alliterative pair of monosyllables (*sed ... sub*) encircling them.

9–10 There is a pleasing mixture of imagery here: his feelings are 'fire' but the verb is liquid (*demanat*) and the flame is *tenuis* – 'slender' but also 'watery' (*OLD* s.v. 'tenuis' 5b).

10–11   The repeated *s* sounds and the assonance of *sonitu suopte* give way to the onomatopeia and *t* alliteration of *tintinant.*

11–12   **twin:** *gemina* must be ablative agreeing with *nocte* rather than nominative with *lumina* as one might expect. This use of hypallage is highly charged and emphatic: his eyes are not simply 'covered in night' but (as there are two of them) covered in 'twin/double night' thus stressing the darkness which has fallen upon them: a darkness which is also strongly emphasised in the oxymoron *lumina nocte* occupying the whole of line 12.

13–16   A stanza often suspected by scholars: it does not appear in Sappho's fragment and might have been part of another poem altogether. It does however fit this context extremely well and surely deserves to be printed as it stands. It has the effect of placing the first three stanzas into inverted commas and looking at what the poet has written with the detached eyes of an observer. Notice the apostrophe to the poet (as at 8.1 etc) and the change of addressee from the girl (*te* in line 3) to the poet himself (*tibi* in line 13): note the polyptoton style of repetition of *otium* – *otio* – *otium* in successive lines calling attention to the way *otium* ruins great cities and small individuals alike. The final stanza is a good example of closure in which the poet signs off his highly emotional words of lines 1–12 with a dismissive explanation of the overwrought state into which his lack of occupation has led him. Lyne puts it clearly: 'Catullus feels uncomfortable about the jealous feelings he describes in the first three stanzas – he feels uncomfortable about the effects of his romantic love – and in consequence reads a moralising lesson to himself: "you've got too much *otium* on your hands, Catullus" (i.e. too much time to indulge in love (cf. Ovid *Rem. am.* 139ff)' (Lyne 1980, 295).

This goes some way to explaining the final stanza, but it still leaves the last two lines as a rather unconvincing 'political' appendix to 'justify' a personal decision. Again, the level of irony must not be underrated: and if the poet in lines 13–14 casts ironic doubt on the value of lines 1–12, then lines 15–16 cast ironic doubt on that doubt. Just as in the closing lines of poem 64 with their moralising sermon on the wickedness of 'modern man', so here the poet adopts the language of the serious in parody of their opinion. The poet describes his emotional and physical weakness in the face of love (1–12), only to explain it away as the fruit of too much *otium* (13–14): but he then turns that sentiment into a parody of itself by couching it in the sort of senatorial moral indignation which would reject *otium*. At the end of the poem we are left no wiser – which is presumably the poet's wish.

13   **nuisance:** *molestum* is a striking word to choose here, more commonly used of personal discomfort and makes the line one of bathetic simplicity after the high style of the previous stanza. It is also an arresting paradox which catches the reader by surprise – one would think it a contradiction in terms.

14–15 the poet justifies his own experience by a generalised observation on the enervating effects of *otium* (here meaning more 'peace' and *luxuria* – having enough wealth to allow citizens not to need to work) on kings and cities, even though Rome was clearly not governed by kings and there were no obvious examples of cities brought low by *otium.* For the philosophical background cf. Sallust *Iug.* 41.1, Fraenkel 1957, 212–3.

What is most striking here is the poet's use of a moralising tone to end an emotional poem: for the fulminating rejection of *otium* as politically dangerous cf. Sallust *Cat.* 16.3.

52

A political poem. Vatinius appears both here and in the following poem: he was quaestor in 64, praetor in 55, tribune in 59 (the year of Caesar's consulship) and consul for a mere few days in 47. He was 'an easy butt because of his personal disabilities, weak legs, and scrofulous swellings.' (*OCD* s.v. 'Vatinius Publius')

Nonius is less easily identified but appears to have suffered similar disfiguring marks as Vatinius (see on line 2). The poem follows a simple pattern with the closural device of the first line repeated as the last line. The offence of Nonius is that he holds any office of high rank, that of Vatinius is to 'swear falsely' by a consulship he has not yet obtained.

Metre: iambic trimeters.

1   **what is it?**: for the outraged question *quid est?* cf. Cicero *Cat.* 1.5.13. The poet addresses himself as often, and then repeats *quid* with the play on words *moraris emori* with *moror* (I delay) juxtaposed with *morior* (I die).

2   the **curule chair** was occupied by a holder of high office in Rome (consul, praetor, censor, curule aedile) and Nonius is sitting on one. Nonius is ridiculed as a 'tumour' or a boil – Vatinius also was mocked for his boils (Cicero *Vat.* 4,39) – and the phrase amounts to calling Nonius a political excrescence.

3   The **Vatinius** of which we know was not consul until 47 B.C. and then only as *consul suffectus* (i.e. consul elected for a small part of the year to replace a consul who had died or retired before the end of his year of office). Such 'substitute consuls' might hold office for a very short time: in 45, for instance, Caninius Rebilus was consul for a few hours. Vatinius was elected consul in December 47 B.C. until the end of the year. If the date of Catullus' death is as generally believed, then the meaning of this line must be that he swears by the consulship which he is certain he will one day hold. Cicero tells us (in an admittedly hostile speech) that Vatinius boasted of his second consulship years before he had obtained his first (*Vat.* 11).

53

Vatinius again, this time in court being prosecuted by Licinius Calvus; Vatinius faced prosecution several times in his career; in 58 B.C. when prosecuted by Calvus, again in 56 when attacked by Cicero as a witness in the trial of Sestius who was being defended by Cicero (whose speech still survives) and again in 54 when defended by Cicero (the sort of flexible attitude towards clients for which Catullus mocks Cicero in 49.7).

The poem is a single comic anecdote. We know right from the first word that it will be funny: it builds up to the climax of the final two words with the colloquial (obscene) word *salaputium* combined with the serious term *disertum*. The joke combines satire of Calvus' stature with admiration for his speaking skill.

Metre: hendecasyllabics

1   **I laughed**: the poem begins with the key idea of laughter, which will be fully explained only in the final words. *corona* here means the 'circle of spectators'.

2   **in fine style**: *mirifice* is apparently the *mot juste* for effective oratory: cf. Arrius in 84.3.

3   **my friend**: the term *meus* indicates close friendship. *explicasset* is a pleasing word expressive of articulate exegesis, also used at 1.6.

4   For raising the hands in a gesture of amazement cf. Cicero *Acad.* 2.63.

5   The joke which made the poet laugh in line 1. There is an obvious oxymoron of *magni* followed by the diminutive *salaputium*: Calvus was short in stature (Seneca *Controversiae.* 7.4.7) and so the diminutive is appropriate. For his eloquence (*disertum*) cf. the story told by Seneca (*ibid.*) that at one point in Calvus' speech Vatinius leapt to his feet and exclaimed: 'I ask you, men of the jury, if I it is right for me to be condemned just because he is eloquent (*disertus*)?'. The term *salaputium* is given the meaning 'penis' in Adams 65 (deriving it from *salax* ('randy') and *praeputium* ('foreskin')) which lends the story more interest, especially when combined with the inappropriate term *disertus*.

54

A poem addressed to Caesar, if the link with 29.11 is sustained: but a text with major textual problems. If there is a topical allusion in the linking of Caesar with the 'warmed-up geriatric', then this is now lost to us.

Metre: hendecasyllabics

1   **head**: *caput* here may mean 'the end of the penis' (Adams 72). *oppido* here is a colloquial term meaning 'very'.

2   The ms reading is: *et eri rustice*, variously emended. Some (e.g. Quinn and Garrison) read Hermes' *Hirri* referring to a certain C. Lucilius Hirrus, cousin of Pompey but not renowned for his unwashed legs, others (Munro, followed by Goold) avoid the name and construct *trirustice* out of *et eri rustice*, coining a word otherwise unparalleled in the language. A genitive case of a name (*Hirri*) fits the pattern of *Othonis* and *Libonis* better, but there is nothing to link the Hirrus of Cicero *ad Q.Fr.* 3.8.4 with this passage and no other Hirrus is known. What matters in this poem is of course the invective directed at Caesar who tolerates such people but becomes enraged at Catullus' poems, and there is no doubt about the 'rustic' poor hygiene of the unknown man behind this textual crux.
     For the attack on 'rusticity' as opposed to 'urbanity' see poem 22.

3   **Libo** is otherwise unknown: he may have been L. Scribonius Libo, father-in-law of Sextus Pompeius. The joke here is perhaps that he was a man who was not known for his subtlety, and that he was 'light and delicate only when he farts' (Garrison).

5   **Sufficius**: *Sufficio* is the reading of the mss: many editors emend to *Fuficio* (Scaliger) referring to C. Fuficius Fango or else to Bickel's *Fufidio*, referring to the Fufidius of Horace *Sat.* 1.2.12–17 and Cicero *Pis.* 35, the friend of Cicero and (like Cicero) native of Arpinum. *seni recocto* probably refers (as Quinn suggests) to the myth of Aeson, Medea's father-in-law, who she rejuvenated by boiling in a cauldron.

6   **again**: *iterum* suggests that the poet's work had already annoyed the *imperator*: for the story of Caesar accepting the poet's apology and inviting him to dinner, see Suetonius *Iul.* 73. *iambis* may denote a style of poetry (invective) rather than a specific metre – cf. 54.4, Horace *Odes* 1.16.24, *hendecasyllabos* in 12.10–11.

7   **commander without equal!**: the honorific title *unice imperator* is taken from 29.11 and saves the poet having to name Caesar. *immerentibus* is strongly emphasised in protest at the undeserved nature of Caesar's wrath.

55

A poem to Camerius asking him to reveal his whereabouts. The artificiality of the poem is immediately obvious – if the addressee is really out of sight then the poem has no chance of being delivered – and the tone of the text suggests that it is primarily a satirical picture of a young man and his amorous adventuring. The interest of the poem is increased by the use of topical names of sites, a device well used in comedy (e.g. Plautus *Curc.* 467–86) and Ovid (*Ars am.* 1. 67–262). Of the 22 lines of the poem, only 8 of them do not contain some sort of a second-person address, and *te* is repeated 7 times as the object of the poet's search. The central exchange between the poet and the women (7–12) purports to show how hard the poet has been searching for his friend but is rather an opportunity for a joke at the poet's expense (line 12). The hedonism of Camerius is well evinced in the text: he has abandoned the public arena and the temple for the *tenebrae*: the *femellae* are well described in erotic terms (*prendi* looks forward to *deprendi* in 56.5: she pulls aside her dress, her breasts are 'rosy', the girls are 'milky-white', and lines 17–20 are an expressive catalogue of pleasure, from *lacteolae puellae* to the 'tongue' of line 18, to the 'fruits of love' in line 19, to Venus herself in line 20. There is, in other words, ample understanding of Camerius on the part of the poet, for all his hard consonantal imperatives in lines 15–16 and his criticism of Camerius' *fastus* in line 14, and the poem ends with the real motive of the text: he wants to 'share' in the pleasure being had by Camerius, pleasure which the poetic text has hinted at and described in verbal terms.

Metre: hendecasyllabics (with some metrical variation as many lines adopt a long syllable for the two short syllables, thus turning the lines into decasyllables by substituting a molossus for the choriamb).

1   **We ask you**: The poem begins in a formal polite style which will prove ironic as the poem proceeds.

2   **hideaway**: *tenebrae* literally means 'darkness' and then 'hideout' (*OLD* s.v. 'tenebrae' 1c) but in this sense the word has a pejorative ring to it ('as typical of squalid or disreputable buildings' *OLD*, citing Cicero *Sest.* 20, Juvenal 3.225 etc). There is a nice paradox here as the addressee is asked to 'show' his 'dark place'.

3–5   Note here the fourfold repetition of *te* to emphasise the single-minded quest of the missing person, and note also the alternation of small (*campus minor ... libellis*) and large (*Circus ... templo Iouis*).

3   **smaller Campus**: the identity of the *campus minor* is not known: clearly a place smaller than the *Campus Martius* but no other reference supports the place mentioned here.

4   The **Circus** Maximus, home of chariot racing in Rome. *libellis* is usually taken to mean 'bookshops' but may mean 'public notices' or 'placards': Martial 5.20.8 makes the former translation more likely to be right, as there the word is clearly intended to signify the place where books were on sale.

5   **temple of highest Jove**: the catalogue of places searched culminates appropriately with the temple of Capitoline Jupiter, dedicated after being rebuilt in 69 B.C., and here given a whole line to itself to mark it as the high point of the search.

6   **walkway of Pompey**: The love-interest begins as the search extends to the Porticus of Pompey (C. Pompeius Magnus, here called simply *Magnus*), a place which Ovid recommends for picking up girls (*Ars am.* 1. 67, 3.387). This porticus was attached to the Theatre of Pompey in the Campus Martius and dedicated in 55 B.C., which provides a convenient *terminus post quem* for this poem. There is also possibly a hint of satire in the manner in which the poet calls Pompey simply *Magnus* (cf. Cicero *Att.* 2.19. 4), placing him above 'Highest Jove'.

7   **tarts**: *femella* is the unusual diminutive of *femina*.

8   *tamen* is used because the poet implies that they would look guilty if they were hiding
     Camerius.
9–12 The ms reading *auelte* is surely corrupt. The simplest emendation is Schwabe's *auens te*
     ('desiring you') but this leaves the direct speech of line 10 without introduction. Camps
     suggests *cette huc* (the imperative from *cedo* with the meaning 'hand over'), a highly
     unusual word which would have been 'corrected' by a scribe which makes much better
     sense and provides a verb for the accusative *Camerium* in the next line. The joke here is
     that the girl answers the poet's question by opening her dress and showing her breasts:
     Copley's suggestion that there is pun on the name Camerius (so that e.g. in Greek it
     meant 'brassiere') is attractive but has no evidence to support it. One can always read
     the lines as ribald humour from the earthy girls teasing the poet with their exhibitionism
     and inviting him to appreciate their charms. He calls them *pessimae puellae* in line 10
     and so they live up to their reputation.
10   **worst of girls**: *pessimae puellae* is nicely alliterative, and *pessimae* is 'mock-indignant'
     (Quinn).
11   The ms reads *quaedam inquit nudum reduc*, leaving three syllables (and sense) to be
     filled in. *nudum reclude pectus* ('unclothe my bare breast') of Friedrich is the smallest
     emendation needed to restore sense and metre but rather steals the thunder of the next
     line. Better sense is restored if we invert the first two words and begin with an
     appropriate *en* ('look!') which would have been omitted by haplography from the
     following line, altering *nudum reduc* to *sinum reducens*: this leaves the line: *en, inquit
     quaedam, sinum reducens* ('Look, said one, opening her dress') which nicely leads onto
     the surrealistic joke of line 12.
12   **hiding**: *latet* had a metaphorical meaning 'has gone out of circulation' (Horace *Odes*
     1.8.13) but a literal meaning 'he is hiding', the former appropriate to Camerius, the
     latter appropriate to the rest of this line; the punch-line is well delivered with the final
     word *papillis*. *roseis* literally means 'rosy' but has a general meaning of 'youthful' and
     'attractive' (*OLD* s.v. 'roseus' 2c) and in this context amounts almost to a sales pitch
     from the street girl.
13   **to put up with you**: 'to carry you' is the literal meaning of *te ferre* and the line carries
     on from the previous one where the girl jokes that Camerius is being hidden in her
     breasts. The poet thus continues the line of humour: 'bearing you is now in fact ... '.
     For the topos of effort as a 'labour of Hercules' cf. Horace *Odes* 1.3.36 Plautus *Persa* 1–
     2, Cicero *Acad.* 2.108; Hercules was the hero of the Stoics and his exploits were well
     satirised by Lucretius (5.22–42). Of his twelve canonical labours, at least three
     involved the carrying off of monsters.
14   **friend ... pride**: a deliberate paradoxical statement: the oxymoron of *fastu* and *amice*
     is split by *negas* giving the additional sense 'you deny your friendship with your pride',
     since real friends do not behave like this.
15–16   **tell ... utter ... share ... publish:** a sequence of four imperatives (with
     enjambement) in two lines, with hard consonants expressive of the poet's stern manner.
     crede luci is of course a reference back to the opening sentence in which the poet asked
     for Camerius' *tenebrae*.
17   **milky-white**: the term *lacteolae* means 'milky', suggesting both their milk-white
     complexion (as in the term *candidus* at e.g. 86.1) and also their full breasts (cf. 64. 65
     lactentis papillas). These girls are presumably the *pessimae puellae* of lines 7–12 and
     their hold on Camerius is well brought out by the verb *tenent*, which in turn looks
     forward to *tenes* in the following line, a repetition which Fordyce wrongly calls
     'accidental'.

18   **tongue ... mouth**: an expressive remark, as the girls' hold on Camerius causes him to hold his tongue, and the 'oral' emphasis in this line shows up the 'fruit' metaphor in the next line in greater light; 'if you keep your mouth closed then you will fail to enjoy the 'fruit' of love'.

20   **Venus**: A gnomic utterance: for the phrase cf. Lucretius 1.39 where Venus is urged *suauis ex ore loquellas/funde*. Note here the repetition of *u*, continued in the following line.

21   **fasten** up: a nice metaphor, appropriate to the poem. If Camerius insists on keeping himself locked away (even if he is not hiding (*latet*) in the girl's breasts), he can continue to 'lock' his *palatum* so long as the poet shares his love.

22   **partaker in your love**: the phrase is vague. Does the poet mean that he wishes to be Camerius' lover and thus 'share' him with the girls (Kroll)? Or in a weaker sense simply that he does not mind Camerius being in love but still wishes to enjoy his close friendship? Or (weaker still) that he wishes to share the knowledge of Camerius' activities?   The previous emphasis on *loquella* supports the last of the three interpretations, but the accent on pleasure throughout this poem suggests more strongly that the poet's real motive for finding Camerius was not mere friendship but jealousy and a desire to share in it.

56

A short poem in two sections: four lines of preface rounded off with the closural repetition of *rem ridiculam ... et iocosam* as *res ... ridicula et ... iocosa*: followed by three lines of anecdote.   The stress in on humour throughout the first four lines: note the repetition of *ridiculam ... iocosam ... cachinno/ ride ... ridicula ...iocosa*. Quinn compares Archilochus fragment 153 LB ('Charilaos, I will tell you a funny thing and you will be glad to hear it ... '). The anecdote itself concerns the 'little boy' of 'the girl' and presents an amusing cartoon-like picture of sexual behaviour, with the youth being sodomised by the poet from behind while he masturbates in front. The identity of the boy (and the girl) are not important.

Metre: hendecasyllabics

1   **Cato** was either the poet Valerius Cato or else the stern moralist M. Porcius Cato Uticensis: the first of these seems more likely in view of line 3 – though there might be a point in dedicating this obscene poem to the stern moralist.

1–3   Four words for laughter and joking (*ridiculam, iocosam, cachinno, ride*) establish the primary response expected of the anecdote, with *ride* picking up *ridiculam* and so ending the sequence with a closural repetition.

3   **laugh as much**: *quidquid amas* is a variant on *si me amas* and suggests that the extent of Cato's laughing will reflect the amount of love he bears the poet. The poet juxtaposes the two names (*Cato, Catullum*) effectively and alliteratively, reinforcing the unanimity of the writer and his addressee through the similarity and closeness of their names.

4   A recapitulation of line 1 to enclose this first section of the poem, with the reinforcing term *nimis* ('too much').

5–6   **the girl's**: *puellae* is taken here to be genitive with*pupulum. pupulus* is the diminutive of *pupus* and means 'little boy' and the poet is clearly stressing his youth and innocence, especially when juxtaposed with *puellae*.

6   **wanking**: *trusantem* is often taken to mean 'screwing' (so *OLD* s.v.) as a version of *trudo* ('push, shove') but can also mean masturbation, as is clear from Martial 11.46.3 (Adams 146 n.1). In this context we have to look for what would be more amusing to the addressee, and more in keeping with the description of the boy as *pupulum*, at an age where masturbation would be more appropriate than sex with another person. The

participle *trusantem* is clearly being stressed here with its position at the beginning of the line and the end of its sense-block.

Dione is the mother of Venus, her name being the feminine of Zeus (the Greek equivalent of Jupiter). She had a cult at Dodona and was sometimes seen as the consort of Zeus (Homer *Il.* 5.370): the phrase *si placet Dionae* here means 'if Dione will allow my boasting', as Quinn glosses it.

7   **banged**: *caedo* ('beat, strike') refers to anal assault by the poet (Adams 145–6) both as a means of taking a sexual opportunity and (more importantly) as form of humiliation of the boy (for this cf. 16.1). Latin texts did not divide words, and so *protelo* could be read as *pro telo* ('as a weapon') or as one word ('one behind the other'): a nice case where *rigida mea* suggests that first interpretation, but the general picture certainly supports the second.

57

A scathing attack on Julius Caesar and his favourite Mamurra, whose 'twin' natures are brought out repeatedly in the poem (*pares utrisque ... altera et illa ... pariter gemelli utrique ... ambo ... non hic quam ille ... riuales socii*). The poem is neatly enclosed by the repetition of the first line at the end, as in 52. The imprecise reference to their 'stains' in lines 3–5 has been taken (by e.g. Lee) to refer to their bankruptcy but the poem is otherwise totally taken up with the sexual misbehaviour of the pair and financial problems would be a distraction. Suetonius, in his life of Julius Caesar, records the defamation of the great man by Catullus:

'Valerius Catullus had also libelled him in his verses about Mamurra, yet Caesar, while admitting that these were a permanent blot on his name, accepted Catullus' apology and invited him to dinner that same afternoon, and never interrupted his friendship with Catullus' father.' (*Iul.* 73, translated Graves)

Metre: hendecasyllabics

1   **good pair**: *pulcre* is colloquial for 'nicely', as in 23.5, 8. *cinaedis* means literally 'passive homosexuals' and thus 'perverts'. For the meaning of the term and the connection of *cinaedus* and *pathicus* cf. 16.2.

2   **Mamurra** has already been satirised in poem 29. Note here how the names begin and end the line, with the descriptive term *pathicoque* inbetween them; the 'misplaced' *que* at the end of *pathico* (= *Mamurraeque pathicoque Caesari*) has the effect of applying the term to both names.

3   **black marks**: *maculae* means simply 'stains' and the point of the sentence seems to be that both Caesar and Mamurra have indelible blots on them arising from their places of origin: this unspecific charge allows the poet to draw attention to the respective origins of the two of them.

4   The line is framed by the two respective terms for the origins (*urbana ... Formiana*). For Formiae cf. 41.4, 43.5.

5   The metaphor of the stains is continued with powerful verbs. *imprimo* indicates the 'stamping' of a seal or the imprinting of a mark, while *eluentur* means to be 'washed out'. Again, the line is made up of three verbal forms, *impressae resident* reinforcing each other.

6   **diseased**: *morbosus* is from *morbus* and means 'diseased': it can have the sense of 'crazy about' (as in Petronius *Sat.* 46.3) but here (as in *Priapea* 46.2) means 'lustful' with the obvious implication that this lust is somehow 'sick'. The rest of the line is entirely taken up with words stressing the equality of their sickness.

7   **couch**: *lecticulus* means both a 'study couch' or a bed: the former is appropriate for *erudituli*, the latter suits the tone of the poem as a whole. Caesar was famed for his

literary works on his campaigns in Gaul and also on the Civil War, and was besides an expert on grammar: Mamurra had literary pretensions, as exposed in poem 105, and may even have been – or been related to – the writer on Architecture Vitruvius (as argued by Rawson 86 n.14). This line is notable for the pair of unusual diminutives juxtaposed, giving the caricature image of two 'small scholars' in a 'small bed'.

8   **greedy**: *uorax* indicates their greed: *adulter* would seem to refer only to heterosexual liaisons, a move away from the homosexuality asserted in lines 1–2 towards the 'nymphets' of line 9. Caesar's appetite for adultery was famous: not for nothing was he nicknamed the 'bald adulterer' in the soldiers' song. Suetonius *Iul.* 50–2 gives a catalogue of his indiscretions both at home and in the provinces, as well as recording the view that Caesar was bisexual ('every woman's man and every man's woman'). No independent evidence exists to substantiate the poet's condemnation of Mamurra (but cf. poem 29.7).

9   **rival mates**: *riuales socii* is something of a paradox, with *riuales* suggesting competition and *socii* suggesting co-operation. *puella* means 'girl' and so the diminutive *puellula* must mean 'little girl' implying that these great men are chasing (comparative) children rather than grown women: Caesar is said to have enjoyed the daughters as well as the wives and mothers of the famous, including Servilia, mother of Brutus, whose daughter Tertia had been 'prostituted to Caesar' (Suetonius *Iul.* 50). *puellula* is used in poem 61, but only to mean the bride – i.e. a young girl old enough to be married but no older.

10   The poem ends with a repetition of the first line, a simple closural device.

58

A short poem of lament about the behaviour of Lesbia. If the identification of Lesbia as the Clodia of Cicero's *Cael.* is accepted, then Caelius' rebuke of her as *quadrantaria Clytemnestra* ('halfpenny Clytemnestra' Caelius *orat.* 23) becomes relevant here. The poem consists of a single long sentence with its main verb the expressive *glubit* in the final line, and yet the text divides up into two time-scales of past and then present. The poet elevates his past beloved by repeating her 'literary' name, just as he ironically elevates her new lovers with the heroic title 'descendants of great-hearted Remus': he names himself in the third person, juxtaposing his name with the significant word *unam* ('her alone'): this *unam* at the end of line 2 contrasts then with *omnes* at the end of the following line, picking up the extravagant *se atque suos*. The past nature of all this is clear from the tense of *amauit* late in line 3: then in line 4 *nunc* alerts us to the present state of affairs where this woman now *glubit* unspecified numbers of Romans in public places.

Metre: hendecasyllabics

1   **Caelius** is usually identified with Marcus Caelius Rufus, the man defended by Cicero in the *Cael.*, but the identity of the addressee (however interesting) is not certain, and indeed he is only mentioned once at the beginning of the poem.

1–2 The poet repeats the name Lesbia three times to highlight the importance which he claims to have attached to her. Note the chiastic arrangement of *Lesbia illa illa Lesbia*.

2–3 For the form of expression cf. 8.5. In poem 72.3–4 he claims to love his girl 'as a father loves his sons and sons-in-law', recalling *suos omnes* here.

4   **crossroads and back alleys**: the setting is important: her sexual misbaheviour is made all the worse for being done in public, and in the streets and back-alleys at that.

5   **grandsons ... Remus**: the mock-epic phrase *magnanimi Remi nepotes* is to expose the degradation to which Lesbia has sunk: men who pride themselves on their pedigree are hardly behaving 'nobly' now (*nunc*). The more normal bathetic technique would be to

put the high-sounding phrase first and then bring it down to vulgar earth with the verb: the poet here gives the verb the initial position to follow on after *quadriuiis et angiportis*.

peels: *glubit* literally means 'peel the bark off, skin' and suggests the 'act of retracting the foreskin by intercourse or masturbation' (Adams 74, 168). The other suggested meaning is 'fleeces' (i.e. takes their money from them) which has considerably less force.

58b

A fragment, possibly belonging to poem 55 (as printed by Goold) or at least a later addition to the theme of that poem, as poem 7 picks up poem 5. The first four lines dart from one swift mythological reference to another, before moving into generalities and natural forces. Even with ease of movement such as all this, the poet says, he would still exhaust himself looking for Camerius. Once again (as in 55) there is an inconsistency in this poem being addressed to an absent person to whom it could hardly be delivered. This is a poem of learning and literary skill: note here the compound adjectives (*pinnipes, plumipedas*), the poetic language (*niueae, bigae*), the allusions to mythology and history, the elegant variation of metaphors for speed (flying, running) and the elaborate description of fatigue (lines 8–9); the peremptory imperatives (*adde ... require*) followed by the variation of the subjunctive *dicares*. Note also the way the poet links swift men/heroes in lines 1–2, swift horses in lines 3–4, swift natural phenomena in lines 5–6 (assuming that Muretus' transposition of lines 2 and 3 is accepted). The *doctrina* of the form creates a mood of artificiality in the poem, assisted by words such as *fingar* (suggesting artistic fashioning of a statue): the hyperbole of the catalogue of swift things and the mythological remoteness of many of them help to convey a mood of unreality which leaves the text as an eloquent expression of literary art and affection but one which is not to be taken at face value, any more than its companion piece 55 was.

Metre: hendecasyllabics

1 **guard of the Cretans**: King Minos of Crete had a giant guard Talos made out of bronze for him by Hephaestus, who ran round the island three times a day and repelled strangers.

2 **Ladas** was a Spartan athlete who won a race at Olympia and died at the finish of the race. His name became a byword for speed in running (Juvenal 13.97). **Perseus** was the hero who was given winged sandals with which he flew to fight the Gorgons. When he beheaded the Gorgon Medusa the winged horse Pegasus arose out of her blood.

3 **Pegasus** was the flying horse ridden by Bellerophon.

4 **Rhesus** was the king of Thrace was the owner of speedy white horses ('whiter than snow, equal to the winds in speed of running' Homer *Il*. 10.437).

5 The long adjectives are here used as substantives.

7 Note the assonance of *Cameri mihi dicares* with the *a – e – i–i–i–i– a– e* symmetry. *iunctos* suggests a harnessing of horses in a team.

8–9 **tired out ... exhaustions**: the poet's fatigue is well e: pressed. Roman poetry often locates fear and cold (e.g. Lucretius 1.355) in the marrow of the bones: love is also felt there in poem 45.16, as it is in 35.15. Here fatigue is spread throughout the bones, as in Plautus *Stich.* 340 In the next line *peresus* literally means 'eaten up', 'consumed' and is an unlikely metaphor with a plurality of *languoribus* (meaning 'many occasions of exhaustion'). The metaphor of 'eating' is more commonly used of love, as in 66.23 ('how deep did emotion eat out the sad marrow of your bones') or the case of Virgil's Dido, for whom *est mollis flamma medullas* ('a soft flame eats the marrow of her bones' *Aen.* 4.66). The poet's use of 'love' metaphors in describing fatigue thus neatly elides the two concepts together into a single idea, whereby the poet shows his love by his tireless searches for his friend.

10 **looking**: the final word is a long-sounding *quaeritando* expressive of the long searching. The addressee, named in line 7, is here simply addressed as 'my friend', which explains the content of the whole poem as an expression of affection.

59

Rufa sucks off Rufulus, steals food from graveyards and pays for it by being banged by the cremator. The poem is mock outrage at Rufa's scandalous behaviour: for similar misogynistic tirades against the female sex misbehaving in graveyards cf. the Widow of Ephesus story in Petronius *Sat.* 111–2. The poem appears to be a rough piece of obscene graffito, but contains artistry of language (note the expressive alliteration of *Rufa Rufulum, saepe ... sepulcretis, rapere ... rogo, prosequens panem*) and a choice of vocabulary which paints a highly realistic picture as the audience is said (*uidistis*) to share the sight of Rufa: her chasing the rolling loaf reminds us of the rolling apple of 65.19–22, her *cena* is in fact a piece of bread (*panem*); the last line either means that her behaviour is too much even for the criminal slave who works there, or else that she numbers him among her sexual partners, giving a neat closure of sex to begin and end the short poem.

Metre: Scazons

1 The opening line reads like a piece of graffito, as Quinn points out (citing some good examples of the genre): a mood of rough abuse is set up which the poet will develop into something more elegant and devastating as the text proceeds. The line is almost all taken up with names until the decisive verb at the end sets the tone for the poem. The two names sound related (Rufulus and his Rufa) and possibly incestuous (Syndikus 286): Bononiensis places Rufa in what is now Bologna.

2 There is further criticism of Rufa (and Menenius: cf. poem 17) in her marital status. *saepe ... uidistis* adds to the assault: her behaviour is not isolated occurences but frequent and not ashamed of being seen either.

3 At funerals Romans used to burn food and drink (along with clothes, arms, ornaments etc) with the corpse, the idea being that the dead person would be able to use them in the underworld: Rufa's theft is thus also sacrilege and unfair to the helpless dead; the poet's indignation is brought out by *ipso* ('the very funeral pyre itself'), the alliterative *rapere.. rogo* and the inflated term *cenam* for what would be only a handful of food. The plural verb *uidistis* implies a large audience.

4 A neat picture of the loaf rolling and being chased by Rufa: *persequens* appropriately follows *deuolutum*

5 **cremator**: the *ustor* was the slave of the undertaker whose job was to burn corpses. By the first century B.C. cremation was more common in Rome than inhumation (cf. Cicero *Leg.* 2.57, Pliny the Elder *HN* 7.187, *OCD* s.v. 'dead, disposal of') and the ashes would then be buried in tombs. *semirasus* indicates a head half-shaven which may indicate that he was a runaway slave (cf. Apuleius *Met.* 9.12), adding to Rufa's degradation. The meaning of *tundo* is uncertain: its basic meaning 'hit' certainly makes sense as the undertaker strove to ward off this thief, but it may also mean 'have sex with' (Adams 148) and thus end the poem with sexual disgrace as it began.

60

A protest at the hardness of heart of the addressee, drawing on the rhetoric of complaint beginning with Patroclus railing at Achilles ('it was the grey sea that bore you, and the high rocks' Homer *Il.* 16.33–5) and continuing with Jason attacking Medea after her murder of their children (Euripides *Med.* 1341–3): Catullus uses very similar language in Ariadne's lament (64. 155–8), as does Virgil when his Dido rails at Aeneas (*Aen.* 4. 365–7). This poem is a single indignant question with internal consistency as the addressee's parentage is seen as bestial in view of the 'savage heart' displayed. Graphic detail is sketched in briefly, with the lion on Libyan mountains and the mythological Scylla barking below her waist. The final two words of the poem enclose the whole, *fero* recalling the beasts of lines 1–2, *corde* recalling the *mente* of line 3. The 'crime' is hardly fitting to the charges brought here: 'despising the voice of a suppliant' evokes a remoter world of Greek culture and hardly merits these monstrous accusations. Commentators usually take this poem as a *cri de coeur* from the poet to Lesbia (e.g. Wiseman 1985, 156–7) but the allusive language of the text and the unspecified nature of the *nouissimo casu* shift attention away from the poet to his poem and the manner in which he has adapted a literary topos to his own poetic purposes.

Metre: scazons

1   **lioness:** for the image of being raised by a lioness cf. Theocritus 3.15–16 ('it was a lion's teat that he (Love) sucked'), 23.19 ('Cruel and pitiless boy, nursling of the savage lioness'), both of which link the lion's savagery with love. The lion imagined here is pictured in the mountains, as often in Homer the lion is 'mountain-bred' (e.g. *Il.* 12.299) *Libystinis* is a variant of *Libycus*: for the location cf. Septimius' wish to meet a lion in Libya (45.6)

2   **Scylla** was loved by Poseidon and turned by her rival Amphitrite into a sea-monster who devoured sailors who sailed near her cave. In Homer (*Od.* 12. 85–100) she has six heads and barks like a dog: in Roman literature she is depicted as a woman with dogs barking around her waist (Lucretius 5.892–3, Virgil *Ecl.* 6.75 etc.). 'Barking' is obvious enough: but doing so 'from the lowest part of her groin' is an odd phrase and suggests the canine shamelessness which is also found in 42.17 and which finds sexual expression in (e.g.) Helen's self-accusation at Homer *Il.* 3.180; cf. also Achilles' insult to Agamemnon as 'dog-eyed' (*Il.* 1.225). Wiseman (1985, 157) well comments: 'The emphasis on Scylla's barking groin is not a commonplace, however: after Poems 58 and 59, and in the metre of invective, it reminds us of sex and shamelessness'.

3   **hard:** *durus* is what the poet wants himself to be in poem 8: *taeter* is an unusual word to use of a mind, meaning 'repellent to the senses' and only then 'morally offensive' – but then it is an odd expression to talk of giving birth 'with a hard and bitter mind'. The poet is clearly eliding his feelings about the attitude of the addressee (which is 'hard and bitter') with the image of that person being raised by a harsh parent.

4   **suppliant:** supplication was a important notion in Greek culture – so much so that a person who was ritually supplicated (with hands clasping knees, chin etc) would feel morally obliged to assist the suppliant, or else face the wrath of 'Zeus Hikesios'. The poet loads the point here with the phrase *in nouissimo casu* which literally only means 'in his latest mischance' but which also carries the hyperbolic sense 'in his greatest need'.

5   **savage:** *fero* is ironic after the opening of the poem: if indeed the addressee was produced by a beast, then it is not surprising that the person's heart is *fero*.

69

A mock epistle to a certain Rufus – who appears again in poems 71 and 77. For all his attempts to buy sexual favours from them, women flee the embraces of this Rufus because of the hideous smell of his armpits.

Scholars have speculated that this Caelius is Caelius Rufus and concluded that the invective is well-aimed: Caelius was 'known to have been a ladies' man' (Goold) and so will have been sensitive to such abuse as Catullus here composes. For a similar abusive poem calling attention to the smell of a successful lover see poem 97.

The goat was proverbially malodorous but also proverbially lustful: Horace (*Odes* 1.17.7) sees 'the goat as the husband of the flock, cf. Theocritus 8.49 'O goat, husband of the white sheep', Virgil *Ecl.* 7.7, *G.* 3. 125 but also Horace *Epod.* 10.23 *libidonosus caper* cf. *Odes* 3.13.3–5.

Metre: Elegiacs

1–2 **Rufus:** The poem begins with a direct address to Rufus. Note the symmetry of the line beginning with *noli* and ending with *nulla* and the ironic juxtaposition of *tibi femina* – ironic as that verbal closeness is (apparently) not matched by sexual closeness in real life.

2. **flank:** for *femur* in a sexual context cf. Tibullus 1.8.26 (*femori conseruisse femur*), Ovid *Am.* 3. 7.10, 3.14.22. The thigh is a 'sexually significant part, in that the space between (the thighs) was the site of the sexual organs' (Adams 51). The reason for using it here is perhaps for the jingle that no *femina* will give you her *femur*. The verb *supposuisse* is interesting: one of its meanings is 'to put at the mercy of, expose to' (*OLD* s.v. 4b), which is perfect alongside the vulnerability implied in *tenerum*. For *tener* used of sexually desirable parts of the body cf. 61.100 (breasts), Virgil *Ecl.* 10.49 (feet), Horace *Sat.* 1.2.81 (thigh). The word is associated with love poetry in general at 35.1, Horace *Ars P.* 246, Ovid *Am.* 2.1.4, *Tr.* 2.361.

3 **shake her resolve:** *labefactare* literally means 'to make unsteady, undermine' and thus serves a double purpose here. Metaphorically it means to 'cause to waver' or 'induce' and is used as such by Cicero (e.g. *Phil.* 4.13); *OLD* lists the present passage under this metaphorical heading (2c). The literal meaning is however not far away, as Rufus seeks to make the women fall on their backs with his gifts.

rarae uestis is again a choice use of words. *rarus* suggests clothing which is expensive and difficult to obtain (*OLD* s.v. 6, listing this passage) but it also means 'of loose texture' found in (e.g.) nets (Virgil *Aen.* 4. 131, Horace *Epod.* 2.33) and basket-work (Ovid *Met.* 12.437) and thus implies the fashionable erotic transparency of *Coae uestes* (see Horace *Sat.* 1.2.101–2, Lucretius 4. 1130 with my note *ad loc,* Griffin 1976, 92) which would make the perfect erotic gift.

4 **gleaming:** *perluciduli* is a word which only appears here in Latin, though the simple form *perlucidus* is relatively common. The line is skilful, being made up of only four words. What sort of stone does Catullus have in mind? 'Transparent, translucent' suggests precious stones as jewels, such as were worn especially as ear-rings. Seneca famously remarked that Roman women carried their dowries on their bodies (*Ben.* 7.9.4). Horace *Odes* 4.13.13–14 has both Coan clothes and precious stones as the equipment of the old woman seeking to attract young men. What both the clothes and the stones share here is the transparency which (in different ways) makes the wearer attractive. For *deliciae* cf. 2.1, 3.4.

5–6 The couplet leads up to the climax of the shocking dissyllable *caper* at the end of 6. Line 5 is drawn out: the 'tale' is given an indefiniteness (*quaedam*) and malice, but the poet distances himself from it by the word *fertur* (it is said).

laedit is well–chosen. Besides the basic meaning ('hurt') it carries the senses 'disfigure' (good for one whose appearance is not working for him) and also 'to wrong in love'.

ualle sub alarum literally means 'under the valley of your arms', the word *uallis* 'chosen for its appropriateness to *habitare*, rather than as the accepted anatomical term'

(Quinn) and the word *ala* having a military connotation; the couplet produces bathos as the high-sounding phrase *ualle sub alarum* is followed by the grotesque caricature of the goat living in the armpit.

7   **this**: *hunc* presumably means the goat, with *metuunt* more appropriate for a wild animal (*bestia*) than a smell. *mirum* picks up *admirari* in line 1, *mala* picks up the *mala fabula* of line 5.

8   **beast**: *bestia* is a strong word, used especially of the beasts in the arena (*OLD* s.v. 2) and placed here for greatest emphasis at the beginning of the line, creating a striking effect in the picture of the pretty girl sleeping with a wild beast. For *cubo* as a euphemism for sex see 78.4, Adams 177.

9   **so ... noses**: A grandiloquent line for a mundane problem. *nasorum* means 'noses' and refers to all the noses of all the women whom Rufus has sollicited. For *pestis* used of persons cf. Cicero *Sest.* 33 of Clodius *illa peste patriae*. *crudelem ... pestem* is a term of epic proportions used at 64. 76 and used ironically here as the evil odour is presented as a monster to be slain (*interfice*) by the addressee.

10   **stop being surprised**: *admirari desine* clearly echoes *noli admirari* in line 1 and produces pleasing closure in the poem.

<h1 style="text-align:center">70</h1>

A short poem which at face value builds up optimism in the first half only to cast heavy doubts on it in the second: in fact there is a dark mood of doubt throughout the text. The opening line is ambiguous, leaving the reader uncertain whether the girl would prefer to stay celibate than marry the speaker or else want him above all others; the mention of Jupiter is also foreboding in view of that god's record of conquest and desertion of a multitude of lovers. When the poet concludes that this sort of language is not to be taken seriously there is literary resonance in the conclusion; the language of love is ambiguous and fluid (like the running water), and there is no such thing as an innocent assertion of love, especially an assertion of the 'poetic' sort which this poem contains. The poet composes a poem in which his lover's words elude his confident interpretation of their sincerity (or even their meaning); this may stand as synecdochic for the opacity of all such poetic texts, whereby the apparently simple emotion being expressed is in fact ambiguous and disquieting, leaving no certain comfort for the poet or for the reader.

Metre: Elegiacs

1   **nobody**: The poem begins with an emphatic *nulli*. *mulier* looks forward to a repetition in line 3, where the poet contrasts his own woman (*mulier mea*) with the general run of women. There is also a jingle of *mulier ... malle*. For the repeated *dicit* Quinn compares Callimachus Epigram 27, a poem of more than passing resemblance to this one:

> Kallignotus swore to Ionis that he would never have a greater
> beloved, male or female, than her.
> He swore so: but they say truly that the oaths
> of lovers do not enter the ears of the gods.
> He is now ablaze with a male flame, and of poor Ionis
> there is, as of the Megarians, not a count or a reckoning.'

Catullus follows Callimachus closely, inserting a more readily understood proverb for the Greek reference to the Megarians, but places his poem in the present tense unlike the past tense of Callimachus.

2   **Jupiter**: for Jupiter's readiness to mate with mortal women see (e.g.) the tales of Alcmene and Semele and *Il.* 14. 313–28 for his own roster of his exploits. Marriage

was not part of the deal, of course, but Catullus uses the topos of Jupiter here (as at 72.2, Ovid *Met.* 7.801, *Her.* 4.36) to indicate the extent of the woman's love.

3–4   An echo of Sophocles Fragment 741N 'I write the oath of a woman onto water' and also Plato *Phdr.* 276c. The choice of adjectives is eloquent: *cupidus* well describes the ardent state found in e.g. 64.86, 374; 107, while *rapidus* expresses *rapio* as well as 'rapid' and has the sense of 'tearing away' as of a hurricane or a river in flood. It is the 'removing' qualities of the water which are apt here rather than simply the speed of the current.

Both the wind and the water take promises away and leave nothing behind: for this image of futility cf. 30.9–10, 64. 142; they derive from Homer *Il.* 4.363, *Od.* 8.408–9 and are imitated at e.g. Virgil *Aen.* 9. 312–3, Propertius 2.28.8, Ovid *Am.* 2.16.45, Horace *Odes* 1.26.2–3 (where see Nisbet and Hubbard *ad loc* for further parallels). What is surprising is the sex of the speaker; we expect the amorous male to make empty promises to his girl – as Theseus did to Ariadne (64. 139–148) whereas here we have the girl promising rashly to the male. As often in Catullus we have gender reversal here as the female plays the lead to his submissive nature.

71

The malodorous armpits of 69 reappear, ascribed to the addressee's 'rival'. The poem builds up to an effective climax in the final couplet: the first couplet sets up the twin sicknesses afflicting an unspecified *sicui ... siquem*, the second couplet concentrates on the wrongs done by the rival, leading to the third couplet which puts these together in scathing summary form. Line 5 is paradoxical: if this rival is enjoying sexual favours, he is also punishing them both, a paradox which creates suspense which the last line releases in a fine caricature of sexual discomfort.

Metre: Elegiacs

1   **rightly**: *iure bono* means 'with good reason' (*OLD* s.v 'ius' 7b) and stands here for the unmetrical *iure optimo*. *merito* in the next line is similar in meaning. *sacer* usually means 'holy' or 'divine' but has the sense here and elsewhere of 'dreadful' or 'fearful' (*OLD* s.v. 2c). For the evil-smelling goat see notes to poem 69. In this line note the juxtaposition of *iure bono sacer* setting up a positive and even 'holy' atmosphere only to block it with the armpit-goat.

2   **gout**: *podagra* is rheumatic foot-disorder, usually translated as 'gout'. *tarda* is apt here; any disease of the feet will cause the sufferer to be slow. *seco* usually means to 'cut' but here means to 'inflict severe pain upon' (*OLD* s.v. 4c). It can also mean to 'castrate' (*OLD* s.v. 3c) and so is apt here in the case of a man whose illness reduces his potency.

3   **rival...yours**: the identity of the rival – as of the addressee – is unknown. For *amorem exercere* cf. 68.69; the sense here is plainly sexual rather than Quinn's bland 'busies himself with your affair' – cf. Plautus *Amph.* 288, *Bacch.* 429, Lucretius 4. 1128 (*exercita*).

4   **wonderfully**: for *mirifice* cf. Arrius in poem 84.3. The ms reading *a te* is wrong – as neither affliction is infectious. Goold conjectures *Quinti* on the evidence of the Quintius who appears in 82 and 100, but Kaster's *apte* makes better sense and also better palaeographical sense (*apte* became *abte* which was then read as *a te* as argued by Nisbet ((1995) 97). *nactus utrumque malum* sounds rather flat, and is clearly leading up to the striking language of line 5.

5   A surprisingly elegant line in view of its content: the correlatives *quotiens...totiens* each have a verb following, and the line splits neatly at the caesura. *ulciscor* usually

means to 'take revenge' or 'avenge' – an odd meaning where no wrong is specified for which revenge should be sought. It is perhaps chosen here because it sounds like *ulcus* (a sore or cancer (cf. Lucr. 4.1068)).

6 **pains**: *affligo* is invested with 'erotic overtones' by Quinn. *pereo* has the sense of both 'be desperately in love' (45.5) and also have sex (Adams 159): note here the effective alliteration of *p*, and the neat division into two halves, with exactly symmetrical structure (person – verb – sickness in both cases).

72

The poem exhibits neat symmetry: lines 1–4 are 'then', lines 5–8 are 'now', the imperfect tense of *dicebas* replaced by the emphatic present perfect of *cognoui*. The verbs in lines 5–8 are all in the present tense, lending an immediacy and vividness to the text. *uelle* in line 2 is picked up by *bene uelle* in line 8, *dicebas* in line 1 is recalled in *inquis* in line 7. The poem is an account of the relationship between 'Catullus' and 'Lesbia' purporting to be addressed to Lesbia in the second person and explaining to her the exact nature of his feelings with psychological subtlety, recording her own words (*dicebas ... Iouem*; *qui potis est?*) and answering them. There is no need to postulate a real setting for this text, the main thrust of which is to foil the reader's expectation with some elegant paradoxes. He draws the fine distinction in the last line between love and liking, with the paradoxical conclusion that *iniuria* can increase love but reduce liking. Given that many people would see 'liking' as a less intense form of 'loving', this conclusion is surprising. Further surprise is afforded by the comparison of the lover's feelings with those of the father towards his male children and daughers' husbands, where sexual obsession (*impensius uror*) is likened to non-sexual affection.

Metre: Elegiacs

1 **knew only**: It was traditional Roman virtue for a woman to be *uniuira*: cf. 111.1–2. *nosse* is seen by Copley as meaning to 'have sex with' in the biblical sense of 'know'. The obvious force of the word is brought out in its repetition in line 5 where *nunc* replaces *quondam* and the poet has 'got to know' Lesbia after her claims to 'know' only him ring hollow. For the sexual sense of *nosse* see Adams 190 citing 61.180, Caesar *B.G.* 6.21.5, etc. The poet names himself in order to juxtapose his name with Lesbia at the start of line 2 (union but also disunion) and also to compare himself with Jove placed in the same final position on line 2.

2–3 **embrace**: *tenere* is literally 'to hold' but here 'to possess'; cf. 64.28–9, Virgil *Eclogue* 1.31. For the hyperbolic use of Jove cf. 70.2. The poet's attitude towards ordinary sexual affection is brought out by the verbal juxtaposition of *uulgus amicam* and the choice of words: *uulgus* is pejorative (cf. Horace *Odes* 3.1.1, Livy 21.31.14) and *amica* has the strong sense of (temporary) sexual partner (cf. Horace *Sat.* 1.3.38) often contrasted with the permanency of a wife (as in Terence *Andria* 216). Line 3 is notable for the strong sequence of alliterative and monosyllabic words.

4 **sons and daughters' husbands**: the designation of 'sons and sons-in-law' has occasioned comment. Catullus presumably means that his love for Lesbia was not ephemeral and was based on ties stronger than transitory sexual attraction (such as the mob might feel for a girlfriend).

5–6 The poet explains that his sexual passion is all the greater for the infidelities of his mistress and despite his poor opinion of her character, as in 85. The poet uses the term *uilis* picking up the cheapness of *uulgus amicam* in 3: the word *impensius* might suggest 'weight' (see e.g. *pensio, penso*) and thus form a neat contrast with the girl being now 'lighter' (*leuior*).

7   **how ...?**: We expect an explanation of the paradox expressed in the previous lines and an account of C's increased passion for a worthless woman, especially in view of the second-person verb *inquis*; instead we get a restatement of the paradox in less passionate terms, with the vocabulary of sexual frenzy (*impensius uror*) replaced by the language of social intercourse: *iniuria* and then *bene uelle. iniuria* is elsewhere used of a woman's unfaithfulness cf. Propertius 2.24b.39, 4. 8.27. The term here is vital: not only does it place all the blame for the poet's feelings on Lesbia's bad behaviour, it also places the situation into the language of *amicitia* as Lyne explains: *iniuria* is 'what, in the language of aristocratic relations, will destroy *amicitia*' (Lyne, ((1980) 39–41), citing Cicero *Fam.* 1.9.20 among others)

8   The line is perfectly balanced, with the contrasting words *magis* and *minus* ending the two halves of the pentameter. The poet stresses the fact that such feelings are not a matter of choice by placing the strong verb *cogit* at the start of the line; the repetition of *amantem...amare* expresses the inevitability of the reaction, while *bene uelle* picks up *uelle* in line 2.

73

Faithless friends figure several times in these poems: cf. 30, 76, 77. Here the text shows a total loss of faith in all friendship (*omnia sunt ingrata*) as a result of the behaviour of one 'friend'. This text is another example of the poet appearing to address himself with a rebuke and an order (cf. 8.1, 76.5) and reasoning with himself: the poem thus becomes an expression of feelings which he simultaneously rejects, ideals subverted by hard practical experience, setting up a scenario of disillusion as extreme friendship (*unum atque unicum amicum*) is betrayed and generates bitterness and trouble. The contrast between the 'unique friendship' and his 'friend's' abuse of this (line 5) is what gives the text its sharp focus and its edge.

Metre: Elegiacs

1   **Stop**: The poem begins with a direct imperative addressed to the poet himself, as in poem 8. *uelle* is important; the poet is no longer even to 'want' to deserve thanks, let alone do anything to earn them. *bene mereri* is a frequent concept in Catullus and other Roman literature: the notion that good deeds deserve recognition and good deeds in return and the contrary notion that there is no point in throwing away kindness on those who do not reciprocate it is found in more depth in 76. The tired quality of the poet's frustration is here well brought out by the repeated sounds of *de–..de...qu–..qu–..bene uelle mereri*.

2   **be made**: *fieri* is important; people cannot be made *pius*. Note the string of three infinitives put together and the striking *p* alliteration of *posse putare pium*.
     pius is an important word in Roman ethical thinking, the classic discussion of which remains Austin's note on Virgil *Aen.* 4.393; it connotes dutiful devotion to others and a recognition of the responsibilities which have to be shouldered and sacrifices which have to be made (cf. 76.2).

3   The line is elegantly shaped, the opening *omnia* being answered by *nihil* after the caesura, just as *ingrata* is answered by *benigne*.

4   The ms reading (*immo etiam taedet obestque magisque magis*) is metrically corrupt. Avantius suggested supplying the verb *prodest* at the beginning and removing the *magisque*: this would complete *nihil fecisse benigne* and restore the metre, a reading adopted by Mynors in the OCT but difficult to explain on palaeographical grounds. An easier reading is furnished by inserting a second *taedet* after the first – an easy word for the scribe to omit by haplography and expressive of the poet's weariness. This also

requires a verb to be supplied after *benigne* and would necessitate reading (say) *benignest* as suggested by Friedrich.

5   **in my case**: *mihi* implies a verb such as *est* – the sentence has no main verb but two relative clauses. *urgere* has the sense of 'press hard upon' often used in military contexts.

6   **the man**: the sex of the faithless friend has occasioned comment. The ms reading *qui* is not suspect on any grounds other than that commentators would like the poem to refer to a faithless female lover rather than a male friend; alternatively, scholars postulate an identification with Caelius Rufus 'who supplanted Catullus as Clodia's lover' (Goold, with remarkable confidence). Goold suggests that the last line points to the *sancta amicitia* of 99 rather than to platonic friendship with any male, ignoring the deep friendship evinced in (e.g.) poems 9 and 11. More striking than anything else here is the degree of elision allowed in the line: *m(e) un(um) atq(ue) unic(um) amic(um) habuit* is hardly coincidental and shows the poet's use of this device at its strongest (cf. Virgil *Aen.* 6. 314 (with Austin *ad loc.*)), evincing a sense that the poet's words are rushing out and finding the constraint of the metre difficult.

74

The poem is the first of seven attacks on Gellius, the others being 80, 88–91, 116. The 'plot' is simple: to avoid censure from his uncle about his sexual misbehaviour, Gellius seduces his uncle's wife, thus making it impossible for uncle to lecture him without the disgrace in his own family coming to light. Uncle is thus reduced to silence, no matter what Gellius chooses to do.

The scenario is absurd and sets up the uncle as a figure of ridicule: first for his opinionated moral lecturing on sexual misconduct (note the all-inclusive *diceret aut faceret* and the young person's term *delicias* used ironically), secondly by being cuckolded by his own nephew, and thirdly by the suggestion of his being himself sexually abused by young Gellius. The irony is total; the inferior youth being lectured becomes the dominant sexual partner, the moralist is himself rendered immoral, the scene set up in the first line is reversed in the final cartoon-like couplet. Note also the poet's use of language to reinforce this: note the five repetitions of the word *patruus* (twice on the last line), with the complex relations in the family well brought out in the repetitions of *patrui ... uxorem.. patruum* in lines 3–4; the ironic 'quoting' of the old man's language in lines 1–2 giving way to the obscene bluntness shown by Gellius' behaviour in *perdepsuit.* The act of Gellius transforms the old man into a Harpocrates – a learned allusion in the style of the *doctus poeta* and not out of place in this parable of comic transformation of the outspoken prude into the silent pervert.

Metre: Elegiacs

1   **Gellius** opens the poem; notice how he had not actually suffered anything to prompt his behaviour, but merely 'had heard' that uncles were 'usually' censuring sexual misconduct. For Roman uncles as stern upholders of morality Quinn compares Cicero *Cael.* 25

2   **naughty**: *deliciae* is a key word in Catullus: cf. 2.4 (*passer, deliciae meae puellae*), 6.1, 45.24 (*facit delicias*), 68.26 (where see my note *ad loc.*). The word denotes the 'darling' itself (e.g. 2.4, Cicero *Att.* 1.5.8, Petronius *Satyricon* 64.5) and also the pleasure created by love, often with a touch of rebellion attached to it against the prevailing *mores* of the day; when Cicero thunders against the *libidinosa et delicata iuuentus* (*Att.* 1.19.8, cited by Fordyce on 50.3) he is using their term against them, just as here the poet is quoting the sort of language most appropriate to the older generation censuring the young for the immorality of which they made no secret; Fordyce (50.3n)

well contrasts the use of *deliciae* and *delicatus* as term of abuse in Cicero but terms of unashamed pleasure in Catullus.

3 **knocked off**: *perdepsuit* only occurs here in Latin. *depso* means 'knead' and is not in itself obscene but must have an obscene sense here and is listed by Cicero as 'more obscene' than *battuit* (Cicero *Fam.* 9.22.4) although only so by context rather than by intrinsic meaning.

4 **wife and ... uncle**: note the juxtaposition of *uxorem et patruum*. Harpocrates 'was an Egyptian sun-god represented as a boy with his finger to his mouth to command silence: cf. 102.4' (Quinn). His name only occurs here and at *CIL* 5.2796; see *OCD* s.v. 'Horus'. The point is the silence and the finger in/on the mouth as both look towards the obscene image of Gellius committing *irrumatio* on his uncle.

5–6 If the nephew actually carried out the *irrumatio* then the uncle would be in no position to utter a word anyway, which is the final image which the reader takes away from the poem.

75

A poem of harsh antithesis, like 72 and 85. The closeness of the poet and his beloved is ironically brought out in the juxtaposition of *tua mea*, while the chiastic opposites *tua culpa.../officio... suo* lay the blame firmly with Lesbia. For the paradoxical contrast between liking (*bene uelle*) and loving (*amare*) see 72.8; the sense of *amare* is clearly passionate love and desire contrasted with 'Platonic' friendship and affection: and yet the poet frequently expresses the wish that his love will be friendship as well as passion (cf. Lyne 1980,25). The first half of the poem sets up the poet's present state as one of loss, the second half leaves the poet helpless in the grip of his passion.

Metre: Elegiacs

1 **misdeeds**: *culpa* is often used of infidelity or at least secret love: cf. 68.138–9, Virgil *Aen.* 4. 19, 172. *mea* is ambiguous in the text: it could be taken either with *mens* or else in the vocative case with *Lesbia*. Syndikus argues that it should be taken with *Lesbia* but this surely ignores the sense of the whole poem which argues that Lesbia is no longer 'his'. The placing of the word brings out the poignant irony that she is now 'his' only by the accident of verbal juxtaposition – a gap which the poem bemoans. *deducta* is also bitterly ironic: the word can connote bringing a bride or a paramour home (cf. *OLD* s.v. *deduco* 10b) and it is thus wryly sardonic that the poet's *mens* is treated thus.

2 **duty**: *officium* is that sense of duty expressed in acts of kindness which induces *gratia* in the other person and also *beneuolentia* as shown (e.g.) in Cicero *Fam.* 13.60. For Catullus' use of the term cf. 68. 12, 42, 150. The implication of the opening couplet is that both the poet and Lesbia have colluded in his demise: her *culpa* is obviously blamed, but then so is his *officium*.

3–4 **become a model person**: *optima fias* is picked up by *omnia facias* in what Quinn calls 'a bitter jingle'. The main verb is *queat*, again stressing that the poet's feelings are beyond any control of his in the chain-reaction of action and emotion. The sentence is structured with neat symmetry, both lines consisting of *nec* followed by an infinitive and a *si* clause, and both lines expressing the powerless state of the poet who cannot alter his response to Lesbia even if she could alter her nature totally. *omnia facias* corresponds, as Syndikus comments, to the Greek *panourgein* (cf. Euripides *Med.* 583, Aristophanes *Ach.* 658), such that 'everything' here means 'all things good and bad' with the stress on 'bad'.

76

A key poem in the collection, and one which merits a lengthy analysis. The argument is that his love is a sickness which the poet endures and prays to be cured of. He claims to have lived a good life and requests that the gods reward him for his good behaviour with the cure he seeks. The poem is structured partly as an interior dialogue in which the poet addresses 'Catullus' (cf. 8.1, 52) and seeks to persuade himself to change his behaviour even if he cannot alter his feelings, and partly as a prayer to the gods. The poem falls into two halves: lines 1–12 describe the poet's predicament; lines 13–26 show him agonising over a solution. The text is usually read as a transparent *cri du coeur* from the poet lamenting his love and wishing to be rid of it.

More interesting conclusions emerge, however, if we examine the style of the poem and the ironic undertones within it. The poet asks to be 'cured' of love, on the grounds that his past good behaviour deserves such a cure: but the examples of his past goodness are unrelated to his behaviour in the relationship and merely demonstrate that he has treated his fellow-human beings without deceit (lines 3–4) and not abused the gods. Does this negative (*nec ... nec ... nullo*) boast qualify him for salvation? Is it any more than he should have done anyway? Later on he says that he has done and said all the good things which anybody can do (lines 7–8) and the following line implies that these good deeds and words have been bestowed on the thankless lover: but his manner of speaking in these lines is bland and vague (*quaecumque homines* is highly unspecific) and puts out a picture of the speaker as one who is struggling to find words to *justify* his feelings, although he is well able to find striking words (*e.g. excrucies* in the next line) to *describe* them.

One theme of the poem is the prayer to the gods: his moral rectitude in relation to the gods (lines 3–4) is used to plead that *they* should help *him*. He rather assumes the gods' opinion in *dis inuitis* (line 12), arguing (presumably) that if the gods favour something it tends to go well, and so (as this relationship is not going well) the gods cannot favour it, a nice example of the classical argument

> if P, then Q
> but not–Q
> therefore not–P.

Lines 17–26 are taken up with a prayer to the gods in characteristic prayer-style: reminder to the gods of what they have done in the past (the poet has already reminded them in lines 1–4 of what he has done for them), followed by the request for help. The place of the gods appears to hold the poem together, explaining the choice of examples of piety at the beginning by looking forward to the prayer at the end: but things are rarely so simple.

There is, in the first place, a slight contradiction between the helpless sickness of the poet in lines 19–26 and his self-addressed determination in lines 11–16, where the poet declares that he can (and must) 'win this battle' even if it is not possible. If he can do it by himself, then he does not need the gods: and if the gods will do it for him, then he need not strive himself. Secondly, the examples of the gods' help in the past are less than relevant here: they have brought help to the dying, but they are not credited with helping the lovesick recover their health (*ualere*). As the poet claims to be seeking health rather than an easy death, and as a quick suicide is something the poet could arrange without the help of the gods (cf. Ovid *Rem. am.* 15--19), the references to the deathbed assistance only serve to render the poem melodramatic and to remind the reader that gods do not (in fact) provide assistance to the lovesick. The prayer is futile and is more a symptom of the malaise being described than a serious attempt to cure it.

This poem, like all these poems, is a text of a performance, with the poetic *persona* being presented in character and with elements of mockery and sardonic humour in the poem. His words to himself (10–16) are (like poem 8) so much rhetoric expended in an attempt to persuade himself of what is needed: his quasi-medical account of his 'sickness' in lines 20–22 is (like 51.5–12 of which it reminds us) another means of grasping the condition and thereby controlling it: his moral posturing at the beginning uses the language of social (*fidem ... foedere*) life to bolster up the collapsed dignity of a failed lover. The final four lines reveal the situation in a nutshell: after all the rhetoric, the medical language and the pious prayers we are left with a man in love with a woman who does not love him and does not care. The language of lines 23–5 is direct and simple and states the truth behind the elaborate moral and religious posture which the first 22 lines of the poem have adopted. Then the final line goes back to the 'moral' picture of the poet praying for justice, just as the final line of poem 8 reasserts the poet's resolve after the previous five lines have seen his pretence of hardness exposed as a sham. At the end of this poem there is no religious faith or piety, no reassurance that the gods will do as they are asked, and no cosy sense that the poet somehow emerges as morally victorious. We are left with an ironic text which shows us an attempt to offset the humiliation of rejection with the posturing of moral rectitude and religious piety: the literary quality of the poem allows us to see behind the rhetoric and the religiosity to the ineluctable sadness which all these words can do nothing to assuage.

Metre: Elegiacs

1   **pleasure**: the word *uoluptas* is emphasised at the end of the line in the sardonic assertion that the only pleasure left to him is the pleasure of his recollection of his former (*priora*) goodness, while the opening word *siqua* indicates that even this pleasure may not exist. *benefacta* recalls the words *fecisse benigne* of 73.3.

2   **a man**: the poet's goodness is not gender-specific, as the gender-neutral term *homini* makes clear; *cogitat* does not imply 'thinks (mistakenly)' but rather 'considers how' or 'reflects', and the word *pius* is a highly charged term indicating both loyalty and integrity: the classic account of the word is still Austin's note on Virgil *Aen.* 4.393. In this context the general term *pius* is given specific justification in the following two lines.

3–4 the lines assert that the poet's behaviour has been honest, in accordance with the wishes of the gods, with appropriate religious vocabulary: *sanctam ... diuum... numine*. The point of the lines is however to underline that he has not broken oaths taken in the name of the gods, using the power of the gods to deceive mortals (*diuum* and *homines* neatly framing line 4 and pointing the contrast). The rhetorical (and alliterative) power of *nec ... fidem ... nec foedere* is augmented by the strong adjective *sanctam* and the sexual metaphor in *uiolasse* (*OLD* s.v. 2c). The 'overstatement' of the poet's case (Quinn) is inevitable in view of its negative nature – where he can only claim *not* to have done wrong he needs all the verbal help he can get.

5–6 **many**: the noun which agrees with *multa* is kept back until the next line to afford a pleasing juxtaposition of *gaudia amore*; love 'ought' to involve joys, but in this case the only way the two go together is in verbal juxtaposition, as is made clear by the signalling word *ingrato*. Anticipation of the word *gaudia* is built up by the pleonasm of *parata manent in longa aetate* which also in turn suggest that the joys available are already here and are all he has to look forward to for long years ahead. *multa* picks up *siqua* from line 1 and rounds off the longest sentence in the poem effectively.

7–8 This is a massive generalisation; whatever good things 'people' can do or say for 'anyone' has been done for the mistress. The words *bene dicere ... facere* are bland to the point of tepidity and are picked up neatly and chiastically in *dictaque factaque*. The tone of the sentence is thus perhaps signalling to the reader the pathetic state of the speaker, whose very command of effective language is (for the moment) letting him down.

9 **They ... mind**: This line is a single line sentence, emphatic after the lengthy sentences which preceded it. *ingratae* picks up *ingrato* from line 6. The metaphor in *credita* is one of a bad investment, as Fordyce notes. *menti* ('mind' rather than 'heart') is surprising at first: while the word can signify an organ of feeling (*OLD* s.v. 6) its more common meaning is one of rational intention and calculation, which paints the mistress as being a creature of unemotional calculation as contrasted with the emotions of the poet.

10 The mss reading *cur te iam amplius* would produce an elision of *iam amplius* which cannot be justified by arguing that *iam amplius* ought to go together. The simple transposition is enough to secure the scansion and the resultant dislocation of phrasing is appropriate in the case of a poet at such odds with his feelings, as is shown in the following line. *excrucies* is a strong term to use: cf. 85.2

11 **and ... yourself**: *atque ... teque* is 'clumsy' according to Quinn: presumably the effect which the poet seeks in wishing to depict a narrator struggling to express unruly feelings. He first uses a metaphor of hardening (*offirmas*) and then a spatial metaphor before declaring his state simply (*esse miser*) in the next line.

12 **the will of the gods**: the poet had never abused the gods (lines 3–4) and is now using their authority to justify his words. *miser* is highly expressive after the elaborate and tortuous periphrases for the poet's misfortune in the poem so far, 'love-sick' is poised at the end of the line, the sentence – and the first half of the poem – in summary of everything which has gone before. The word *miser* is used later on in line 19, as it is used of the love-sick romantic lover in Lucretius 4. 1179 and of the deserted Ariadne at 64.57, 71.

13–14 **long ... suddenly**: the juxtaposition of *longum subito* brings out the difficulty of the task, as does the repeated *difficile est*.

15–16 **this ... this ... this**: note the anaphora of *haec ... hoc ... hoc*. The poet depicts the struggle with his feelings in quasi-military terms as a battle he must win at all costs, with the effort of the struggle evoked by the long syllables of the fifth-foot spondee *peruincendum*.

17 **o gods**: after the reference to the poet's pious behaviour in lines1–4, he now directly invokes them in typical prayer formula (o gods, if ever you help people ...now do this). The prayer is couched in terms which suggest a degree of irony: the poet is not after all close to death, and the gods' assistance in easing an inevitable death is therefore irrelevant in his emotional crisis; even if his love is a sickness, then he should be praying for a recovery from it rather than a gentle demise into oblivion. The language of *extremam iam ipsa in morte tulistis opem* is also overblown and has the effect of casting the poet as the object of his own gentle self-mockery.

19 **look at ... decently**: 'the self-righteous note troubles the modern reader. Is Catullus still too close to things to have regained his sense of proportion? or does he draw too uncritically upon the clichés of tragic rhetoric?' (Quinn). This is again to miss the point; *puriter* is hardly a declaration of sexual chastity but a traditional term (see Fordyce) in sharp contrast to the uncleanness of the affliction (*pestem perniciemque* alliteratively stressed). There is thus built up a contrast between the poet's life and his present condition, exactly as was explored in the opening nine lines.

19–21 **me ... me**: note the repetition of *me ... mihi... mihi*. This plea is nothing if not egocentric.

20–22 **creeping like paralysis**: the language is that of disease, with appropriate symptoms of lethargy and depression; contrast the more physical symptoms of poem 51, which is subtly echoed here. For the language of medicine to treat a bad case of love cf. Propertius 1.1.26–7.

23 **I am not ...**: the poet runs through the various 'solutions' and dismisses the first two (which require the mistress to change) in favour of a restatement of the prayer for himself to be changed and thus cured. The first alternative (that she should love the poet) is possible and presumably reflects an earlier – or imaginary – state of affairs; he dismisses any possibility of her wishing to be chaste with *uelit* stressed at the end of the line.

26 **goodness**: the word *pietate* picks up *pium* in line 2, the theme of the poem being restated as the poet's sense of his moral worth being poorly rewarded and deserving of better.

77

A savage attack on Rufus, on whom cf. 69. The poem recalls the poem immediately preceding in its phrasing: *credite* (*credita* 76.9) *subrepsti* (76.21) and *pestis* (76.20) and it has tempted some to suggest that Rufus stole the mistress lamented in poem 76. More plausibly the ordering of these poems casts ironic doubt on both as some of the same terms are used in both for very different ends. Rufus is here called the *pestis* of the poet's relationship, whereas in the previous poem the relationship itself was a *pestis*. The poem sets up a medical theme in line 3 which is developed and exaggerated: Rufus has caused an internal fever (*intestina perurens*) because he is a 'poison' and then a 'sickness' which blights the poet's relationship, while in the previous poem the poet himself was seen as sick. The text uses neat epanaleptic links from line to line (*frustra ... frustra: eripuisti ... eripuisti: heu heu nostrae ... heu heu nostrae*) and is also notable for having eight elisions in six lines.

Metre: Elegiacs

1 **Rufus**: the poem begins with the name addressed. Note the expressive tautology of *frustra ac nequiquam.*

2 **nothing**: the word *frustra* is qualified; hardly for nothing, as it cost him dear – and trouble.

3 **burning ... insides**: the violent metaphor *intestina perurens* is notable, depicting an intestinal fever, and sets up a medical/poisoning theme which the rest of the poem will pursue in *uenenum* and then *pestis*. For the phrase cf. 108.6. The use of 'burning' as a metaphor for sexual passion is common: cf. 72.5, 64.91–3.

4 **lovesick me**: *ei misero* recalls 68. 92–3 in the context of his brother's death.

6 **life ... friendship**: the line begins with *uitae* and ends *amicitiae*, suggesting that for the poet his relationship was his life. For the use of the political term *amicitia* see 109.6. Lyne 1980, 28–9 and note how in this context the poet's false *amicus* Rufus has poisoned his *amicitia*.

78

A tale of incest, elegantly told by the poet. The structure of the poem is extremely symmetrical, with each couplet beginning with *Gallus* followed by a dissyllabic word beginning with 'h'. The excessive use of polyptoton and chiasmus (see notes) is intended to display the parallel nature of the contorted and unnatural relations between these family members; the final line (uncle shows uncle's adultery) forces the reader to think out exactly who is meant by the two 'uncles' and thus conveys well the poet's moral distaste coupled with his adept manipulation of language and obvious enjoyment of the paradox. The poem uses simple 'storybook' style to narrate this tale, whereby we suspect nothing sinister in the story of nice (*bellus* is used a lot) people in a nice family until line 4 – and even then we have to infer the incest from the simple terms *puero ... puella*. It is only at the very end of the poem that we have a pejorative word (*adulterium*); and one of the poem's notable features is thus the clash of form and content as the text conveys obscene events without itself being in the least obscene: this expresses the poet's 'moral' pose of disapproval which will not lower itself to spell out the salacious details while allowing him to enjoy the scandal.

Metre: Elegiacs

1   **very charming**: *lepidissima* is generally a term of approval (cf. 1.1) applied to women in e.g. 6.2, 10.4.

2   Note the chiasmus of *alterius lepidus filius alterius*.

4   **pretty ... pretty**: note the polyptoton of *bello bella* (picking up *bellus* from line 3) and the chiastic placing of *puero ... puella*. The term *puella* suggests that Gallus' sister-in-law is young. The short word *cubet* is bathetic after the grand periphrasis *dulces iungit amores* of the previous line.

5   **fool**: for the stupid (i.e. cuckolded) husband cf. 17.12–22; the point here is that if Gallus' nephew can cuckold one uncle he could well cuckold his other uncle, Gallus himself. Uncles generally figure in Roman literature as upholders of stern morality (74.1, Cicero *Cael.* 25)

6   **uncle ... uncle**: note the polyptoton of *patruus patrui* and the interesting overtone *monstrum* possibly lurking behind the verb *monstret*.

78b

This is clearly a fragment of a longer poem – or the misplaced ending to poem 80 (as Bergk suggested). The addressee is polluting a young girl, whose purity is stressed as much as the pollution of the addressee; the poet threatens the addressee with reprisal for his conduct: and the best punishment a poet can inflict is the notoriety which a poem can publicise and further. The young girl will be avenged by an old woman (*anus*), as the addressee' oral abuse is punished by oral repetition of his misdeeds (*loquetur*). The poet emerges as the champion of the innocent, with suitable exaggeration of his powers (*omnia saecla*).

Metre: Elegiacs

1   **innocent ... innocent**: notice the polyptoton *purae pura* next to the word *puellae* all reinforcing the purity of this girl.

2   **kisses**: the sweetness and purity of the girl is evoked by the term *suauia* for 'lips' – being sharply polluted with the phrase *comminxit spurca saliua*. The verb *comminxit* is a conjecture of Scaliger and has the right obscene force and originality. For the scathing use of a term of urination for unclean sexual contact cf. especially 67.30 ('who pissed in his own son's lap'); the idea is given additional force here by the application of urinary terms to saliva, recalling the dental hygiene of Egnatius in 39.

4   **old woman**: for the metaphorical 'old woman' (*anus*) cf. 68.46

79

Lesbius is usually taken to refer to Publius Clodius Pulcher, the radical tribune of the plebs in 59 B.C, rabid enemy of Cicero, and brother of the Clodia who is usually identified with the poet's mistress Lesbia. Her brother would naturally take the masculine form of the name.

    Clodius is often said to have had incest with at least one of his sisters (incest going right back to their childhood according to *Cael.* 36 and certainly during her marriage according to Plutarch *Cic.* 29.3; cf also Cicero *Pis.* 28, Wiseman 1985, 83, 85).

The epigram is neatly structured with repetition (*pulcer... pulcer: cum ... gente, Catulle ... cum gente Catullum*) and the style reminds us of the preceding poem. The theme of the 'family' holds the poem together, as Lesbia prefers her brother to Catullus and his family, and Catullus would wager his whole family if his assessment of Lesbius is wrong. The poet's family thus loses out both times, being rejected in line 2 and wagered in line 3: this stress on the family is of course highly appropriate in the context of the incest between Lesbius and Lesbia.

Metre: Elegiacs

1   **pretty**: the poem begins with a play on Publius Clodius' *cognomen* 'Pulcher' (beautiful), a device often used in correspondence by Cicero (*Att.* 1.16.10) who refers to his arch-enemy as *pulchellus* ('little beauty').

2.   **Catullus**: for the self-address *Catulle* cf. 8.1, 76.5. The poet jokingly asserts that as Lesbia cares so much for her own family she would reject all Catullus' family outright.

3–4 Clodius is welcome to put all of Catullus' family up for sale as slaves if he can find three acquaintances to greet him with a kiss: three standing for an insignificant number (*OLD* s.v. 'tres' b). The poet is so sure of his statement in line 4 that he is prepared to risk the freedom of all his family as a wager on it.

80

The opening couplet is in an artificially high poetic register to create bathos when the obscene truth is revealed in lines 6–8. Even here however the language is vague: *tenta* means 'tense, taut' (*OLD* s.v. 'tensus' b), and even the final word *sero* only means 'sperm' by innuendo as its primary meaning is 'whey' – this is the only case where it means 'semen'. *uorare* signifies 'devour' and is therefore obviously metaphorical. Catullus has managed to create a poem of high obscenity without ever using an obscene word to do so, his invective all the more effective for the restraint of its language.

Metre: Elegiacs
1–2 **rosy lips**: the lips are delicate in description – diminutive *labella* coloured *rosea*, a term often applied to the youthful and/or the female mouth (cf. 63.74, Virgil *Aen.* 9.5). The term *candidus* is also a term of beauty (8.3).
3–4 **the eighth hour**: the Roman day was divided up into twelve hours from sunrise to sunset, the length of the hours depending on the time of the year. The eighth hour would be two thirds of the way through the day, in mid-afternoon, as Gellius was getting up after his siesta (*quiete e molli*).
4 **long day**: *longo die* refers to summer time when the days are long, in contrast to the winter snow with which the whiteness of Gellius' lips is compared. *mollis* often denotes effeminacy.
5 **rumour**: the poet distances himself from the gossip which 'whispers' (with neat personification) the news of Gellius' activity; the line forces the reader to wait for the climactic truth in line six.
6 **middle**: *medii* is perhaps unnecessary, but puts the meaning of *tenta* beyond doubt. *uorare* is a common enough term to use for oral sex, also used for the self-fellation of 88.8 and the cunnilingus of Martial 7.67.15, and affording a pleasing alliteration here with *uiri*.
7 **that must be how it is**: the doubts of line 5 are dispelled here. We know nothing of 'Victor'. For the term *ilia rupta* some explanation is needed; the verb *rumpo* is more commonly applied to the effects of sexual intercourse on a woman, but is also used of the 'bursting' of male desire, as in 11.20, Horace *Sat.* 1.2.118, Propertius 2.16.14. Here the excessive indulgence of male lust is seen as 'bursting the loins' of the hapless (*miselli*) Victor, as Lesbia allegedly does in poem 11. After the grandiloquent description of the male groin as *grandia medii tenta uiri* the term *miselli* is perhaps ironic, and the strong verb *clamant* is perhaps hypallage – it is more probably Victor himself who is shouting rather than his ruptured loins. *emulgeo* properly means 'to milk' and so is perfect here for the sense of drawing the white fluid. *labra* reminds us of *labella* in line 1 and thus closes the poem as it began with the picture of Gellius' lips.

81

Iuventius is taunted for his latest lover: the poet sets up a mocking portrait of the man as being from a 'dying' Pisaurum with a face matching the sickness of the place. The joke is of course on the poet: this sickly man from a sickly place is still preferable to himself in the youth's eyes: and it is hard to imagine this poem being taken as a serious plea from a jealous lover with its mock-heroic language (*moribunda ab sede*) and its hyperbolic ending (*facinus facias*) which is exaggerated both in sense and in sound. The description of the man in line 4 is deliberately overdone, and suggests that the poet is seeking to use his poetry both to put Iuventius off this man and also to demonstrate his own (attractive) poetic gifts: he is also not above using rhetorical tricks such as anaphora (*qui ... quem*) to hammer home his points.

Metre: Elegiacs

1 **nobody ... so great**: the juxtaposition *nemo ... tanto* is clearly effective pleading. Note also the alliteration of *p*.

2 **nice**: for *bellus* cf. 78.3–4.

3 **Pisaurum** – an Umbrian town on the Adriatic, the modern Pesaro. A new body of settlers was sent to revive it in 43 B.C. The place is not in itself as important as the adjective *moribunda* which goes with *sede*, the phrase suggesting a sickly place to live. *iste* indicates contempt.

4 **visitor ... statue**: the man in question is a visitor to the city (*hospes*) and his complexion is pale perhaps from sexual excess (cf. Theocritus 2.88–99, Propertius 1.5.21f etc). The point of this is that the man does not need any more sexual activity: note also the poet's use of a high style of writing to express a low form of comment.

5–6 **who is now your favourite**: the poet finally gets round to the point of the poem; Iuventius prefers this stranger to *him:* note the indignation in *audes* and the patronising assumption that if Iuventius knew what he was doing he would refrain: and note especially the etymological play of *facinus facias*.

82

This neat little poem is held together by the constant repetition of *oculis* and *carius*, especially the repetition of *quid carius est oculis* at the end of lines 2 and 4. The poet will owe him whatever is 'dearer than eyes' if Quintius will not steal what is to the poet 'dearer than eyes', a technique reminiscent of the repetition of *gente* in poem 79. For the phrase 'dearer than eyes' cf. 104.2. The poet offers his eyes (or anything which is dearer than them) for the privilege of keeping what is *much* dearer than eyes: he would give up anything in the world, in other words, sooner than give up this one thing. The poem thus sounds both like a warning and also like an expression of friendship at the same time: if Quintius were minded to steal his beloved, the poet is at his mercy as he has offered him anything in the world to pay him for not stealing his best beloved. Editors all assume that the poet means his mistress by *quod carius ... oculis*, but the poet is careful not to be so specific, and the biographical 'background' may well be of more interest to scholars than it was to the poet.

Metre: Elegiacs

1 **Quintius ... Catullus:** The line is framed by the two names of poet and addressee. Note also the assonance of *i* in *si tibi uis*.

2 **eyes**: For the use of eyes as the dearest thing to a person cf. 3.5, 14.1, Aeschylus *Sept*. 530: for the amatory importance of eyes cf. 45.11, 48.1.

3 **remove:** *eripere* often means 'to steal', but also had the meaning 'remove, get rid of' in 76.20 and the two passages nicely contradict each other. Whereas in 76 the poet begged the gods to *eripite* the disease of his love, here he seems to be offering anything for Quintius *not* to *eripere* the same thing: the slippage between two closely placed poems shows the extent to which each of these texts stands alone and should not be read as fragments of an autobiography.

83

The poet deduces from Lesbia's constant talking about him, even though it is all insults, that she cares about him. The poem is interesting in many ways: there is psychological subtlety in the remark that attention – even hostile attention – indicates interest and thus that apparent dislike may in fact mask love, on the grounds that any interest is better than no interest and that love and hate are both sides of the same coin (cf. 85), the opposite of both being indifference. There is then the comic figure of the husband, being cuckolded and too stupid to see through his wife's words as the poet does: but against this there is the *persona* of the poet himself who may well be deluding himself with wishful thinking: far from it being *her* helpless love which is revealed here, it is the helpless love of the poet who cannot resist interpreting everything she says as evidence of her love for him. The text is thus ironic, as the 'mule' of a husband at least enjoys Lesbia's favours while the poet has to sit there and watch and listen as he is abused: he rails at the 'ass' of a husband in imaginary dialogue but has to admit that the man enjoys the greatest joy. A similar tone is found in Ovid *Am.* 1.4 where the poet affects superiority over the husband but is helpless and jealous of the rights which this man has over his beloved.

Metre: Elegiacs

1   **Lesbia ... me ... husband**: Quinn assumes that all three are present, Lesbia, the *uir* and the poet: this is not necessary here, as other third parties might relay Lesbia's words to the poet, but is made more likely by *obloquitur* in line 4.

2   **joy**: *laetitia* suggests that Lesbia's husband finds her criticism of Catullus reassuring and a source of joy, because he feels that the poet is a threat: or else simply that her presence and animated conversation fill him with the same joy as they fill the poet and this man has more than he deserves. The line is thus double-edged: it purports to assert the poet's superiority but in fact may assert the reverse.

3   **You donkey**: the poet pretends to be addressing the husband directly, although obviously he does not do so in reality: the poem becomes ever more the wish-fulfilment of the poet daydreaming rather than a report of 'real life'. For the common comic image of the foolish man as a mule cf. Terence *Heaut.* 877, *Ad.* 935, Plautus *Mostell.* 878.

4   **free of love**: *sana* means 'free of the sickness of love', as in Lucretius 4.1075. The word *gannit* suggests the snarling of a dog, a term appropriate for Lesbia: cf. Helen's self-image as 'nasty bitch evil-intriguing' in Homer *Il.* 3.180.

5   The line ends with a monosyllable, giving the rhythm a bumpy and forceful sound, and the key word *irata* is held over by enjambement onto the next line.

6   **that's it**: *hoc est* 'that is to say', the poet supplies his own conclusion from the evidence. The poem ends with *loquitur*, reminding us of *dicit* in line 1 and *loquitur* at the ending of line 4, all three stressing the speech as the key indicator of Lesbia's feelings: the text concludes with two simple verbs in parallel, the causal connection between them having to be inferred by the reader as it is inferred by the poet.

84

Arrius and his aitches: a brief sketch of a man who thinks he is speaking well (*mirifice*) when in fact his manner of speech is comic. The poem is neatly organised: four lines outlining the situation, two of family background to reinforce this, then three lines of calm and rest as Arrius goes to Syria before the final three lines bringing word back of his relentless aspiration. The poet uses aspiration himself to reinforce the point: he shows how Arrius misuses the sound, then alludes to this aspirate-merchant simply as (a suitably aspirated) *hoc* in line 7: all is peacefully unaspirated until the messenger comes who is himself aspirated (*horribilis*) bearing news of the final aspiration of the poem, which thus both begins and ends with a false aspirate. The poet also manages to suggest the oratorical force of Arrius in the choice of words to illustrate his habit – *commoda* and *insidias* are words one might more easily find in oratory than in conversation – as well as in the adverb *mirifice* to describe his delusion of oratorical grandeur.

The practice of aspirating words was comparatively new in Catullus' time. Earlier Romans had transliterated Greek aspirated words without the aspirate (e.g. Aciles for Achilles), but now the Greek style of aspirating was taking off both in words which needed it (Greek words such as 'theatron', for instance) and also in words which did not – so that *pulcer* becomes *pulcher*. There are good examples of people unsure whether or not to aspirate and adding an unnecessary *h* as in the grave-inscriptions to a *maritho*. Initial aspiration is also a matter of some variation – one notes the freqeuncy of both *arena* and *harena*, for example. Arrius was clearly trying to be thoroughly *à la mode* and only succeeded in sounding ridiculous.

Metre: Elegiacs

1   The poet uses epanalepsis (*chommoda … commoda*) to render the inelegance of Arrius in an elegant Latin poem The force of the imperfect tense *dicebat* is to suggest that he did this repeatedly.

2   **Arrius** is not known: he may have been the orator Q. Arrius mentioned by Cicero (*Brut.* 242).

3   **hoped**: The element of uncertainty is there in *sperabat*, and the inflated rhetoric is well evinced in the term *mirifice* (itself a word with rhetorical force) and the descriptive phrase *quantum poterat* which tells us that Arrius' speech was not an unconscious slip but deliberate policy.

5–6 All the relatives mentioned are on the mother's side of the family, *credo* adding the right note of authorial uncertainty. *liber* is surely wrong: there is no point in mentioning that uncle was 'free' and accusing the whole family of servile status is hardly assured by this partial and cryptic route. Nisbet (1995, 97–8) suggests reading *semper* which makes good sense and adds the point that the family always spoke like this.

7–8 **ears … heard**: note the juxtaposition of *aures audibant: leuiter* here means 'unaspirated'. *haec* is cleverly handled: it refers to words which Arrius would aspirate and it begins with an *h* itself, but this initial aspirate is elided and so the poet manages to recreate the dropping of aspiration which is what the sentence is describing.

9   **fear**: *metuebant* is hyperbolic, as mispronunciation is hardly something to be feared.

10   **dreadful**: the messenger is appropriately *horribilis* – a word which both means 'dreadful' and which begins with an aitch – and his arrival is like to that of the messenger in a Greek Tragedy bringing dread news..

11–12 The climax of the poem, elegantly repeating *Ionios* three times with the aspirated version to conclude the poem. The joke is again one of hyperbole: that Arrius changed the name simply by being there, and the poet manages to end the poem as it began with a false aspirate.

85

One of the most famous poems in Latin, its fame in inverse proportion to its size. The paradox of the opening three words is not explained but simply stated: what is striking at once is that the turmoil of the mental state described is conveyed in a couplet of elegant and controlled Latin verse. As in poem 83 the apparent opposition of love and hatred is here corrected by the statement that they may in fact be two sides of the same coin, the opposite of both being indifference. The words on the page seek understanding and imagine an interlocutor seeking understanding, but end up simply stating feelings without any attempt to understand. The poet is unable to explain his state and can only describe it: the poem is notable for having eight verbs or verbal forms in a short compass, all of which assert what is happening but without the explanatory adjectives which might render the situation less stark.

Metre: Elegiacs

1   **you**: the imaginary interlocutor is put there to give the poet the opportunity to state his inability to explain his opening words and to stress the need for intellectual understanding of what seems to be a contradiction. The harsh alliteration of *f* adds to the tone of dissonance.

2   **I don't know**: intellectual knowledge may be lacking (*nescio*) but the poet is all too aware of his feelings (*sentio*) – and they are torture (*excrucior*) to the extent perhaps that they blot out all possibility of rational thought.

86

Quintia is compared unfavourably with Lesbia. This poem is not primarily harsh invective against the other girl, as is poem 43, where Ameaena is held up to ridicule and the comparison with Lesbia is not explored so fully; here the other girl is praised as being attractive, but not in the same league as Lesbia. This poem thus works as praise of Lesbia more effectively than poem 43. The poem is held together by the word *formosa* which occurs in lines 1,3 and 5 and dictates the argument of the text: Quintia is called *formosa* – wrongly in the poet's view – while Lesbia really is *formosa*, with line 5 answering line 1 as closely as possible.

Metre: Elegiacs

1   **to many**: the poet distances himself from the views of the masses by placing *multis mihi* side by side; *they* think this, but *I*...
    The list of adjectives is interesting in determining what exactly counted for terms of approval of female beauty; *candida* denotes the sort of pale white skin which is not browned and beaten by the sun, and thus implies that the girl is of a class which does not have to work in the fields or the market-place, just as Lucretius mocks the 'swarthy' girl (4. 1160) and just as Catullus tells Fabullus to bring a *candida puella* in 13.4. *longa* suggests that the Romans favoured tall girls over short ones: cf. how Lucretius mocks the *paruula pumilio* ('stunted pygmy') in 4.1162, and how Ovid regards tallness as the attribute of goddesses and heroines (*Am.* 2.4.33, cf. *Met.* 3.181–2) while *recta* indicates the importance of deportment. Horace matches the Catullan list almost word for word in *Sat.* 1.2.123–4.

3–4 The contrast is strongly drawn between the size of the girl (not a point against her) and the lack of any tiny grain of *salis*. For the meaning of *sal* cf. 13.5n and also *salsus* in 12.4, 14.16, and see how its opposite *insulsa* is used at 10.33 and 17.12. Lucretius (4.1162) mocks the way little women are described euphemistically as *tota merum sal*. What Quintia lacks is *uenustas* – because Lesbia has stolen all the *ueneres* in line 6.

5–6 **and what's more**: the correlatives *cum...tum* mean virtually 'both ... and ...' here. The final word of the poem is (as often) highly charged and emphatic, intensified by the juxtaposition of *omnibus una omnes* (she alone has stolen all of the *ueneres* from everybody). The meaning of the word *ueneres* is still in dispute: does it mean 'all the embodiments of Venus' i.e. qualities which lend a woman sexual attraction? Or could it even mean that she has purloined other men's penises (for *uenus* meaning penis cf. Lucretius 4.1270, Martial 1.46.2., 3.75.6, Juvenal 11.167, Adams 57) and so end the poem on the far less complimentary note that Lesbia has stolen other women's partners? This sort of sting in the tail might well conclude the poem and cast ironic doubt on what has gone before: but one hesitates before recommending it as a valid interpretation.

87

In the mood of poem 76, a protestation by the poet that he has deserved better treatment than he has received from Lesbia. The poem consists of two couplets, each beginning with *nulla* and each ending with *mea est,* each having the correlative (*tantum ... quantum: tanta ... quanta*). The first couplet however describes the situation as if to a third party in general terms of 'true love', while the second turns to address Lesbia directly (*tuo*) in order to point the contrast between *tuo* and *mea* and (more importantly) to explain what he means in more typical terms of 'social bond', using the language of social obligation (*fides ... foedere*) to express his integrity in his sexual relationship (see 109.6, Lyne 1980, 37–8). Three of the four lines describe the relationship with a part of the word for 'love' (*amatam ... amata ... amore*) while the third line shifts the emphasis to 'trust' and 'bond'.

Metre: Elegiacs
1–2 **no woman ...**: cf. 8.5, 58.2–3. Notice the repetition of *amatam ... amata* and also that of *a me ... mea.*
3–4 The poet builds up the intensity with *ullo ... umquam* and with the harsh *f* alliteration, before turning to address Lesbia directly in the final line (*tuo*) and restating the 'love' element after describing the relationship in more 'social' terms in line 3.

88

The first of four consecutive Gellius poems. We last met Gellius engaging in oral sex in poem 80: this poem ostensibly describes an un-named third party, but most readers assume that *is* refers to Gellius himself. Again, the poem is a good example of an obscene poem with no overt obscene words in it: the poet manages to describe in some detail a scenario of incestuous abandon but tries to preserve his own detached and 'respectable' stance towards it all. Notice the use of bathos, as the poet's lofty allusion to sea-deities in lines 5–6 leads to a disgusting caricature of sexual contortion and perversion: notice the mock-scandalised tone of line 2, the mock-legal tone of line 4, the oratorical repetition of words (*suscipiat ... suscipit*) and names (*Gelli ... o Gelli*). This poem is a study in prurience and a parody of the very tone it adopts.

Metre: Elegiacs
1 **mother**: actually his stepmother, if Valerius Maximus (5.9.1) is to be believed. Similarly the sister in question has been conjectured to be the mother's sister or the wife of the uncle he cuckolds in poem 74. Gellius is addressed in person (as again in line 5) as if he were in court.
2 **all night ...**: it is not enough that he commits these acts, but he does them all night long and naked, the poet dwelling pruriently on such details to bring the sordid facts to life. For this use of *prurit* cf. Martial 9.73.6.
3 **does not let ...**: Gellius does not allow his uncle to be a husband in the sense that he (Gellius) sleeps with his uncle's wife and so usurps his place. The phrasing confuses the reader who is suitably bewildered at the complexity of the incestuous arrangements, which are thus brought out by the verbal confusion as much as by the sense of the words.
4 **crime**: *sceleris* is putting it mildly, as adultery and incest together constitute a double crime; see Treggiari 281. Note again the forensic tone of the words used.
5 **undertaking:***suscipit* picks up *suscipiat* in the previous line. The couplet uses mythological information – Tethys was the wife of Oceanus, called 'furthest' as the Ocean was thought to be at the very rim of the world. Their daughters are Oceanids.

The style of this couplet is deliberately high and scholarly to make the bathos of the final couplet all the more effective. For the notion of sea-water as washing away crime cf. Euripides *IT* 1193, Sophocles *Aj.* 654–6, Apollonius Rhodius 4.663.

7 **crime**: *sceleris* recalls line 4, the speaker once again using forensic language to accuse his victim.

8 As often, the punch-line is powerful; we leave the poem with the caricature of a man practising autofellation; for the strong verb *uoret* cf. 80.6. The sense of the ending is that this man has had sex with everybody he could, leaving only himself to be seduced.

89

Another poem of deeply disturbing content expressed in words which are not themselves obscene. The poem is held together by repetition of *tam* and the theme of being thin (*macer*). The opening statement of Gellius' thin physique is followed curiously by a catalogue of his relatives: it is only when we reach the verb *attingat ... tangere* (cf. Adams 185–6) in line 5 that we suspect the link between the thinness of the man and the plethora of relatives. The first four lines are rounded off with closural paraphrase of the opening remark, as if the initial question *quid ni?* had by now been answered: the final two lines simply confirm the answer and add a further twist that the villain does not merely *include* his relatives in his sexual life, but rather he *excludes* all others: in other words he neatly inverts the 'normal' taboo on incest by his behaviour.

Metre: Elegiacs

1 For the style of the opening cf. 78, 79.1.

2 **hearty**: *ualens* has the sense of 'energetic' in the sexual sphere: cf. 61.227–8. Note the effective alliteration here with *uiuat ... uenusta*.

3–4 **obliging**: Uncle is 'obliging' presumably in allowing his wife to be seduced: and the *puellis* are presumed to be simply 'girls' (slaves etc) – until the following line tells us that they too are related to him: notice the effective emphasis provided by the enjambement and the word *cognatis* falling at the end of the phrase but the beginning of the line – and the rest of the line encloses the first four lines of the poem with a closural reminder of the opening phrase.

5–6 The concessive phrase is ironic: Gellius may not have a vast number of sexual partners, as he only touches untouchable relatives, but there are enough of them to keep him thin. Gellius thus reverses the usual taboo by refusing to sleep with any woman who is *not* related to him.

90

A further study of Gellius' improprieties, couched in a parody of the language or oracular utterance, with suitable doubts about the truth of the Persians' religion (line 4) if it espouses such perversion. For Roman scepticism about eastern priests and their habits cf. Juvenal 6.548–552. For parody of oracular language cf. Aristophanes *Lys.* 770–776

Metre: Elegiacs

1 **magus**: for the practice of incest among Persian *magi* cf. Strabo 17.735. The office of *magus* was hereditary and so Catullus assumes that the incest must have been mother and son. *nefandus* is a strong term; cf. Virgil *Aen.* 4.85 (with Austin's note). The term *magus* meant a 'magician of oriental cast' (Rawson 309).

2   **union:** *coniugium* here can only mean 'liaison' as mother and son could not get married.

3–4   Note the repetition of *magus* from line 1 and the *figura etymologica* of *gnato gignatur,* as well as the surprise that this monstrous incest is right and proper (*oportet*) if the religion is true.

5–6   We are left with a picture of the young Gellius taking part in the rituals: the paradox being that one born from so perverse a family ought not to be *gratus* to the gods. The detail of the religious rite with which the poem ends is a sketch of the priest going about his task, the solemn language well evoking the solemn pomposity of the young man as he melts the fat caul – the fatty membrane covering the intestines – in the flames, the final couplet giving closure as it marks the end of what line 2 (*discat ... haruspicium*) began.

91

A repetition of accusations of incest made in the previous three poems, but this time couched in lament rather than sheer mockery. The first six lines make up a single sentence, whose sections are clearly signposted by *non ideo ... quod ... sed,* the purpose of which is to assert both Gellius' moral obligation to the poet over against his propensity for incest, the positive and negative reasons for the poet's hope that Gellius would not touch his beloved. There is of course irony in the opening sentence with its 'heavy, measured syntax' (Quinn), just as there is sardonic wit in the logic of lines 7–8 where the poet (having said that Gellius only fancies family-members) wonders if Gellius thought that long friendship made one honorary family and so 'justified' going for Catullus' woman. Gellius' 'joy' is contrasted with the poet's sorrow, the high ideals of loyalty (1, 3) and long years of friendship (7) were thrown aside in a brief half line (*tu satis id duxti*). The poet exaggerates and heightens the mood with his choice of words – the epic-sounding phrase *magnus edebat amor,* the plangent repetitions and elisions of line 2, the pejorative language of *turpi ... probro ... culpa ... sceleris.* A mood of sad and plangent accusation is set up.

        And yet, if Gellius had stolen the poet's girlfriend, he would not be committing a crime in doing so – unless she were married, in which case the poet would be as guilty as he. Gellius would be committing a crime in having sex with a close relation, but the poet's girlfriend is emphatically not a relation of his and so the charge of *scelus* is unfounded: ironically, the poet's beloved would save Gellius from committing *scelus* with his sister. Furthermore, one wonders why the poet has been such a good friend for so long (the phrase *multo coniungerer usu* indicating long intimacy) with one who sleeps with all his female relations. If his disapproval of Gellius' enjoyment of wrongdoing (line 10) is so genuine, why has he not distanced himself from him before now? There is a disturbing note of petulance in the text which rebounds on the *persona* of the poet: the reader begins to judge the wisdom and the worth of this hopeless lover who befriends perverts and then wonders why they betray him, who falls in love but seems unhappy about it (*misero ... edebat amor*) and who then watches another man get the *gaudium* he wanted for himself. The text is, in other words, hardly the transparent document of a real situation which it is often taken for but rather a speech of unwitting irony and self-criticism which paints Gellius as the villain – but the poet as the fool.

Metre: Elegiacs

1   **would be loyal:** *te mihi fidum* are neatly juxtaposed to show the bond of loyalty between the two of them: *sperabam* is ominously in the past tense, inviting us to expect disappointment.

2 Notice the three elisions in this line as the poet describes his forlorn love-affair, and the assonance of all the *o*'s in the line. For *miser* meaning 'lovesick' cf. 8.1: for *perdito* cf. 45.3, 105.3.

3 **know you well**: *bene* goes with *cognossem* but is juxtaposed with *constantem* and so lends extra strength to that word also. The subjunctives give the strong signal that the poet is saying 'I did not think you would be loyal because I knew you *as I did not* and because I thought you reliable *because I did not*'.

4 **scandalous disgrace**: after the false generalities of line 3, this line spells out the poet's specific fears of Gellius' conduct, with the decisive words emphatically placed at the end of the two halves of the line, *turpi* at the caesura and *probro* at the end of the line. The same phrase is used at 61.99.

5 Notice the hyperbaton of *neque quod* for *quod neque* and the poet's change of verb: after the forlorn hopes and thoughts of Gellius' character we have a decisive verb 'I saw' to suggest that if the positive reasons for Gellius' good behaviour were uncertain, the negative one was not.

6 Note the alliteration of *m* and the striking epic-sounding image of love 'eating' him away (cf. 35.15, Virgil *Aen.* 4.66, Horace *Epist.* 1.2.39).

7 **intimacy**: the long association is described as *usu*, a word which sounds trite and legalistic but which was used of close friendship (e.g. Ovid *Tr.* 3.6.19) and sexual intimacy (Tibullus 1.9.55): the juxtaposition with *coniungerer* heightens the sense of 'intimacy'. The point Catullus is making is that:
Gellius always goes for relatives:
their association goes back so far that they are now 'related' by intimacy
therefore Gellius will go for Catullus' woman.

8–9 Notice the epanalepsis of *satis*, the alliteration of *c*, and the juxtaposition (over the line-break) of *tibi tu* with the variation of vocabulary from *credideram* to the more emphatic and colloquially contracted *duxti* (for *duxisti*). The poet's considered opinion takes up a whole line 8 but is dismissed by Gellius in half a line, the immediacy of his response being effectively brought out in the abbreviated *id duxti* with its harsh repetition of *d*. Gellius' *gaudium* is bought at the expense of the poet's misery, and the reader is reminded of line 2 where the poet's love-affair is described as *misero* and *perdita*.

10 The line is framed by words for 'offence': *culpa* (cf. 68.139, Virgil *Aen.* 4.19, 172) denoting a moral flaw, *scelus* denoting a criminal offence. The poem thus ends with the word *sceleris* ringing in the ears.

92

A continuation of the theme of poem 83. The poem is structured very simply, with the symmetry of the relationship mirrored in the symmetry of the verse: so 'her' *dispeream nisi amat* becomes 'his' *dispeream nisi amo*, 'her' *mi dicit semper male* becomes 'his' *deprecor illam assidue*. Similarly, the phrases referring to incessant talking employ enjambement to indicate the unending stream of words (line 1–2 and 3–4), just as the tautology of *dicit semper ... nec tacet umquam* also expresses Lesbia's ceaseless verbiage in poetic form.

Metre: Elegiacs

1 **always ... and never**: The poet says the same thing twice here: she always speaks and is never silent. The repetition underlines the way in which Lesbia constantly repeats herself.

2 **may I perish**: For *dispeream* cf. 45.5.

3   **evidence**: the poet sets up an imaginary dialogue with the reader. *signum* is the equivalent of the Greek *semeion* meaning material which justifies a philosophical point of view (*OLD* s.v. 'signum' 4) and denotes here simply 'evidence'.

criticise: *deprecor* has been misunderstood (as 'pray for relief from' for instance): if the poet means what he says in *sunt totidem mea* then it must be his equivalent to Lesbia's *male dicit semper*, and so must mean 'to express disapproval of, deprecate' (*OLD* s.v. 'deprecor' 1c).

4   **all the time ... love**: the line is framed by the key words *assidue* and *amo*.

93

A suitably tiny poem to indicate minimal regard for Caesar: the poet only has enough regard for Caesar to write this shortest of poems to say so. Both lines of the couplet begin with a negative and the poem ends with a phrase of total disregard for the great man. Elsewhere the poet shows interest in the behaviour of Caesar (see 54, if *unice imperator* there refers to Caesar), his friend Mamurra (see the next poem) or both (poem 57), and this poem is of course ironic in the sense that genuine indifference does not compose poems. Quintilian discusses this poem (11.1.38) and judges the sentiments 'madness' for a poet to say to Caesar but arrogance for Caesar to say to the poet: this is hardly an 'odd comment' (Quinn) but perceptive – this poem is, in other words, turning the tables on the *imperator* by treating him with the scornful indifference with which he treated 'lesser' men.

Metre: Elegiacs

1   **not overkeen**: *nil nimium* is a nice example of alliteration and litotes, and the pleonastic use of *uelle* further indicates the poet's studied indifference rather than active dislike (which would at least show that Caesar had made some impression on him). *studeo* has a political meaning 'to be a partisan supporter of' (*OLD* s.v. 'studeo' 3, used by Caesar himself in this sense (*B. Civ.* 3.35.2)) and the reader who stopped at *tibi* would understand the Latin to mean 'I do not support you overmuch'.

2   **white...black**: the phrase sometimes simply means 'not to know anything about one' (cf. Cicero *Phil.* 2.41) but also has a further sense of 'bright and gloomy' as at Horace *Epist.* 2.2.189 which suits this context well: the poet does not want to know whether Caesar is in a good mood or a bad one as he doesn't care about either.

94

A short satirical sketch of somebody unknown hiding behind an obscene nickname. The point of the epigram is contained in the use of the 'proverb' with which it ends, a phrase which sums up the behaviour of *Mentula*, for the Greek tradition of epigrams working up to a climactic quotation of a proverb or idiomatic saying Syndikus cites *A.P.* 5.93.4, 5.127.6, 5.130.6, 9.749.2, 11.5.2, 11.141.8, 11.417.4.

Metre: Elegiacs

1   **Prick**: the word *mentula* refers to the male organ, and is often taken to be a nickame for a well-known man. Mamurra is described as a *diffututa mentula* in 29.13 and most scholars assume that the unkind soubriquet refers to this henchman of Caesar's. The line sets up an imaginary dialogue with the reader (cf. 92.3) by having the opening statement inverted and turned into a question, and then answered (*certe* – i.e. 'what do you expect of a *mentula*?').

2   **what they say**: there is no record of the phrase as a well-known proverb, and its basic meaning is simply 'people do what comes naturally to them'. Adams (29) discusses the

possibility of the phrase being a sexual *double entendre* (first suggested by Buchheit *Hermes* 90 (1962) 254f) with *olla* implying the *cunnus* and *olera* the penis but decides that the evidence is not sufficient to justify this reading.

95

Cinna the poet was a friend of the poet's and one of the circle of poets whom we call collectively 'Neoterics'. His short poetic masterpiece *Zmyrna* is here contrasted with the inflated and (to Catullus) worthless bombast of a Hortensius, a Volusius or an Antimachus. This poem is a testament to the Callimachean aesthetics of the Neoterics, whereby the perfectly-formed miniature is contrasted favourably with the turgid epic, and whereby the small coterie of connoisseurs is approved over the mass tastes of the wider public: see the Introduction for more on these topics. More interesting still is the way in which this poem not only expresses these ideas but also embodies them: the text is one of neat literary skill and artistry as the opening couplet conveys the long passage of time in the repetition of words denoting seasons, as the title of Cinna's poem is repeated at the start of three lines, as the poet brings in the learned allusion to the exotic river Satrachus (contrasted bathetically with the parochial Po), as he employs the elegant metaphor of Volusius' poetry being transformed into 'tunics' for fish as his poems will 'die', while 'white-haired' ages will long read Cinna.

Metre: Elegiacs

1–2 **nine**: the poem took nine years to complete – as Horace (*Ars P.* 386–90) recommended that a poem should – and Catullus appropriately spends a whole couplet on this to stress the lengthy genesis of this poem, the passing of the years indicated by the alternating seasons of fertile harvest and winter.

3 Meanwhile Hortensius produced half a million lines, his rate of productivity being many times that of a Cinna and his quality (according to Catullus) so much the poorer. The line is clearly incomplete on its own and editors have to assume a lacuna of at least one line after this one. Q. Hortenius Hortalus (114–49 B.C.) was most famous as a florid 'Asianic' orator who was also famous for his extravagant culinary tastes: Cicero regarded him as one of the *piscinarii* (aristocrats more bothered about their fishponds than anything else). Ovid (*Tr.* 2.441) lists him along with Catullus, Cinna, Memmius and Calvus as a writer of 'naughty poems' (cf. Pliny *Ep.* 5.3.5): Velleius (2.16.3) remarks on his *Annales,* which may be the target of the criticism here, but he is usually seen as very much in sympathy with the neoterics and has poem 65 addressed to him in a most friendly manner. It is quite possible that the name Hortensius is corrupt.

5 **Satrachus**: the line appears merely to be asserting that the poem will travel far, but of course the name is not chosen at random. Satrachus was the river in Cyprus where Adonis and Aphrodite made love: and Adonis was the son of the princess Smyrna, whose passion for her father Cinyras was the subject of Cinna's poem. *canas* is the unmetrical ms reading and is clearly 'borrowed' from *cana* in the following line: the usual emendation *cavas* is hardly convincing and is well disposed of by Nisbet (1995, 98–9) who suggests *suas.* Better sense is however provided by Morgan's *sacras* (see Morgan) as the Satrachus was the 'bride-bath' of the goddess Aphrodite.

6 **hoary**: for personified time cf. the personification of rumour as an old woman in 78b.4.

7 **Volusius**: Poem 36 describes Volusius as the 'worst of poets' and wants to see his *Annals* burned. His poetry will not even get beyond the river Po, Volusius' local river to contrast with the exotic river Satrachus. Note here how the poet juxtaposes the three proper names in the first half of the line, linking the author, the work and the place as all belonging together.

·

8 **loose**: there is a nice point to *laxas* which is that the plentiful nature of Volusius' poetry will provide plenty of paper and so the wrapping may be loose. It is possible that the paper was used as a jacket for cooking the fish in rather than simply as a wrapper for them to be bought and carried in (see Thomson). The point of the line is the caricaturing bathos by which the great works of literature are 'tunics' for mackerel.

9–10 The Oxford text of Mynors prints this couplet as a separate fragment but it fits neatly at the end of this poem. Note here the description of *Zmyrna* as *monimenta* – a word more commonly used of the marks of greatness associated with generals (cf. 11.10) and here provocatively used of the short miniature epic whose fame will outlast the bombastic epics (cf. Horace *Odes* 3.30.1).

10 **Antimachus** of Colophon wrote a lengthy *Thebaid* and was admired by Plato (cf. Cicero *Brut.* 191) and later critics (see especially Quintilian (10.53) who praises him as 'second to Homer' but calls attention to his lack of 'emotion, charm and arrangement'). Callimachus (frag. 398 Pf.), however, called his poem *Lyde* 'fat and inelegant' which is very much the sentiment expressed here.

96

A *consolatio* to Calvus on the early death of Quintilia. Propertius talks of Calvus writing an elegy on her death (2.34.89–90), and we have two fragments of this poem, one of which appears to be Quintilia speaking of her future state as 'ashes' and the other saying that 'perhaps the ashes themselves might rejoice at this' which suggests that Catullus had this line in mind when composing the last couplet of this poem. If this poem is a deliberate echo of Calvus' own elegy then we may inevitably misinterpret this text in the absence of the Calvus poem: but on face value this poem seems rather odd as a *consolatio*: the first couplet expresses doubts about any life after death, the second mentions the longing felt by the living, and the last one speculates that (despite all this) the dead might be happy after all. The chief area of controversy is lines 3–4: many editors see this as the poet reminding Calvus of his infidelities to his late wife (translating *missas* as 'thrown away'), as urged powerfully by Fraenkel (1956). This theory is surely wrong. For one thing, it would be the height of indiscretion to mention such things after Quintilia's death ('you must be feeling guilty now, Calvus?') especially in view of the couplets which surround it, the first one doubting that the dead feel anything and the last affirming Calvus' love for her. If lines 3–4 mean that Calvus has been deliberately cold to her and thrown away their relationship, then *amore tuo* in the final line is nonsense or else a sick joke. In the second place, lines 3–4 are in the first person plural, and yet the poet has not thrown away Quintilia's love. Better sense of the lines is made if we read them at face value: the *dolor* which Calvus feels at the loss of his wife is the sort of longing (*desiderio*) with which all of us face personal losses, some which can be assuaged while others cannot – old love-affairs which can still be revived we renew out of longing for things past (and presumably are happy to do so), while friendships which have once been destroyed we can only weep over as they cannot be restored. Quintilia falls into neither category, nor does Catullus ever suggest that she should: the pain is that Calvus (no doubt) would be able to revive an old love-affair – but cannot revive a dead wife; and that she is as unreachable as a friendship which has been destroyed for ever. His relationship with her is both *amor* and *amicitia* and the poet can identify with the longing for the old sexual excitement of the former as well as bewail the permanent loss of the latter. Neither image sets out to do justice to Calvus' grief, but both of them allow the poet to claim to be able to share it in the first person plural.

Metre: Elegiacs

1-2 **If ...**: any poem relating to the dead must contain this *caveat* that the words spoken may be of no worth to the dead themselves, who cannot speak (*mutis*) to confirm their feelings even if they have any: cf. Servius Sulpicius writing to console Cicero on the death of his daughter (Cicero *Fam.* 4.5.6): 'if there is any consciousness even among the dead ...'. The poet here makes this point even more sharply by referring not to the 'dead' but to the 'tombs' – reminding us that after cremation there really is almost nothing there except a tomb, and tombs (by definition) are silent and unresponsive, and by strengthening *si quid* ('whatever') into *si quicquam* ('if anything at all'), as well as by putting *potest* emphatically at the end of the sentence.

3-4 For the interpretation of these lines see above. Note here the 'old-new' juxtaposition of *ueteres renouamus* and the heavy pathos of *olim* and *flemus* in this context of mourning for what has ceased to be.

4 **let slip**: *missas* is often taken to mean 'lost' (i.e. with the death of Quintilia) but Fraenkel 1956 argues that it must rather mean 'thrown away' and refers to Calvus' guilt at his infidelity to Quintilia and rejection of her affection, relying on Ovid's remark (*Tr.* 2.431-2 that Calvus 'revealed his love-affairs (*furta*) in various metres'.

5-6 This couplet is the conclusion of the conditional which the poem consists of. For the pathos of early death see e.g. Virgil *G.* 4.476-7 = *Aen.* 6.307-8. The poet asserts confidently (*certe*) that Quintilia is happy (*gaudet*) at Calvus' love more than she is sad to be dead so young: but this confidence rests on the considerable qualification in lines 1-4 which must make the ending of the poem less of a consolation than it might seem. The final couplet is built on antitheses – *tanto ... quantum, dolori ... gaudet* – and the final line is neatly framed with the wife and husband at either end.

97

A scathingly obscene poem describing a certain Aemilius; the first of three poems on the theme of the 'dirty mouth' and a startling contrast to the previous poem. From studied indifference at the beginning, as the poet expresses detached comparison of Aemilius' mouth and anus, we pass to a highly charged caricature of the man's mouth (lines 5-8) before being told (surprisingly) that he has many sexual partners and thinks himself charming. The two themes are joined at the end with neat closure: such girls as Aemilius enjoys must be indifferent to his appalling personal defects: and in particular the similarity of his mouth and his anus (with which the poem began) is finally alluded to with the image of the girl kissing an anus. The poem charts the growing recognition of the disgusting facts about Aemilius: it begins with the poet saying 'I thought it made no difference' only to find that in fact it *did* make a difference as (contrary to expectation) the anus was cleaner than the mouth: and so the poem passes from detached indifference (lines 1-2) through detailed description (lines 3-10) to final and total disgust.

Metre: Elegiacs

1 **So help me gods**: the opening line gives no indication of the savagery to come. For the invocation to the gods (bathetic in this case) cf. 61.189-90, 66.18.

2 **Aemilius** is otherwise unknown.

3 **no cleaner ... no dirtier**: note the balanced symmetry of the line, with *nilo/nihilo* followed by *mundius/immundius* and then *hoc/illud*, with the break between the two phrases falling neatly at the caesura.

4 The poet surprises us by declaring that the *culus* is in fact cleaner than the *os*, with *mundior* picked up from the previous line and joined alliteratively with *melior*.

5 **no teeth**: the poet begins with a surreal remark that 'at least his *culus* has no teeth (and so is preferable (*melior*) to his mouth)' before turning to look at Aemilius' teeth which

are described in ludicrously exaggerated terms. *sesquipedalis* is used by Martial of a man's *mentula* (7.14.9), by Horace of inordinately long words (*Ars P.* 97): only Catullus uses it of teeth in this grotesque manner. Note here the repetition *dentibus ... dentis*. For bad or missing teeth as an object of satirical attack cf. 64. 315, Horace *Epod.* 5.47, 8.3, *Odes* 2.8.3, 4.13.10f: Ovid advises girls with 'black or enormous or crooked teeth' to avoid laughing (*Ars am.* 3.279–80.)

6   **gums ... wagon-box**: an odd-sounding line, but *ploxeni* was clearly read by Quintilian (1.5.8) and so the corruption (if it is corrupt) was an early one. *ploxeni* is a dialect word for a 'carriage-box' and editors think of a 'wagon-box ... large, clumsy, battered, covered in dirt' (Quinn). Such carriages often had 'toothed axles' which may be what gave the poet the idea for the imagery here.

7–8   The teeth and the gums lead naturally to a picture of the grin (*rictum*) and the poet continues the theme of comparison between the mouth and the anal region by comparing the smile with a 'cunt' (*cunnus*), postponing the word until the next line. The phrase is grotesque in the extreme: to compare a man with a 'she-mule' is bad enough, but to add that his mouth is like the animal's *cunnus* and then add that it is 'pissing' in summer (when the heat dehydrates and so the urine would smell even worse than usual), and to cap it all by using the violent verb *diffindere* ('split open') of the *cunnus* all amounts to a couplet of enormous savagery and vicious imagination. The phrasing is also elegant in style, however, with the alliteration of *m* and the effective juxtaposition of *meientis mulae cunnus*.

9   **fucks lots**: despite his alleged imperfections, Aemilius is said to enjoy an energetic sex life, although *se facit* suggests that his 'charm' is in his own imagination.

10   **mill and the donkey**: *pistrinum* ('mill') was a place of punishment for slaves in Greece and Rome, as in Lysias 1.18, Terence *An.* 199, *Phorm.* 249–50 (other exx. in *OLD* s.v. 'pistrinum' b); the hard labour of pushing the pole around the millstone was usually done by animals, and Quinn assumes that the slave drove the ass who drove the mill-wheel. The point of the line is bathetic: after the previous line in which Aemilius is seen as a galant man-about-town the poet wonders why he is not sent to work with the lowest slaves: and *asino* picks up *mulae* from line 8.

11–12   The final couplet gives us shockingly neat closure: if Aemilius has many girlfriends (as stated in line 9) but is as disgusting as is stated in lines 1–8, then these girlfriends must be capable of anything however disgusting. Nice girls (the implication runs) would not associate at all with a hangman, let alone do what the poet describes here. Once again the disgusting imagery is postponed until the final line and is concentrated there in four words. The disgust is (as in 7–8) cumulative: not just *culum lingere* (though that is bad enough) but to do it to a hangman (worse) and one who has dysentery at that. The final couplet is highly appropriate in this poem which began with the comparison of the mouth and the anus and ends with an anus being licked.

98

Another poem on the theme of the unclean mouth addressed to a man of verbose habits and recreating that verbosity in the text. The poet delays the point of the opening sentence for a long three lines, lengthening the sentence with unnecessary qualification such as *si usus ueniat tibi* and thus making the obscenity of line 4 all the more shocking. The repetition *omnino ... omnes ... omnino* also suggests the prolix style of Victius. The point of the poem is that the poet makes the metaphorical dirt of Victius' mouth into real dirt, and (presumably also) his metaphorical 'boot-licking' into real licking of real boots (for *lingere* used of degradation cf. Pliny *Ep.* 8.18.9); and so this 'foul' mouth could destroy all by simply opening, both in the metaphorical sense (by speaking: cf. the exaggerated effects of Arrius' speech in

84) and in the literal sense (by the smell). The final phrase perhaps alludes to the pomposity of the man who thinks that his effective speaking is all he needs.

Metre: Elegiacs

1   **Smelly**: *putide* cf. 42.11–12, 19–20 where it is applied to a whore. Here the word has a figurative meaning of 'tedious' or 'affected in manner of speech' (*OLD* s.v. 'putidus' 3b) which is appropriate to the speaker Victius as well as a more literal meaning ('stinking') which the rest of the poem will make clear. Victius is not known.

2   **gasbags**: *uerbosis* is not particularly pejorative (cf. Ovid *Tr*. 4.10.18) but *fatuis* is, as in 83.2.

4   The climactic line to finish the sentence. Notice the alliteration of *c*, the obscene image of *culos lingere* (as in 97.12) and the additional detail of *crepidas carpatinas* (*carpatinus* ('made of hide') only occurs here and is presumably added for the sound and the graphic realism).

5–6 The final couplet is held together by repetition of *omnino*, the balanced use of *uis ... cupis*: note also the emphatic placing of *hiscas* at the end of the phrase but the beginning of the line.

99

The poet describes stealing a kiss from Iuventius and being made to feel guilty for doing so. The punishment of Iuventius' wrath was greater than the pleasure of the kiss. The tone of the poem is superficially self-critical – it ends with a firm resolve never to repeat the crime – but also contains hints that Iuventius has been excessively hard of heart in his treatment of the poet. Look, for instance, at the indignation with which the poet sees Iuventius wipe his 'soiled' lips as if they had been kissed by the 'foul spittle of a pissed-on whore', look also at the strong term *saeuitiae* and the torture relentlessly (*non cessasti*) inflicted on somebody whose only crime is to be 'lovesick' (*miser* 11, 15). Thus what appears to be a love poem is also a poem recounting bitter experience and how the poet has learned from it: the sweet kiss soon turned to bitter hellebore, love was 'hostile' (*infesto*) and tortured him in his 'sad' state and the object of his adoration treats him like the lowest of the low (lines 7–10). What seemed part of a game (*ludis* line 1) turned into serious trouble and the punishment so outweighed the crime that the reader is left feeling that the boy was clearly not worth it after all. For Iuventius cf. poems 15, 21, 23–4, 48, 81.

Metre: Elegiacs

1   **playing**: *dum ludis* suggests that Iuventius was 'asking for it' as the verb *ludo* has the meaning 'frolic' in a sexual sense at 17.17. For *mellite* cf. 48.1 where it is also used of Iuventius.

2   **ambrosia** was the legendary food of the gods, and the comparison of this with kisses is well paralleled in e.g. *A.P.* 12,68,10 (and cf. the similar treatment of nectar at Horace *Odes* 1.13.16). Both kisses and ambrosia give 'divine' oral pleasure. Note the repetition *dulci dulcius* and the balanced abab construction of the line.

4   The line is notable for the alliteration of *s* and *m*. The poet's description of his torture is expressive: the phrase *in cruce suffigere* leaves no doubt that it is crucifixion which he has in mind (cf. Cicero *Pis*. 42.) For a cross as a means of execution of slaves, criminals and enemies see many reff. in *OLD* s.v. 'crux': it was one of the methods by which criminals were executed in the arena. The relevance here is the slowness of the death – a feature which made it less attractive to the audience in the arena also – and which makes it comparable to the slow (*amplius horam*) pain of the poet.

5   **tears**: *fletibus* suggests that the poet weeps: and later on (lines 7–8) Iuventius wipes away *his* tears. *purgo* is a strong word, suggesting the cleansing away of pollution, and is nicely alliterative with *possum.*

6   **savagery**: Iuventius' reaction is not stated until the decisive and emphatic final word *saeuitiae.*

7   **lips**: the poet focuses on the lips (*labella* placed at the end of the line) as the place of his crime and the part of the body which needs washing: the soft liquid sounds of *diluta labella* continue the theme of the poet's affection for the boy.

8   *omnibus* is the reading of V but is surely wrong, if only for metrical reasons as it produces a hiatus after *abstersti*: Lee's conjecture *mollibus* has found favour with many editors and makes excellent sense suggesting the rather effeminate youth with his 'soft knuckles'.

9   **infection**: *contractum* has the sense of 'infectious'.

10   **disgusting ... tart**: the crude phrasing reminds the reader of 78b.2: *lupa* literally 'she-wolf' was a common term for a prostitute (*OLD* s.v. 'lupa' 2).

11   **lovesick**: *miserum* (here and in line 15) suggests that the kiss was not the mere seizing of a sexual opportunity but an act born of infatuation. *amori* is best understood as *Amori* the god of love to whom the poet has been handed over for torture, with *excruciare* picking up the *cruce* of line 4 and reminds us of the poet's *excrucior* in 85.2. *infesto Amori* is hardly an oxymoron (as Garrison suggests) but reflects the painful love expressed in (e.g.) 8, 76 (especially 76.12 *dis inuitis*), 13–14. The sweetness is maintained as long as possible (*ut ... suauiolum*) with the ending of the couplet concentrated bitterness. Note the affectionate diminutive *suauiolum* (picked up from line 2) with its hint of the word *suauis* ('pleasant') suddenly transformed into the unpleasant *tristi,* the verbal arrangement mirroring the transformation being described. The couplet is framed by the two substances, ambrosia at one end and hellebore at the other, and the reduplicated *tristi tristius* recalls *dulci dulcius* in line 2.

14   **hellebore**: also used at *A.P.* 5.29 as a metaphor for bitter love: 'sex is sweet: who denies this? But when it demands money it becomes fouler than Hellebore.' The Hellebore plant was used as treatment for insanity in the ancient world, which may be a further reason for its description as *tristius* here and also for the poet's mention of it in his account of his insane love.

15   Note the alliteration of *q* and *p*.

15–16   the poet draws the conclusion with no pathos and plangent lament but in a tone of quiet resignation. The accumulation of *numquam iam posthac* emphasises that the kiss will 'never now again' be repeated, and *surripiam* ends the poem with the word with which it began.

100

The poem begins by describing the situation in the third person: then the poet turns to address Caelius in the second person for the rest of the poem. The poem ranges widely in its picture of the 'life of love': here are two brothers in love with a brother and sister, here is the poet himself remembering the madness of passion in his own life. The violence of the love is apparent beneath what appears at first to be a gentle (*flos ... dulce sodalicium*) atmosphere – notice the strong term *depereunt* in line 2 and the insistent 'fire' imagery in lines 6–7 (*igni ... torreret flamma*). Similarly the neat and sure symmetry of the love in line 1 (the language and word-order mirroring the symmetry of the siblings) gives way to madness (*uesana*) and doubt (why else wish Caelius 'potency' in love?). The ambivalence of love is again explored here.

Metre: Elegiacs

1 The line is notable for its fifth-foot spondee and its symmetrical balance as the names of each pair take up one half of the line.

2 **flower**: for the phrase *flos Veronensum* cf. *flos gymnasii* in 63. 64: for *depereunt* cf. 35.12, 45.5.

3 The line is remarkable for the repetition of *hic ... ille ... hoc ... illud* showing again the perfect equilibrium of the relationships.

4 **fraternal unity**: the line is framed by the key words *fraternum ... sodalicium* and the line caps the first half of the poem with a comic citation of a common turn of phrase, just as in poem 94. The Latin term *fratres* can denote 'siblings' such as Aufillenus and Aufillena.

5 **Who ...?**: the narrator turns to the reader and then to Caelius in the second person, exactly as he did in poem 1.1–3

6 The ms reading *perfecta exigitur* is surely corrupt and has been emended to *perspecta ex igni est*: for the phrase cf. *Post reditum* 23, Cicero *Fam.* 9.16.2. The word *igni* is important in the following line with its talk of *flamma*.

7 **crazy flame**: the phrase *uesana flamma* is bold: *uesanus* is used of madness and lust at 7.10, while the notion of flame scorching the bone-marrow recalls 45.16. *uesana* is thus used predicatively as a transferred epithet: the flame of love scorched the bones and turned him 'mad'.

8 The two halves of the line both begin with *sis. potens in* + ablative means 'capable of' as in *OLD* s.v. 'potens' 3. The suggestion may be that Caelius suffers impotence and needs the poet's good wishes.

101

A famous poem in a long tradition of Greek elegies addressed to the dead (Book 7 of the *Greek Anthology* is full of them), but a poem very much in Catullus' own style. The text reads like a somewhat formal performance of prescribed ritual (note the emphasis on the rites to be performed which occupy half of the poem) and there are elements of overlap with the actual words of the valedictory (*aue atque uale*): the poet's own feelings for his brother come out in the interstices of his performance of his duty (5–6, 9) and in the strong use of adjectives such as *miseras, fraterno, tristi* and adverbs such as *nequiquam*. More striking still is the emphasis on the family: obviously a poem over a dead brother will mention the fraternal bond, but there is also emphasis on family tradition in *prisco more parentum tradita sunt* which recalls the Roman emphasis on the continuity of the family and its history in their funerals (see e.g. Hopkins 201–2). This is some comfort to the poet and there is psychological realism in his clinging to the familiar pattern to control his grief, the emotion being contained in the ordered structure of the poem. The poignancy of the poem is that this highly Roman text spoken to a dead Roman with all the trappings of a Roman funeral (*inferias*) is imagined as being delivered on a far shore: the poet elsewhere (poem 68) seeks out and exploits the associations of Troy and the Trojan War in expressing his grief, but here the place is not named and could be anywhere. The point we are faced with from start to finish is the distant separation of the brothers and the futility of the words and actions performed here to overcome the distance between them.

Metre: Elegiacs

1 **Through many ...**: the long journey to Troy is well evoked in the repetition of *multas per ... multa per* and also in the juxtaposition over the line-break of *uectus aduenio*. Conte ((1986) 32–39) finds here an echo of the opening of Homer's *Od.* (1.1–4: 'many

were the cities, ...many the pains..') which is ironic in that Odysseus travels far from Troy to go home, whereas Catullus travels far to Troy.

2 **sad burial-rites**: *miseras* and *inferias* go together, the former at the caesura, the latter at the end of the line: and *miseras* is effectively juxtaposed with *frater* for added pathos. The poet addresses his brother, as again in lines 6 and 10. The rites consisted of an offering to the spirits of the dead: milk, wine, honey and flowers were often given.

3 **final**: *postremo* is positioned early for emphasis. *munere mortis* is strongly alliterative: the word *munus* occurs again in line 8 and *mortis* here must mean 'connected with death, death-gift' (Fordyce) rather than its superficial meaning 'gift of death'.

4 **silent**: just as the poet referred to the 'silent tombs' in his poem on the death of Quintilia (96.1) so here the ashes are 'dumb'. The address to them is accordingly futile (*nequiquam* well juxtaposed with *mutam*).

5 **me ... you**: the poet juxtaposes *mihi tete* for emphasis: such verbal closeness only underlines their present separation.

6 **alas ...**: the phrasing reminds the reader of 68.20: note the emotion breaking through in *heu* and the adverb *indigne* and the strong participle *adempte*. The poet stresses his personal loss in the placing of a stressed *mihi* at the end of the line.

7-8 **at any rate**: *interea* does not mean 'meanwhile' here, implying that this is an interim ceremony looking forward to a later effort, but rather means 'at any rate' (i.e. 'even though it is futile (*nequiquam*), this is something I can do'). Note the way the poet, after the strong personal emotion of line 6, now comes back to the protocol of funeral ceremonies and alludes to the tradition as expressed in *prisco more parentum tradita sunt* (for *prisco* cf. 64. 159). *munere* picks up *munere* in line 3, just as *inferias* at the end of the line picks up the end of line 2.

9-10 **brother**: the emphasis on 'brother' in *fraterno ... frater* is obvious and effective: so is the chiastic alliteration of *f... m... m... f* in line 9. *fletu* is the first (and only) mention in the poem of weeping, kept to the end of the poem and the line for emphasis; the eternal nature of their separation (already hinted at in *postremo*) is similarly made finally explicit in *in perpetuum. aue atque uale* seems to have been a part of the traditional funeral rites: editors compare Virgil (*Aen.* 11.97-8) and sepulchral inscriptions (Fordyce cites *CIL* ii. 3506, 3512, 3519). The term has especial poignancy here in that it suggests a reunion with a long-separated person ('hail') which is simultaneously a 'farewell' to him.

102

The poem has not fared well in the hands of critics: 'The lines are clumsy and crabbed even for Catullan elegiacs. As they stand, they are little more than doggerel ... ' (Fordyce) This is to ignore the literary skill with which it is composed: *tacito* is placed early in the first line, the last line ends with the silent Harpocrates, the poem splits into two halves (if anyone ... then I ...) with the final line framed by the two names of the addressee and the sun-god. *fido* is picked up by *fides*, and the sense of religious sanction in *sacratum* is turned into the caricature of the poet as a sun-god in the climax of the poem.

Metre: Elegiacs

1 **silent**: the use of *tacito* (emended by some scholars to *tacitum*) is effective in setting up the idea of two friends bound together, the one loyal and the other silent: their reciprocal trust is brought out by the simple device of the single *amico* to unite the two of them, just as *fido* is picked up by *fides* in line 2.

2   **spirit ... fully**: *penitus* and *animi* are strictly speaking unnecessary, but both add intensity to the line.

3   The ms reading *meque* meaning 'me also' is weak and much improved by Vossius' emendation *me aeque*. *iure sacratum* is a strong phrase: *sacro* means 'bind with an oath' (*OLD* s.v. 'sacro' 3b, citing Livy 9.40.9, 23.9.3 as parallels) but has the primary sense of 'consecrate' 'dedicate to a deity', while *ius* is the 'system of rights and duties' (Fordyce) with a strong sense of legal right (e.g. *ius intercessionis, ius prouocationis*): the phrase thus has the sense of political, legal and religious compulsion which guarantees the silence promised.

4   **Cornelius** is not known; there is no reason to assume that it refers to Cornelius Nepos (the addressee of poem 1). The line builds up slowly with the phrase *factum esse* and the parenthetic *puta* (let's say') to delay the final climactic word, the poet depicting himself (comically) as being turned into the Egyptian sun-god. (For Harpocrates see on 74.4).

103

Both couplets end with the same phrase *saeuus et indomitus*: 'please' begins the first line (*sodes*) and ends the third (*quaeso*): the decisive term *leno* is placed for emphasis at the start of the last line – until then we have no idea what the money was for. The whole poem is a series of orders (*redde ... esto ... desine*).

Metre: Elegiacs

1   **Please**: *sodes* = *si audes*, 'please'. 10,000 sesterces was the sum demanded by Ameaena in poem 41 and was a 'tidy sum' (Quinn): the alliteration of *s* in this line is effective.

2   **brutal and wild**: note the intensification of the expression *saeuus* by the addition of *indomitus*.

3–4   The expression is unclear: the poet would hardly gain by telling Silo to keep his money if he stopped being a *leno*. What he means is made clear by the ending of the poem: if he wishes to carry on being in business ('if the money pleases you') then he had better improve his attitude towards the customer and not think that he can get away with being *saeuus atque indomitus*. Note again the alliteration of *delectant desine*.

    pimp: The figure of the *leno* is common in Roman Comedy (see Segal 79–92) and is always seen as sinister and greedy: Cappadox, for instance, in Plautus *Curculio* is viewed as greedy for money, and he responds to Curculio's criticism (494–504) with a telling comparison with the life of the banker, thus confirming Catullus' assumption here that a *leno* is one who likes money: but see also Ovid *Am.* 1.8 for the female equivalent (*lena*). It is plain from all these sources that to call Silo a *leno* was hardly a compliment.

104

An unusual epigram with no named addressee. The poem is built around the verb *possum*: *potuisse ... potui ... possem* all reflect the poet's sheer inability to insult his beloved, and *maledicere* is placed in contrast to *carior*. The poet appears to protest too much, especially when we reread poems such as 11 and 58 which would qualify as *maledicere* to most people. Furthermore the logic of poem 92 would seem to contradict this text; in that poem the *maledicere* of Lesbia proved her love for the poet, whereas here his love does not allow him to do the same. The echoes of earlier poems of Catullus make one wonder how ironic this text is: and the final line is certainly bathetic after the desperate protestations of love in the rest of the poem.

Metre: Elegiacs

1 **love of my life**: for *mea uita* as meaning 'my darling' cf. 45.13, 109.1, 68.155: *maledicere* reminds the reader of 83.1, 92.1

2 **dearer than ... eyes**: for the phrasing cf. poem 82.

3 **love ... desperately**: *perdite amare* is reminiscent of 45.5 and also 91.2

4 **the clown**: *tappo* is something of a mystery: the name existed as a real Roman name, but it has also been suggested that it is a nickname derived from a character in farce and that in this context it means simply 'clown'. There would be something odd about an epigram not naming the addressee but naming a third party like this, and Lucilius (1307M) seems to have known and used the term The final phrase is unclear: it may mean 'you exaggerate everything' (and so your belief that I can insult my beloved is also exaggerated), or else 'you are capable of all manner of evil' (and so nobody would believe you).

105

The opening of the epigram ('Prick is trying to ... ') leads us to expect something obscene: our expectations are foiled as his ambitions are literary. The poet implies by this method of writing that for Prick to write is even more obscene than the activities which earned him his nickname.

Mentula's literary ambitions are mocked as much in the style of this epigram as in its content: the first line sets up his pretensions (with long spondees indicative of his mock-grandeur) as one who wishes to climb the mountain of the Muses – only for the Muses bathetically to pitch him out with forks in a phrase which was itself banal. The rise and fall of the two lines of the couplet match the rise and fall of Mentula, especially as the rise of the hexameter is answered by the pentameter.

Metre: Elegiacs

1 **Pipla** was the name of a spring in Pieria on the slopes of Mt Olympus and was associated with Orpheus and the Muses. The term was unusual and somewhat *recherché*, used by Callimachus (*Hymn* 4.7) and later on by Horace (*Odes* 1.26.9). In case the reader does not understand the literary connotations of Pipla, the next line makes it clear with the Muses taking part in the action. *scando* carries the obscene overtone 'mount' (used of animals (Adams 205).)

2 **pitchforks**: *furcillis* is a down-to-earth term: after the pretensions of line 1, these hardy rustic Muses use rustic tools to eject him. The phrase was something of a cliché in literature (cf. Cicero *Att.* 16.2.4, Horace *Epist.* 1.10.24) and thus neatly completes the poem describing Mentula's failed literary exercise with a banal literary topos.

106

A tiny joke of a scene: a pretty boy with an auctioneer and the poet's judgement on what he sees (*uidet ... quid credat nisi ... ?*). The point of the poem is that the boy is using the auctioneer to auction his (the boy's) sexual favours to the highest bidder, and the intense word *discupere* suggests that the boy is ardent for the sale to be carried out. The criticism of the boy is thus twofold: in the first place he is promiscuously selling himself as a rent-boy on the open market, in the second place he is shamelessly enjoying the sex.

Metre: Elegiacs

1 **pretty boy**: the opening words *cum puero bello* invites us into the world of boy-love and we imagine that the epigram is going to proceed as a typical expression of homosexual desire on the part of the poet: the word *praeconem* comes as a shock after that and then sets the reader wondering how the combination of pretty boy and auctioneer is going to work out in the following line.

2 **wants**: the poet saves his final criticism of the boy for the final word of the poem: *discupere* is a stronger version of *cupere* and suggests that the boy is passionate to be bought. Sex for him is pleasure as well as business.

107

Lesbia is addressed as having returned to the poet's embrace. The poem is a breathless text of high excitement, with lots of verbal repetition and with eight elisions in as many lines. The metre is also bumpy (e.g. *ipsa refers te* at the end of line 5 and *magis hac res* at the end of line 7), suggestive of the sort of excitement which the text describes.

Metre: Elegiacs

1 **If anything ...**: for the opening phrase cf. 96, 102. The line as it stands has a hiatus at the caesura and the insertion of *que* after *cupido* restores the metre. *cupidoque optantique* is not tautologous: *opto* is a weaker word ('wish') whereas *cupidus* expresses strong desire (cf. *discupere* at the end of the previous poem). Note here the assonance of *o*.

2 **dared not hope**: *insperanti* is stressed by being placed at the beginning of the line but the end of the phrase in enjambement. *proprie* here means 'in the real sense of the word' and goes with *gratum*.

3 **this is pleasing**: *hoc est gratum* is repeated from the previous line. For *carius* applied to his beloved cf. poem 82. The problem with the text as it stands is that it depends on punctuation after *quoque* to make it make sense. Much better understanding is reached with the small emendation of *quoque* into *que est* as printed.

4 **longs for you**: *cupido* picks up from line 1.

5 **give yourself ...**: *restituis ... cupido* is repeated from the previous line, while *insperanti* is picked up from line 2. The line ends with an uneven rhythm: the final monosyllable in particular forces an extra stress into the last syllable, as in the end of line 7.

5-6 **yourself ... to me**: *te/ nobis* is effective juxtaposition: the closeness of the words indicates the closeness of the poet and his beloved, while the separation over the line indicates the distance between them which has existed until now.

6 **whiter mark**: for the phrase 'with a whiter mark' cf. 68.147-8: the Cretans used to drop a white stone into their quiver to mark a happy day, a black stone to mark an unhappy day (Porphyrio on Horace *Odes* 1.36).

7-8 The couplet is framed by *quis ... quis* and the poem ends with a closural repetition of *optandas* (picking up *optantique* from line 1). The text is uncertain, but the best emendation so far suggested is Lachmann's as read in the text.

108

A fantasy of popular justice being gruesomely exacted from an unknown old man Cominius, complete with graphic details of his mutilation. There is a strong resemblance between this poem and Ovid's *Ibis* 165-172, suggesting that both Catullus and Ovid borrowed from the Greek text of the lost *Ibis* of Callimachus.

Another significant 'borrowing' is however Homer *Il.* 22.66–76 where the old Priam foresees the fate of his own corpse: 'my dogs will rip me raw ... who will drink my blood in their anger ... ; when an old man is dead ... the dogs mutilate the grey head (cf. *cana senectus*) and grey beard and the private parts.' Catullus has taken the pathos of Priam's words and created a poem which is both pathetic and bloodthirsty at the same time. It is also striking that this poem of brutality should be placed in between two sentimental love-poems.

Metre: Elegiacs

1 **will of the people**: *populi arbitrio* the poet imagines a consensus opinion of the whole people that Cominius should be executed; the purpose of this is to reassure the reader that the hatred is felt generally and is not merely the poet's private aggression, but the phrase is more suggestive of lynch-mob justice than judicial condemnation. *cana senectus* draws attention to the old age of Cominius, but the effect here is not pathos but rather delight in the degradation whereby the old man will not be strong enough to resist.

2 **polluted ... habits**: the phrasing justifies what is to come; note the juxtaposition of the two pejorative terms *spurcata impuris*. For *spurcata* cf. 99.10.

3 The line delays the 'action' with a legal-sounding phrase suggesting that the angry and vicious punishment to be exacted is being calmly considered by the poet: there is thus a contrast of the violence and the calm thought which reflects it.

3–4 **enemy of the good**: *inimica bonorum/ lingua* tells us that Cominius' primary sin was to speak against *boni*; the tongue is therefore to be cut out, as is often threatened to slaves in comedy (Plautus *Amph.* 556, *Aulul.* 189, 250 etc). The punishment consists in the cutting of the tongue: the additional remark that it will then be given to a greedy vulture merely adds insult to the injury. In the Ovid *Ibis* (169) the vulture 'will drag at your groin with his beak and claws': the ripping out of the tongue is Catullus' addition.

5 The word-order presents us first with the mutilation *(effossos* with effective *f* and *s* sounds) and then the picture of the raven who will eat them. Again, the primary pain will be in the eyes and the type of bird or the colour of its throat will hardly increase that but will increase the threatening effect of the poem as one imagines that the black throat of the bird will be the last thing that the hapless Cominius will ever see. The assonance of *o* in the line is striking, as is the delaying of the word *coruus* until the end of the line (as with *uolturio* in the previous line).

6 The previous two lines had birds attacking the head; now the dog-like creatures attack the rest of him, the pace of the poem picking up considerably as whole line units become half-line units. The Ovid passage has it that: 'greedy dogs will tear your faithless heart, and your body ... will be made a fighting ground for insatiable wolves'. Catullus is more explicit and more gruesome: the *topos* of dogs eating at the flesh of corpses is common enough but there is also a clear allusion to the phrase *hac lupi hac canes* ('between the devil and the deep blue sea' Plautus *Cas.* 971 cf. Horace *Sat.* 2.2.64) which allows the poet to take a proverb and make it all too real for Cominius. For him there is no escape: and the last line contains no verb, the action being implicit in the nature of the animals mentioned and the body parts which they attack.

109

After the violence of the wolves this poem begins with *iucundum* and sees the poet musing about the future. The poem addresses the beloved as 'my life' *(mea uita)* and projects an everlasting future of happy love throughout their life *(tota uita).* The hopes are transparent, however: the poet no sooner reports the mistress's promise than he is doubting her ability to make a promise at all, and the final line is brilliantly expressive of the inner impossibility of what he is looking for: *amicitia* is in Rome a political alliance based on self-interest which may last (but often did not), and the hyperbolic accumulation of *aeternum sanctae foedus amicitia* is eloquent of the doubt that this can ever be achieved. Did any *foedus* last for ever? Or any *amicitia*? And did the gods ever intervene in the love-lives of humans to guarantee fidelity? In the context of the other poems in this book it is hard to imagine any reader being reassured by this text that eternal happiness was a realistic prospect: the very idealism of the words on the page subvert themselves and create a dramatic irony in which the *persona* saying the words is being silently examined by the poet and is understood all too easily by the reader as deluded.

Metre: Elegiacs

1   **love ... pleasant**: the line is framed by the words *iucundum* and *amorem*: the beloved is addressed as *mea uita* (cf. 104.1) which is more than merely an affectionate term in this poem as the whole text is concerned with the 'whole-life' nature of their relationship (*perpetuum ... aeternum*).

2   **of ours ... between us**: *nostrum inter nos* stresses the point that the relationship is to be mutual.

3–4   **Great gods**: the poet turns from addressing his beloved to addressing the gods: note the repetition of *uere ... sincere ... ex animo* which all in different words express the same thing. *possit* is stressed by its alliteration and its position at the end of the line and might be seen as something of an insult to the girl ('is she even *capable* of making a real promise?').

5   **carry on**: the intensive prefix *per–* is important in *perducere*: the sequence of words *tota perducere uita aeternum* strongly emphasises the hoped-for 'whole-life' quality of the relationship.

6   **friendship**: the poem ends with the strong word *amicitia* which has a primary meaning 'friendship' (cf. 96.4) but a more usual political sense of 'political alliance' (see Brunt). Lyne 1980, 36–8) sees this line as the poet aspiring to the 'marriage-pact of friendship' as the best of the two worlds of marriage (more permanent but not loving) and friendship (more loving but less permanent): but *foedus* by itself does not mean 'marriage' (and Lyne's examples (64.335, 373) only mean marriage in their context). It is at least as likely that the line has more political overtones: 'an everlasting bond of sanctioned alliance' is more the surface meaning of the words to a Roman reader and shows the poet attempting to find vocabulary to express his feelings and his hopes: but there is also the undertone of doubt in the hyperbolic language chosen.

110

A girl who takes the money and then goes back on her word. A distinction is assumed between the *meretrix* who 'puts her whole body up for sale' and the *bona amica* who will agree to serve the wishes of the man who puts up the money. Aufillena, the underlying tone suggests, would hate to think of herself as a *meretrix* but she is in fact worse than this: and the poem begins with her name and ends with the pejorative word *prostituit*. The poem thus contrasts the different sorts of girl: the chaste girl who does not even promise, the 'good' or 'generous' girl who obliges as she has agreed, and the thief (*furis*) Aufillena who says that she will oblige and then goes back on her word. The text brings this out by the double use of *facere*; Aufillena 'does' wrong because she does not 'do' it (*facis ... facere*) and her motive is put down as greed (*corripere ... auarae*).

Metre: Elegiacs

1   **Aufillena** was last encountered in poem 100. *amica* here means 'mistress', and *bonae* has the sense ('obliging') which it carried in 89.1

2   **get … undertake**: the line is framed by the two verbs

3–4   The sentence needs to be read more than once to see where the several examples of *quod* fit in: the first is taken to be 'because', the second is a relative pronoun, the third is another causal preposition, and the main verb is *facis*. This means that line 3 is to be read as: *tu, quod inimica mentita es quod promisti* and so the line as it stands is a good example of hyperbaton. The repetition of *quod* is highly effective in the damning catalogue of Aufillena's faults and the juxtaposition of *mentita inimica es* allows us to read it either as 'you have lied, you enemy' or as 'you are my enemy because you lied'. The verbs *das et fers* are short and simple and allude to the girl's ability to take (*fers*) without giving (*das*). Note the *figure etymologica* of *facis facinus*.

5   **does it**: *facere* picks up *facis* from the previous line. The line neatly summarises the two acceptable positions of honest compliance with the paying customer or else chaste refusal to take any part in the deal and looks forward to Aufillena's option of being a *fur* in line 7.

6   **snatch**: *corripere* is a violent word – to 'snatch' and adds to the accusation of theft (*fraudando.. furis*) and greed (*auarae*).

7   *officiis* is Bergk's correction of the ms *efficit* and is accepted by most editors: Munro's reading *est furis* is however a better reading and the one adopted in the text: it gives excellent sense and a pleasing alliteration of *f*. *meretrix* is a woman who earns her living by prostitution – possibly a slave owned by a pimp (*leno*) – whereas the *amica* may well be a freedwoman who is free to enter into sexual relations for money if she chooses and with whom she chooses. (On this topic see Lyne 1980, 8–17)

111

More on Aufillena. To be faithful to one man throughout her life is high praise for a wife: but it is better to sleep around than to sleep with uncle. The praise of the *uniuira* which is built up in lines 1–2 is to allow the bathos of lines 3–4: far from being the paragon of wifely chastity, this woman is a monster of immorality. In line 3 we see a woman of promiscuous ways, in the final line we see a twisted maze of incestuous parenting. The *uniuira* idea of the first couplet is solely to provide a foil to what follows.

Metre: Elegiacs

1   **one man only**: even in the racy world of Rome in the first century B.C. it was still conventional to praise a woman who was faithful to one man throughout her life: for *uniuira* see parallels in *OLD* s.v. 'uniuira', esp. Propertius 4.11.36, and Treggiari ch. 8.

    praise: *laus ex laudibus* is high praise indeed. The line builds up the theme of praise and merit in order to make the next couplet all the more shocking.

3   The repeated –*uis* words strongly suggest that the girl may sleep with whoever she wishes. *succumbere* is a passive word, indicating the 'giving in' to male desire rather than seeking it out herself.

4   The ms read simply *patruo* and leave the line three syllables short: the simplest addition is Doering's *parere*. The line is effectively confusing, the juxtaposition of the three sorts of relations (*matrem fratres ex patruo*) showing the twisted morals which produce 'cousins' from an 'uncle' as a 'mother'. *fratres* here means 'cousins' (as in Plautus *Poen.* 1069).

112

A neat epigram satirising Naso. The reader does not understand the precise sense of *multus* at the start, and is thrown off the track with the repetition later in line 1 (where *multus homo* simply means 'many a man'): it is only in line 2 that the sense of 'large' makes sense with the paradox that this big man prefers to be penetrated and thus let his 'largeness' go to waste. The poem is thus held together and given its rhythm by the threefold *multus*. The writer connives at the (fairly typical) Roman attitude which had no objection to homosexuals who pursue and penetrate others (such as Iuventius) but have nothing but contempt for the 'pathics' who are 'fake men who try to attract men' in Ovid's caustic phrase (*Ars am.* 1.524).

Metre: Elegiacs
1   **great**: *multus* means 'much', 'big' or else 'much in evidence, tedious'. The line is defective in the ms and Schwabe's *est quin* is needed to make sense.
2   *descendit* is the ms reading and is accepted by many editors (taking it to mean 'go down into the forum'): much more sense is made by Haupt's *te scindat*, with its clear obscene sense (for which see Adams 150). The paradox is that Naso is well endowed himself (and so would be good at penetrating others) but is the sort who prefers to be penetrated (a *pathicus*).

113

Pompey was consul twice in his career: first in 70 B.C., and again in 55 B.C. The point of the epigram is that Maecilia's list of lovers has grown from two to two thousand and two over the fifteen years, an astonishing increase in number. The fact that the increase is in sexual activity allows the poet to make the joke about the fecundity of adultery in the final line, and the naming of Pompey in this manner gives the text an air of 'mock-solemnity' (Quinn) which the behaviour of Maecilia duly undermines. (The epigram has even more point if we emend Maecilia to Mucilla as Goold does: Pompey divorced Mucia in 62 B.C.)
        No high moral ground is being claimed by the poet in his 'condemnation' of adultery: such condemnation would hardly sit with the glorification of adultery which we find in poem 68.143–8. The epigram is a piece of fun poked at a woman whose adultery ran into four figures.

Metre: Elegiacs
1   **when ... consul**: it was normal to date a year by naming one of the consuls for that year. Note here the juxtaposition of *primum duo* and the way the infinitive to describe what the two were doing to Maecilia is left to be supplied by the reader.
2   **Maecilia** is placed for emphasis at the start of the line and the end of the sentence. *nunc* may suggest that this poem was composed in the year of Pompey's second consulship (55 B.C.).
3–4   **the two have stayed**: the original two are still active: the implication of *manserunt* is that Maecilia never lets lovers go as she has never got enough of them. The accumulation of numbers in the line spilling onto the next line in enjambement gives a good impression of the multiplication of her lovers. The poem ends with a 'mock-proverb' playing on the senses of *creuerunt* and *semen*: *crescere* is used for growing seed (*semen*), but is also used to mean 'grow to manhood' (Horace *Odes* 2.8.17–18) and *semen* obviously in this context has the meaning of 'sperm'.

114

A neat epigram in two halves: lines 1–3 set up the image of the rich estate with a catalogue of its wealth: while lines 4–6 demolish the image of the wealthy owner by the simple statement that he spends more than he earns. This Micawberish point is of course orthodox Epicureanism (cf. Lucretius 5.1117–9) and had been stated by Democritus before that (283–4DK).

Metre: Elegiacs

1 **Firmum** (Fermo) is on the Adriatic in Picenum. The pseudonymous Mentula last appeared in poem 105: we expect anybody with this nickname to be ridiculed for sexual behaviour and the charge of poverty in wealth here is something of a surprise.

3 **meadows**: *prata* are meadows, while *arua* are ploughland: *feras* indicate deer and wild boar. The poet gives us a catalogue of sources of food to prove that Mentula need never go hungry.

4 **All for nothing**: the second half of the poem begins with the stressed single-word sentence *nequiquam* to highlight the inanity of all the lavish wealth which he has just recited.

5–6 The poet indulges in some paradoxial writing: he may be called rich so long as he has nothing, and his estate may be praised so long as he is poor: all explained by the three-word phrase *fructus sumptibus exsuperat*. *saltum* in the final line recalls *saltu* in the first line. *modo* in the final line cannot be correct, as it would create a hiatus for the pentameter to scan: of the suggestions made, Richmond's *modio* is the neatest and would nicely end the poem on a note of concrete poverty, as the *modius* was the standard dry measure of (e.g.) corn, and especially next to *ipse* meaning 'the master' (cf. 3.7).

115

A variation on the previous poem with much of the same material, but this time ending in a punch-line more appropriate to the man's nickname. The pretensions of Mentula are well brought out with the ironic recital of his estates – something like the recitation of Trimalchio's estates in Petronius 53 – although the estates are hardly worth boasting over: note also the grandiose pretension of his 'outdoing Croesus' and having lands which spanned the earth from Ocean to Hyperboreans. All this is set up to allow the poet to finish the text with a caricature of the man himself as bigger even than these big estates – but only massive in terms of his 'prick.' The poem is held together by Mentula as a nickname in line 1 and as a rude anatomical term in the last line.

Metre: Elegiacs

1–2 the ms reading *instar* would not allow the line to scan, and would be improved by emendation to Scaliger's *iuxta*. The figures which the poet quotes are not impressive: one *iuger* was two-thirds of an acre and so Mentula's estate is 20 acres of meadow-land and 27 of ploughland, while the rest of his 'land' is swamp. If his estate runs to many acres, in other words, it is mostly worthless.

3 **Croesus** was the proverbially rich (cf. Horace *Epist.* 1.11.2) king of Lydia in the 6th century B.C. who was defeated by Cyrus. Legend had it that after his defeat – and as reward for his piety -- Apollo took him off to live among the Hyperboreans (cf. line 6). To compare Mentula's poor holdings with this man is mockery indeed.

5 The poet provides a list of the types of land, just as in the previous poem he gave us a list of the types of food available. *prata* and *arua* are worth having: *siluas* will at least

allow one to hunt in them: but 'huge marshes' are of course no use to anyone. (The ms reading *saltusque* is surely wrong and the text is much improved by Pleitner's *uastasque*. Goold points out that the corruption entered the tradition to 'correct' the haplography of *–uas uas–*.)

6 **The Hyperboreans** lived in permanent sunshine beyond the North wind and were idyllically happy worshippers of Apollo, who was said to spend the winter with them every year. Here the term reminds us of the myth of Croesus (see above 3n.) and also to indicate the furthest possible distance which a human could traverse northwards. The Ocean is the river which encircles the world and where the sun and stars rise and set: its significance here is that the estates run right to the ends of the earth, in all directions.

7 **great**: *magna* sums up the previous lines and the estates they describe, to be capped by *ipse maximus* as the Greatest Master, who is a *mentula magna*.

8 Note the alliteration of *m* and the caricature of the man as a great threatening prick: for the colloquial phrase *non homo sed ...* cf. Cicero *Att.* 1.18.1, 7.13a.2, Petronius 38.15 ('not a man but a dream'). Syndikus speculates that Mentula is being presented as a Priapus guarding his massive estates (as in e.g. Horace *Sat.* 1.8.3–7).

116

'No more Mr Nice Guy'. The poet looks back on his attempts to produce Callimachean poems to soften the anger of Gellius and reflects on the futility of this exercise: from now on he will produce invective to answer Gellius' hostility. The poem is at first glance an odd text with which to end a collection, and many see it as proof that the poet did not consciously order his collection. Macleod shows, however, that the poem deserves its place here as a 'inverted dedication': dedicatory poems speak of the work which goes into the poetry (e.g. Lucretius 1.52, 140–5), 'of the poet's desire to honour (e.g. poem 1) or acquire (Lucretius 1.140–1) a friendship' (Macleod 308), whereas this poem looks back on such efforts as a waste of time and determines to hit back. There is some ring-composition in the echoes of the first poem in the collection: Nepos thought that Catullus' 'trifles' were something, while Catullus here claims that his efforts were 'pointless': both refer to the effort of presentation (1.2 – *studioso animo* 116.1) and the Callimachean aesthetic is implicit in 1 (*lepidum novum libellum ... expolitum*) and explicit in 116 (*Battiadae*); in poem 1 the poet praises the 'hard work' of Nepos, while in 116 the poet speaks of his own *labor*. What distinguishes 116 from other 'epilogue-poems' (e.g. Horace *Odes* 3.30) – which openly defend and describe the poetry collection which they conclude – is that it does so obliquely, with some retrospection but with an upbeat note of looking forward to poetry to come, even though examples of the sort of invective Catullus refers to can be found (74, 80, 88–91) earlier in the collection of which this is the conclusion. This sort of 'false-closure' epilogue is not unknown in later poetry (Macleod (1973) compares Horace *Epod.* 17 and Virgil *Ecl.* 10) but is something of a pioneering move by Catullus.

The text is thus typically Catullan in that it foils our expectations of a conclusion while still providing one. We expect a summary of his achievement and a sense of closure as he looks back on his work and instead we find work very much still in progress: the reader is invited to recall two key elements and attitudes of the book she has just read – the twin poles of the 'aesthete and the mudslinger' (Macleod 307) referring to the Callimachean work in poems such as 66 and the invective of many of the short poems – but the poet is not going into retirement just yet and the poem makes this abundantly clear, not least by the sentence-structure which has him still 'searching' (*requirens*) in the present tense.

Also striking is the artistry with which this *apologia* for abandoning the Callimachean style is composed: Gellius' 'rustic' manner of speech is mocked in the spondaic rhythm of line 3, but the poet takes pains to contrast his own performance with Gellius, such that his efforts are elegant and serious (line 1) while Gellius has a rough *conarere* attributed to him, Catullus delivers *carmina* while Gellius delivers *tela*, Catullus comes as a peace-maker (*lenirem*) with prayers (*preces*) while Gellius is a warrior (line 4) with weapons, Catullus (line 2) uses *mittere* of poems, Gellius (line 4) of weapons. If at the end of the poem the poet resorts to the same tactic and the same language – and the archaic elision *dabi'* is studiedly un-Callimachean – then we have by then been persuaded that he had no choice but to do so.

Metre: Elegiacs

1   **you**: the addressee is not named until line 6. The accumulation of the adjective and the participle agreeing with *animo* is indicative of the earnestness which the text expresses. The metaphor 'hunting' is also striking: it looks forward to the firing of missiles later in the poem and also reminds the reader of the difficulty of translating difficult Greek poetry into Latin (Macleod compares Propertius 1.7.6 and Lucretius 1.143 for this image of 'seeking' the words).

2   **Battiades** ('son of Battus') refers to Callimachus as in 65.16. Battus was the legendary founder of Callimachus' native city of Cyrene, and Callimachus calls himself *Battiades* in Epigram 35 (Pfeiffer). The line is framed by the key words *carmina ... Battiadae*.

3   The line is entirely made up of spondees: and although the neoterics were famous for their fifth-foot spondees, only found elsewhere once in Homer (*Od.* 15.334) and in Ennius (33, 623f Vahlen).

4   **hostile weapons**: *tela infesta* is picked up later on by *tela ista* in line 7. The line as it stands in the ms (*telis infesta mitteremusque caput*) is corrupt and defective and Muretus' insertion of *meum* is suitable to fill the metrical gap.

6   **Gellius** was last adressed in highly unflattering terms in poems 88–91.

7   The ms read *euitabimus amitha*. Baehrens reads *acta* ('those missiles of yours launched against me').

8   Goold points out that the elision of *s* plays on Romulus' threat to murder Remus in Ennius: *nam mi calido dabi' sanguine poenas* ('you will pay me the penalty with your hot blood'): the conscious archaism also adds a note of uncouthness which serves to mock the speech of Gellius: is is also significant that Cicero (*Orat.* 161) records that the 'new poets' shun the suppression of a final *s*, thinking it *subrusticum* ('bumpkin').

The collection began with a more formal dedication: it ends *in mediis rebus* and leaves us with a continuous text which invites us to go back to the beginning and start all over again.